Pelican Books

The Psychology of Learning

Robert Borger was born in Vienna in 1927
and took a degree in mathematics at the University
of Wales. After some postgraduate work in
statistics at Cambridge he spent two years working
as a statistician in Paris. He returned to take a
degree in psychology at Oxford and then taught
for some years at Manchester University. He is
now Senior Lecturer in the Department of Psychology
at Brunel University. His current interests
lie in the explanation and simulation of goal-directed
behaviour. He has also published papers on serial-choice
responses and various aspects of skill.

A. E. M. Seaborne was born in Chicago in 1930
and educated in England. He qualified as a mechanical
engineer and subsequently studied psychology at
University College, London. After graduating he spent
two years on the staff of the University of Edinburgh
and was then for some years at Brunel University. He is
now a lecturer in psychology at the London School of
Economics. He is interested primarily in the field of
perceptual learning and has published papers on social
influences on perception and on the use of inspection skills
in industry.

Robert Borger and A. E. M. Seaborne

The Psychology of Learning

Penguin Books

Penguin Books Ltd, Harmondsworth,
Middlesex, England
Penguin Books Inc, 7110 Ambassador Road,
Baltimore, Maryland 21207, U.S.A.
Penguin Books Australia Ltd, Ringwood,
Victoria, Australia

First published 1966
Reprinted 1967, 1969, 1970
Copyright © R. Borger and A. E. M. Seaborne, 1966
Made and printed in Great Britain by
Hazell Watson & Viney Ltd,
Aylesbury, Bucks
Set in Linotype Times

Contents

Editorial Foreword

To place this book in its historical setting we need only to recall the three main phases through which psychology has passed in the course of the last hundred years. Until the mid nineteenth century psychology was a branch of philosophy. After Darwin and throughout the last half of the century it became increasingly influenced by biological concepts and preoccupied with laboratory methods. Early in the present century it had established its position as a natural science without philosophical commitments. In its new-found independence psychology then split into a variety of 'schools' – Behaviourism, Psycho-analysis, Gestalt Psychology and others. By the next mid century, however, sectarianism in psychology was on the wane. When Roger Russell succeeded Sir Cyril Burt to the chair of psychology at University College London he made a significant remark, 'Today it is not so much a matter of schools of psychology in general: it is rather that there are schools of thought in special fields, e.g. Learning Theory.' So it was, and so it has remained. 'Learning Theory' was an apt example to choose. This has been a major preoccupation of experimental psychologists for at least the last thirty years. There are several important schools of thought concerning the basic principles of learning and each school has a formidable body of experimental evidence in support of its theory. The theories and the experiments adduced in support are not in principle difficult to understand, but out of concern for precision these schools have developed also a rather formidable technical terminology. Hence the need for restating the facts and the theories in language understandable by students of psychology, by teachers, and by 'ordinary' readers. To provide such a restatement is what the authors of this book have set out to do. And this is what they have, in fact, done.

C. A. Mace

Acknowledgements

We are indebted to Professor C. A. Mace and Professor B. M. Foss who read the manuscript and made many helpful suggestions; to our colleagues in the Brunel psychology department for their interest and criticism; and especially to Professor Marie Jahoda whose moral support in the early stages of the book was invaluable.

We are grateful to Professor James Olds of the University of Michigan who kindly allowed us to reproduce plate 2 and to the National Aeronautics and Space Administration who supplied plate 9. Plate 1 is reproduced by permission of *Life Magazine* © 1965 *Time Inc.* and plate 4 by permission of William Vandivert. Plates 3 and 5 were photographed in the laboratory of the M.R.C. Unit for the Experimental Investigation of Behaviour at University College, London, and are reproduced by courtesy of Mr G. A. Tolliver.

1. Introduction

People are continually engaged in some learning activity or other – learning to ride a bicycle or speak a foreign language, to dance, swim, cook or play the latest card game, to handle a pneumatic drill, manage a shop or administer a Government department. For each person, a selection of such experiences, and especially the universal one of school, goes to make up his idea of what learning is about and what sort of questions need to be answered. They help to produce some more or less clear expectation of what this book will be about. We might as well ask at the very beginning: what is the relationship between the reader's questions about learning and those that psychologists try to answer? When psychologists talk about learning, do they mean the same thing as the reader?

The examples of learning that have been quoted cover a wide range of human activity. How does one deal with such a varied and complex field? Is it all just one topic to be dealt with under a single title?

Many people who have written about human learning have done so as a result of long experience in teaching children. They have grappled with the task of producing learning in others, have reviewed and reconsidered both what they were doing and what they were trying to do, and have arrived at insights and theories about the learning process as they saw it. Ideas developed in this way can be valuable and are certainly often influential. Suppose, however, that we want something more systematic, an experimental investigation of learning that not only produces conclusions, but can present the evidence and the reasoning on which they are based. Where should one begin?

Two broad approaches are possible. We can, on the one hand, concentrate directly on 'real' situations – people learning mathematics or languages or particular skills – and gradually build

11

up a sort of mosaic made up of knowledge about individual cases. Here we are asking not so much, 'what happens when people learn', but rather, 'in what circumstances and by what methods do people best learn mathematics or French or typing?' This approach has been characteristic of much educational research. We can, on the other hand, set out to look for principles that apply to learning in general. After all, we talk about 'learning' in every instance that has been mentioned. Could this be significant? Why do we label all these situations in the same way? We may be tempted to suppose that they have something in common, that there is something similar in what happens to the learner. If so, if we can clarify what it is and distil from our everyday language some sort of working definition, we might then be able to set up comparatively simple and controlled situations to demonstrate some basic rules of learning. On the whole, this has been the approach of experimental psychology, and it has led to an interest in many problems that may seem a long way removed from the classroom, the training school or the library.

What is it about learning history or algebra, about learning to operate a lathe or to play chess, to recognize a faulty paint-finish or a case of Parkinson's disease, that makes us use the same word 'learning' in every case? What is the common feature? Certainly the procedures and situations are very different, as are the actual achievements involved. The only similarity lies in that in each case the learner *changes* according to criteria specific to the situation – the history student can talk about the factors leading up to the outbreak of World War I, whereas this was previously impossible, the budding chess player finds that he is beating his father with increasing frequency. These are the sorts of observation which we would in fact use in deciding if learning was taking place. We would point to such changes if challenged to explain what we meant by saying that this or that individual had learnt something.

These examples of learning are of a special kind. Usually they involve the explicit recognition by the learner of some objective he wishes to attain, and often specially created circumstances – such as schools or industrial training schemes – are available to help him do it. We spend quite a considerable part of our lives in this sort of deliberate and self-conscious learning situation, and it provides the most obvious examples; but it is a feature that is not essential. Children, for example, learn a great many things even though they may have no particular intention of doing so. Nor need there be intention on anyone else's part – no stage-managing is necessary for the proverbial child to find out about fires and learn to avoid them. The essential features of this situation are an interaction between learner and environment, and a subsequent change in the pattern of his behaviour. Of course, if the circumstances have been deliberately engineered to bring about such a change, we are more likely to notice it and label it as a learning situation. But had they been like that 'by accident', or arranged for some quite different purpose, their impact on the 'learner' would have been the same – though we must obviously recognize the intention of the learner as a factor in the situation. If we are concerned with learning as a *process*, we must include this case with the rest. And we must not leave out those cases where the change that takes place is not a particular *achievement*, not something that we should normally comment on, or even recognize as a behavioural entity. Such a conception of learning will include, say, developing the habit of taking a particular route to work, of wearing certain clothes, of smoking, speaking with a certain accent, refusing certain foods, being friendly to certain people. All these represent changes of behaviour brought about in some way by the interaction of the environment with the individual. We might not ordinarily think of the development of food preferences as a learning phenomenon. Yet having once started to group together, under the heading of 'learning', the process of becoming a doctor and that of gaining proficiency on a bicycle, it may become appropriate to include all conceivable aspects of behaviour, important or trivial, simple or complex, deliberately contrived or brought about 'by accident'. To consider learning is to consider how the interaction between an individual and his environment brings about changes in the way in which he tends to behave.

We can go further. So far we have considered human beings – but changes in the pattern of behaviour under the influence of the environment obviously take place in animals other than man. Indeed, the capacity to change in response to properties of the 'external world' seems to be, in various degrees, a basic characteristic of all living organisms.

Compared to man, earthworms are, of course, rather limited in what they can achieve. But if we consider, as a provisional definition of an instance of learning, *any more or less permanent change of behaviour which is the result of experience*, we find that we must regard even these primitive animals as capable of some learning. This opens up the investigation of learning processes in dogs, cats, octopus, chimpanzees and a host of others – including, of course, the ubiquitous white rat.

It may seem that our attempt to turn the idea of learning into a working concept has had the effect of greatly complicating the issue. Certainly it looks as though we shall have to deal with a much wider range of situations than we started out with. But it has also had certain advantages. It is becoming clearer what are the defining features of the phenomenon we are trying to come to grips with. This means, particularly once we have brought animals into the picture, that we can construct comparatively simple experiments to serve as possible models for a whole range of more complex learning situations. We can introduce an animal into an environment whose properties we can specify and control. We can observe the ways in which its behaviour changes, and attempt to discover any systematic relationships between what happened in the animal's environment and what happened to its behaviour. The use of animals makes possible types of experimental set-up, degrees of control and kinds of measurement that ethical and legal considerations, as well as sheer inconvenience, would rule out in the case of human beings. It has the added advantage that it decreases the similarity between the investigator and his subject – a situation peculiar to psychology – and thus helps the attainment of the sort of objective attitude that is usually regarded as being essential in scientific work. All this, and the fact that many people either just like working with or are specifically interested in animals, accounts for the large volume of animal research done by learning psychologists.

Needless to say, there is also a great deal of work done on learning in human beings. While some experimental procedures are ruled out, many others are only possible with people – all those involving verbal material, for example. A great deal of human learning is, or appears to be, vastly more complex than anything to be found among animals, and this raises serious problems for experimental method. Some psychologists try to meet this challenge directly, while others may take the view that they should start by attacking those parts of their subject matter that are relatively simple. In either case, they are usually concerned with trying to make a contribution towards some comprehensive account of the learning process.

For the moment, let us recapitulate. We started off with a look at what learning might mean to most people who are not in fact professionally concerned with it. We indicated that within psychology the term learning was not used in quite the same way, and we tried to arrive at a more technical working definition of the area to be investigated: more or less permanent changes of behaviour that are the result of experience. This view of learning includes a wide range of situations that might not ordinarily be thought of under that heading – in particular it extends the topic quite explicitly to both human and animal behaviour, without making any sharp distinctions. We suggested that while inevitably methods and materials differ according to the type of learning situation being investigated, psychologists are essentially concerned with a search for rules and principles of wide application. It is important to appreciate this general aim in order to understand the choice of some of the particular problems being studied.

How far have we really moved from our starting point – how adequate is the definition and the type of inquiry that has been outlined in dealing with a normal everyday conception of learning? Consider a number of possible objections.

Introduction

To begin with one might feel some misgivings about the emphasis that has been placed, in everything that has been said so far, on behaviour. This may be all right for animals, or when dealing with the learning of manual skills. But if someone is learning history, say, surely he is gaining knowledge and understanding, not acquiring some new way of behaving.

Just what sort of distinction is this? To find out what progress is being made in learning to operate a lathe we must look at some aspect of performance, at something that the learner *does*. And when he is learning history? Unless he does *something*, in writing, or speaking, or by giving some other sort of sign, we shall be unable to study how he is getting on. Indeed our judgement of whether any learning has taken place at all must ultimately rest on making some sort of observations. If pressed to explain what we mean by saying that someone *understands* a certain mathematical theorem, we must do it in terms of an account of various things he can *do* – reproduce it, explain it, apply it in different situations.

There are two differences between this case and the one involving some routine manual task. One is the difference in *type* of behaviour – speaking or writing words or symbols as compared to making comparatively straightforward movements. The other is a difference of complexity. We can contrast understanding with rote learning both in mathematics and in lathe operation. Judged from the point of view of *criteria* this amounts to contrasting a wide and flexible range of behaviour with a more limited one.

These are important differences and any comprehensive account of learning will have to deal with them – but, as far as the basic *data* of any investigation are concerned, they are differences in behaviour. Perhaps now that it has been said, it may seem an obvious point, but it needs to be made. We cannot study even the most profound knowledge except by making observations on the behaviour that it produces. In fact we should put it the other way round. It is because we observe particular sorts of behaviour that we start talking about knowledge in the first place.

Still, there would be something odd about *identifying* the results of learning with changes of behaviour. To be considered an expert on the French Revolution, a man need not be talking about it all the time, and an industrial inspector is not regarded as losing his competence while he is watching television. The change which learning has brought about in these people is a change in a disposition or tendency, or ability to behave in certain ways. To say that a man has the ability to recognize certain faults in paintwork is, in one sense, just another way of saying that when you put appropriate surfaces in front of him, he *does* as a rule make a correct judgement. However, the individual who *can* and the one who *cannot* must in some specific way be different, even at a moment when neither is in fact demonstrating his competence. The fully trained lathe operator is somehow different from the novice, even before he switches on his machine. Whatever the change which the training period has brought about, it is one which must continue in some form during the tea breaks as well as during actual work periods.

Essentially the same point can obviously be made in the context of the animal laboratory. But what exactly is it that endures? Something needs to be put between the learning experiences and the eventual demonstration. One thing we can do is to fill the gap with *words* – terms like 'memory' or 'knowledge' that serve a very useful function in communicating with other people; but if one is confronted with a demand for explanation they lead you back to the associated behaviour. They provide a shorthand but do not themselves add anything new to the situation. Later we shall meet a number of technical terms of this sort – concepts that link the events making up the learning experience and the eventual behaviour.

There are, however, a whole range of observations of a different kind that may help to fill the gap. If there is a change in the way in which a mechanical or electronic system functions, we would naturally consider looking *inside*, i.e. at aspects of the machine's state and behaviour that are not normally observable – either because they are simply hidden under a

17

cover, or because they require special techniques or instruments. Now living organisms, even the simplest, are very complex when compared to existing machines – and we are still a long way from being able to relate in detail observations made, say, on the nervous system of an animal, to any but the simplest aspects of its behaviour. Nevertheless, there must obviously be continuity between what is outwardly observable and that which goes on 'under the bonnet'. Lasting changes in the capacity to act must in some way be reflected in lasting changes in the physiology of the organism. And although psychologists are divided on the extent to which it is necessary, or useful, to bring physiology into an account of learning, *at the present time*, it is important to remember that the organism does have an 'inside', and that whatever explanation we put forward to account for changes of behaviour will, in the long run, have to fit in with what we can discover, by different means, about the workings of that inside.

In our provisional definition of learning we referred to change *as a result of experience*. This is an important qualification and we must try to make it more explicit. Small children cannot open doors or handle heavy objects, whereas adults usually can. This is a change of behaviour, yet in part at any rate it is somehow different in kind from those we have so far considered. The behaviour in question requires the attainment of a certain height and muscular development, and these are called *maturational* changes, emphasizing the fact that they are controlled by factors *within* the individual, and are relatively independent of the environment. Many of the more obvious physical characteristics of people and animals are genetically determined – eye and hair colour are well-known examples, and, of course, that complex combination of characteristics that we tend to take for granted, which makes the offspring of people into people rather than into chimpanzees or polar bears. These characteristics appear and develop in a way that is within limits unaffected by the circumstances in which the individual matures. It is as if there is in the organism, right from the moment of its conception, a blue-print or programme that lays down the course of development of the characteristics in question.

Such blue-prints must also affect behaviour. An animal's anatomy will determine the kind of movements of which it is capable and to what aspects of its surroundings it is capable of responding. But quite apart from such general and indirect influences, quite complex and detailed patterns of behaviour can be determined by the genetic programme. Such behaviour is called *instinctive* or *innate*, and develops within wide limits irrespective of the animal's experience.

We will consider later the interrelationship between innate and environmental factors in bringing about changes of behaviour. Strictly speaking we can never entirely separate hereditary and environmental factors. The environment produces its effects by acting on a particular sort of organism, and the properties of that organism will obviously play a part in determining what those effects will be. On the other hand, all maturational processes need *some* restriction of the environmental conditions to allow the normal development to take place. This is not to say that it is pointless to make a distinction between innate and acquired characteristics – in our case behavioural characteristics. By saying that the nest-building behaviour of certain birds is innate, we draw attention to the fact that a wide range of different circumstances – including isolation from other members of the species – leave the nest-building pattern unchanged. If we wish to understand how it develops, it is not on the animal's environment that we must primarily focus our attention. If, on the other hand, we are interested in how it comes about that a particular cat frequently taps a certain window before running to the adjacent door, a consideration of the events leading up to the development of this behaviour will be found to be relevant. We will gain more by looking, in the first instance, at these events, than by looking at the properties of cats.

Nevertheless, in trying to formulate rules about how the environment leads to changes of behaviour, and particularly long-term changes, we cannot leave the behaving organism entirely out of account. And this brings us back to what is a source of frequent puzzlement – the psychological interest in animal behaviour. Does it really make any sense to consider learning as a single process? It may be very nice and orderly to find an all-embracing definition that places the cat alongside the college student, but will a search for common principles pay off? We may class together horses and motor cars as forms of transport, which does not mean that by becoming a horse doctor one necessarily furthers one's understanding of the internal combustion engine.

Animals facilitate systematic experimentation. But is this enough? There is the story of the boy who was peering about under a lamp-post, looking for a sixpence, which had, however, been lost in a different part of the street. He was looking under the light, because here he could see, whereas it was too dark in that part of the street where the coin had in fact been dropped. Does this story not have some application in the present context?

This is an issue that is often raised, particularly by non-psychologists, and it deserves to be given some space. To begin with, one can be interested in the behaviour and learning processes of specific animals even without having any ulterior motives, as it were. An understanding of human beings is no more the only objective of psychology than it is that of physiology. Just as in physiology, we may expect to find some continuity between species, and be able to develop concepts that are useful even when applied to animals of very different degrees of complexity. The ability to change the pattern of its responses to the world in which an animal lives, as a consequence of being exposed to it, is to be found at all levels of development, and although many aspects of the changes produced may differ from species to species, we may nevertheless find common patterns in the interaction between environment and organism that leads to such changes. At the same time, it is important to realize that generalizations made, say, on the basis of observing the learning behaviour of the rat, need not apply to dogs or human beings – they can provide general hypotheses which then have to be independently checked. If we do find that a particular account of the learning process is successful in a variety of different species, we have greater reason to believe that we are dealing with a basic set of principles.

Explanatory rules that have been developed mainly as a result of work on animals like rats, cats and dogs, have found useful application when translated into terms of some human learning situations. The first part of this book deals with what we may call 'the search for common principles', and rests heavily on animal experimentation. In the final chapters we consider the impact of some of these ideas on two rather different practical fields – that of education, where such an impact might have been expected, and the treatment of the mentally disturbed, where it comes perhaps as more of a surprise. It provides a measure of encouragement for a line of inquiry if the ideas which it develops are found to span in this way areas of application which are not normally associated.

The fact that principles of learning developed in the animal laboratory are found to be useful when dealing with some aspects of human behaviour should not, however, be taken to mean that the subject of learning is all neat and coherent. Scientists *aim* to keep the number of their explanatory hypotheses as low as possible, and look for relationships between them wherever they can – it is a way of going about things, but does not guarantee the attainment of immediate order. Apart from what we have called the search for basic rules, there are many investigations of comparatively complex learning which are not as yet well integrated with the main body. As we might expect, they concern mainly aspects of human learning, especially those involving verbal and symbolical material. These have been given a special place in the middle chapters of this book.

2. An analysis of simple learning situations

One of the authors has a cat that scratches at the kitchen window to be let in – not through the window itself but through a door some distance away. The sequence of events usually runs something like this: cat scratches window – runs to door and waits – the door is opened (sometimes) – cat comes in. From here on things are more variable – she may head straight for a chair by the fire, or hang around her plate on the floor or just sit down and wash. A second, equally unremarkable characteristic of this particular animal is that the handling of newspaper tends to produce loud miaows, rubbings against legs and general following around of whoever has the paper. Quite often the newspaper is subsequently put down on the floor with a plate of food on top of it.

This sort of thing will obviously be familiar to anyone who has ever had a domestic animal. Dogs even more noticeably than cats will develop in time patterns of behaviour that are in some way adapted to the way things work in their particular surroundings, from 'begging' for biscuits to fetching leads or walking sticks as a preliminary to going for a walk. How do we explain this sort of behaviour?

It is worth while pointing out again that if an explanation is called for in everyday conversation it is usually of a kind that is different from the sort we shall pursue. Thus it may be that a visitor who has just opened *The Guardian* asks 'why is your cat so excited?' He will be quite satisfied with the explanation that the paper frequently serves as a sort of feeding mat. The cat thinks she is going to be fed. What puzzles him is not the familiar general fact that experience gives rise to expectations, or that expectations lead to various forms of appropriate action – but only the way this particular animal is behaving. The explanation he gets meets his particular state of perplexity at the time and is in this sense a perfectly good explanation. A study of learning on the other hand may ask questions about precisely those familiar facts which we normally – and quite rightly – take for granted. Whenever we make the transition from everyday problems to an attempt at systematic study, it is important to appreciate the change in the nature of the questions being asked, before trying to evaluate the answers that are being offered. Nowhere is this so important as when dealing with behaviour, this being a field where there is an abundance of everyday problems and corresponding answers.

Our inquiry then will be concerned with the *general* features of the way in which experience affects behaviour – the history of our cat forming a special instance. But how does one go about inquiring into 'general features'? We shall have to set up situations which are in some way abstractions from a wide variety of individual cases which bring out and emphasize certain common aspects. Consider two well-known early experiments on animal learning.

The Russian physiologist Pavlov, in the course of some investigations of the digestive system in dogs, decided to investigate in detail the anticipatory behaviour of his animals. He noticed that some features of their behaviour which had at first occurred only when the dogs were being fed, began to make their appearance when they were *about to be* fed, apparently in response to the feeding preparations. Instead of taking this familiar phenomenon as self-evident and putting it down to the expectation of food, he set about trying to discover just what the phenomenon amounted to and on what features of the situation it depended.

Dogs were placed in a harness, in a soundproof room with constant temperature and constant illumination. The reason for taking these precautions was to ensure that accidental variations of position, noise etc., would not affect the course of the experiment. A small operation made it possible to tap one of the salivary ducts in the dog's mouth and to obtain an accurate measure of the amount of saliva being secreted. Salivation is one of the aspects of an animal's eating behaviour and Pavlov singled it out for scrutiny because it was comparatively easy to quantify.

When the animals had acclimatized themselves to the experimental situation, the following sequence of events was introduced. A buzzer was sounded, and after a short interval, with the buzzer still sounding, a small measured quantity of dry food was delivered to the animal. The buzzer-food sequence was presented over and over again. Gradually the amount of saliva produced began to increase as soon as the buzzer sounded, anticipating the arrival of the food. The animal could now be said to salivate in response to the buzzer, whereas at the start of the experiment it had not done so.

Pavlov called the presentation of the food the *unconditioned stimulus* (UCS) and the salivation which it evoked the *unconditioned response* (UCR). The repeated pairing of the buzzer with food turned the originally 'neutral' stimulus into a *conditioned stimulus* (CS) which now evoked salivation as a *conditioned response* (CR). The whole process was called *conditioning*. Pavlov and his collaborators concerned themselves with the relationships that existed between the various measurable aspects of stimuli and responses such as their intensities, amplitudes and times of occurrence.

At about the same time, E. S. Thorndike in America used cats in another simple though somewhat different learning situation. He put a hungry cat into a cage, food being available outside and visible through the bars. The cage was so constructed that a given operation, such as the pulling of a string hanging from the top, or the pressing of a lever, would open the door of the cage. At first the animal struggled against the sides of the cage, reached out its paws towards the food, bit the bars – i.e. it engaged in behaviour consistent with the descriptions 'trying to get out', 'trying to get the food'. In the course of its activity the cat would now sooner or later operate the escape mechanism 'by accident', leave the cage and eat. After an interval, the cat was put back into the cage, escaped, and so on. Thorndike observed that as time went on, the animal's general activity shifted increasingly towards the vicinity of the 'door latch', and that the period between arriving in the cage and getting out got progressively shorter. After a large number of trials the cats would operate the escape mechanism as soon as they were put in the box, struggling, reaching etc., having completely dropped out.

Thorndike expressed the results of his experiments in terms of his 'Law of Effect': 'Acts followed by a state of affairs which the individual does not avoid, and which he often tries to preserve or attain, are selected or fixated.' Such desirable states of affairs were also called *satisfiers* and the learning process *trial-and-error-learning*. At the present time, the term *positive reinforcement* is normally used, to correspond to Thorndike's satisfier and *instrumental learning* or *operant conditioning* replaces the term trial-and-error learning.

Thorndike's work, like Pavlov's, may be regarded as the ancestor of a long line of experimental investigations tending to preserve the basic difference in structure between the originals. Thus the ingredients of Pavlov-type or classical conditioning experiments are essentially a stimulus (UCS) that evokes or elicits a (preferably measurable) response in the animal, and another stimulus or signal which is neutral, in the sense that it does not at first elicit the particular response evoked by the UCS. Many unconditioned stimuli, including food, bright lights or air puffs directed at the eye, and electric shock, have been used, with interest focused on such responses as salivation, eyeblink, pupillary constriction, changes in heart rate or respiration, or in the electrical resistance of the skin. The conditioning procedure then pairs the neutral stimulus with the UCS. Changes of response pattern are observed but do not, typically, affect the course of presentations. In this respect instrumental learning presents an important contrast. The 'Skinner box' – a much used piece of laboratory apparatus named after Professor B. F. Skinner – can be taken as a prototype of the instrumental learning situation. The box is constructed so that the selected piece of behaviour – pressing a bar, pushing a door open, pecking a key – produces a reinforcement such as delivery of a food pellet, access to water and/or other signals such as the turning on of a light, the sounding of a tone etc. In this situation also, the animal's response pattern changes in the course of the experiment, but although the overall way in which the box works is arranged by the experimenter, the animal's activity forms an integral link in the sequence of events that make up the experimental session.

What are the particular features of ordinary learning that are emphasized by these two types of experimental set-up? We may begin by looking for correspondences between the case of the domestic cat that we started with and the laboratory situations. Taking first the window scratching, we note that this is a situation of the instrumental learning type. Certain events, i.e. the opening of the door (and the opportunities that this presents), depend on a particular response being made by the animal.*

If we consider the circumstances leading up to the cat's excitement in response to newspaper rustling, we find similarities to the structure of Pavlovian conditioning experiments. A pattern of sights and sounds is followed, though not as regularly, by the presentation of food. The newspaper-food sequence forms only one aspect of a more complex and variable situation in which the cat's behaviour develops – but it is this aspect on which the conditioning experiment focuses attention.

The particular world in which our cat lives – i.e. the world as it impinges on her – is characterized by many more or less stable features. It is for example a world in which, as a matter

* It must, however, be recognized that the relationship between window scratching and door opening is looser than any we have considered so far. There is also the difference that the *embodiment* of the relationship between the animal's activity and the reinforcement is a mechanism in the case of the Skinner box, and involves human intervention in the case of the author's cat. But this does not matter as far as the impact on the animal is concerned. It does not make any difference to a rat in a Skinner box if the lever which it presses activates the feeding mechanism *directly*, or whether it happens only via the activity of an observer who notes the lever press and then, independently, operates the feeder. True, the animal might be affected by differences in the speed, or by the reliability with which pressing produces food delivery. The point is that the animal is affected by the characteristics of its immediate environment, not by the particular machinery, organism or causal chain generally that lies behind the workings of that environment.

of *fact*, window scratching leads (fairly often) to door opening, and newspaper rustling precedes feeding. The world of most infants is such that raising their arms is often followed by their being picked up, the sound of the mother's voice occurs in regular conjunction with a variety of particular visual and tactual experiences. If certain buttons are pressed, this event is followed by the sound of a bell and usually, after an interval, by the opening of a door. Thunder follows lightning. There may be many different types of explanation for the conjunction of particular events – the laws of physics when we let go of a heavy weight, particular human customs when we try to drive on the wrong side of the road, or the properties of animals when we sit on an ant heap. But for whatever reason, the experience of individual people and animals is *structured*, involves different patterns of regularity – some events following each other swiftly, others after a delay, some every time and others only intermittently, some always in the same form and others with variations from occasion to occasion.

Apart from the events themselves, the *manner* of their hanging together constitutes an important variable in the description of our environment. Thus if an animal spends some time in circumstances in which, for whatever reason, A occurs in conjunction with B, any change that takes place in the animal's behaviour as a result of being exposed to this state of affairs can be seen as a function partly of the way A and B taken separately relate to the animal, and partly of the pattern of association between them.

From this point of view we can see that both instrumental learning and conditioning experiments essentially present an animal with a simple type of relational property – A is followed by B. This property characterizes the animal's environment during the experimental sessions. In the case of Pavlovian conditioning both A and B are events initiated outside the animal. Food follows bell, a loud noise follows a light, a buzzer is paired with a shock. The experimental situation represents that aspect of our experience which involves relationships between 'external' events. Typically, one of the events is chosen to be of 'significance' to the animal – i.e. it is an event, like the presentation of food, to which the animal responds in a definite way.

The instrumental learning experiment also presents an animal with a situation in which there is a simple relationship between A and B. This time, however, A is not an external event but involves a specific act on the part of the learner, a movement, a sequence of movements, an operation; and B is the consequence of that act. Thus the experiment isolates another important aspect of experience. Typically again, B is an event to which the animal is not indifferent.

In both types of situation learning takes place. Before looking at some of the features of this learning, we may very briefly consider two questions. Firstly, are we dealing here with two different types of learning, or are they both instances of the same fundamental process? Certainly, there are here two types of *circumstances*, two aspects of the world with which an organism has to cope, giving rise to different forms of adjustment. On the whole conditioning experiments involve responses which we would normally describe as involuntary or reflex – salivation, pupillary constriction, changes of heart rate – responses which are often also of an 'emotional' character. Instrumental learning experiments, on the other hand, involve movements, operations on the environment. But we hardly know at this stage what might be meant by a difference in *type of learning* as distinct from a difference in learning situation and type of response. This question will have to be clarified before it can be answered and we are going to shelve it for the moment.

Secondly, can the two aspects of the environment which are emphasized respectively by the two types of experimental set-up claim to exhaust the ways in which organisms are affected by their surroundings? They are after all very simple situations which hardly do justice to the complexities of real life. Here we must distinguish between particular experiments and approaches to a problem. The approach to learning that has been indicated regards the learner as exposed to various kinds of relationship and this obviously allows one plenty of scope for going beyond the experiments of Thorndike and Pavlov. Even so, important aspects of learning may be ignored and this also we shall have to consider later. For the moment we shall look at a number of other features of *simple* learning situations.

Timing

We have been talking of relationships between events in terms of their following each other with some regularity. What of the interval that separates them? When someone pushes a bell, the noise is instantaneous. Quite a long time can elapse between a seed being put into the ground and a shoot appearing above the surface. Touching something hot is immediately followed by pain, but it may be quite a while before eating an excessive amount of sweets and ice cream produces a feeling of sickness. How does the interval that separates related events affect the extent to which behaviour is modified?

If we tried to train a dog to beg by arranging to feed him consistently every time he got onto his hind legs, but postponed the actual presentation of food until, say, a quarter of an hour after the selected response had occurred, we would not anticipate much progress. 'Food follows begging' may be an invariable rule of the animal's environment, but if the time gap is too large, the relationship fails to make an impact on behaviour. People become aware of the connexion between two happenings much more readily if they follow each other closely than if they occur at widely different times. This is not of course an explanation, only another instance of the way in which organisms react to regularities in their environment. Pavlov found that best results were achieved when the conditioned and unconditioned stimuli were separated by about half a second. In instrumental learning also the rate of learning falls off rapidly if anything but a very short interval intervenes between the response-to-be-learned, and reinforcement.

Secondary reinforcement

Often when we want to reward a child for something it has done, we promise to give it something that it likes. Although the reward itself may be some way off, the promise alone produces pleasure at the moment at which it is made, and the effect of giving the reward is thus in some sense brought forward in time. Although we are here dealing with the use of language and an altogether more complex situation than the sort of thing we have been considering, there is a corresponding phenomenon at a primitive level.

The food-delivery mechanism in a Skinner box usually makes a click as it operates. If the experimenter operates it repeatedly, click being paired with food presentation, we are exposing the animal – pigeon or rat, say – to a Pavlovian conditioning situation in which the click becomes a conditioned stimulus. So far no particular activity has been required from the subject. Suppose now that, after many such pairings, we change the rules. We arrange that pressing a lever or pecking a key near the food tray will operate the feeding mechanism. At the same time, we remove the food supply, so that when the lever is pressed there is only the click, but no food. Under these circumstances, although the animal has never pressed the lever before, it begins to learn to do so, much as when food is actually presented. The click is thus acting as a reinforcer for lever pressing. It is referred to as a *secondary* or *conditioned reinforcer* to distinguish it from a *primary reinforcer* like food. A primary reinforcer is one that requires no special conditioning procedure to make it effective. A secondary reinforcer – which can be any event whatever – acquires its reinforcing property through being paired with a primary reinforcer.

Obviously we do not want to draw too close a parallel between promises and clicks. They are similar only in the (important) sense of deriving their power from their relationship to another and more fundamental event which they announce. Clicks, like promises, lose their effectiveness if they repeatedly fail to be honoured.

We can see now that the instrumental learning situation inevitably involves secondary as well as primary reinforcers – for example, the sight of food is a secondary reinforcer, even though this property will have been developed outside the experimental situation. We can, however, make deliberate use of secondary reinforcement by pairing a suitable signal with food presentation. The advantage of this is that a signal, like a click, can be made to follow a desired response immediately, whereas there is inevitably some delay before the presented pellet of food is seized and eaten.

What happens when we look at behaviour in situations which are different in various ways from those in which the original learning took place? This is obviously an area of great importance, since in 'real life' situations rarely repeat themselves exactly. We normally expect that the effects of a learning experience will not be confined to just one particular set of conditions – indeed judging by the great contrast which usually exists between the setting, content and procedure of formal education and the circumstances in which we hope to benefit from it, we appear to have great faith in the possibility of a very general extension of learning to new situations, at any rate when we are dealing with human beings. Are there any parallels at a more primitive level?

Extinction

Suppose that, having consistently followed the sound of a buzzer with food, and having established a conditioned salivary response, we change the situation so that food no longer follows the buzzer. Since the conditioned response *precedes* the arrival of food, it will obviously occur the first time the buzzer sounds under the new rules. There is no way so far in which the change could have communicated itself to the animal. As we repeatedly present buzzer *without* food – conditioned without unconditioned stimulus – the conditioned response continues to occur, but to a decreasing extent, until eventually it disappears. Like the impact of the original rule, the impact of the changed rule is gradual in its effect. The process is called *extinction*, and has its counterpart in instrumental learning, when a response established by reinforcement eventually ceases after repeated non-reinforcement. In both cases, a response comes about gradually when B repeatedly follows A, and ceases gradually when this is no longer the case.

We cannot, however, think of extinction as a simple reversal of the original learning. Although the response may appear to have ceased, it will tend to start off again after an interval such as that separating two experimental sessions. This recurrence is called *spontaneous recovery*. It is only if the extinction procedure is repeated several times that spontaneous recovery finally fails to occur. Even then we do not have a return to the animal's original state, in that the time taken to re-establish the response, if the A-B rule comes once more into operation, tends to be less than the first learning period.

Generalization and discrimination

Another way in which we may depart from the initial learning conditions is to present instead of the conditioned stimulus A something that differs from it in various respects.

Thus the cat mentioned earlier is conditioned to eat off *The Guardian*. How will she respond to the pink *Financial Times* or to a piece of brown packing paper? She would seem to be affected by both, though it is difficult to assess any qualitative or quantitative differences in the response. The phenomenon is technically known as *stimulus generalization*, and has been extensively investigated. Many such studies take the form of establishing a conditioned response to a precisely specified stimulus, such as a given wave-length of light, or a tactual stimulus applied to a specified part of the body, and then obtaining measurements of the response when we present stimuli that differ from the original along some dimension. For example, having conditioned salivary flow to a pure tone of 800 cycles/sec., we might plot the amount of saliva produced when presenting tones of different pitches. The curve obtained in this way is called the *gradient of stimulus generalization.* The range of stimuli affected depends, as we might expect, on whether a single stimulus, or a variety, was used in the original conditioning; but this is an area in which much work remains to be done, especially when we move away from variations along a simple dimension, such as wave-length of sound or light, and begin to look at generalization across 'qualitative' differences.

Generalization occurs also in instrumental learning, but before considering this, we must take another look at our model. We have represented the instrumental learning situation as one in which a particular response A is followed by an event B, i.e. an animal is exposed to circumstances in which this rule holds. These circumstances, however, must have other characteristics also – reinforcement follows a given action in a particular setting, be it Skinner box or classroom, and this setting must, strictly speaking, enter into a description of the conditions involved in bringing about the final behaviour. If we train an animal to press a lever in one sort of box, will it do so in another? (Will behaviour learned in the classroom generalize to situations outside?)

Boxes, not to mention classrooms, are very complex settings and can differ from each other in an enormous number of ways. We might expect that changes that are more salient, more pronounced, will have a more disrupting effect on a learned performance than those that are less so. There is some evidence that this is so. But what constitutes a 'pronounced change'? To some extent this will depend on the kind of animal involved – smells, for example, are likely to affect dogs more than pigeons and different species generally tend to be susceptible to different aspects of the environment. Differences of this kind have been studied by ethologists, who have been primarily concerned with the innate behaviour of organisms. Differences in the susceptibility to the environment are certainly also relevant to learning and generalization, though in this context they have tended to be neglected as an explicit object of study.

Discrimination and stimulus control

Aspects of the environment can become relevant to an animal's behaviour as a result of learning. Suppose for example that a pigeon has learned to peck at an illuminated key by repeated reinforcement. A change in the colour of the light will not normally make any difference to this behaviour once it has become established. If, however, we arrange that pecking the key is reinforced only when the light is green, and never when it is red, then the response becomes established in the first, and extinguished in the second situation, i.e. the colour of the key becomes a critical factor in the occurrence of the response. Our model has become quite explicitly 'A is followed by B, in the presence of stimulus 1, but not the presence of stimulus 2.' Skinner uses the symbol SD to denote a stimulus that signals the occasion for reinforcement and $S_\triangle$ for a stimulus that announces non-reinforcement. By means of this sort of *differential reinforcement* we bring about discrimination where there would otherwise be generalization.

Discrimination involves *stimulus control* – in the sense that SD, the stimulus associated with reinforcement, brings about the appropriate response, whereas $S_\triangle$ inhibits it. Children learn to recognize the occasions on which requests of different kinds are likely to be met. Our cat, observed from another room, will lie quietly on the kitchen window ledge, and will begin to 'ask for admission' only when someone enters the kitchen. The use of a term like 'stimulus control' does not announce a discovery, except insofar as it highlights a principle. Its recognition makes it possible to develop special stimulus situations with the explicit purpose of exercising control over behaviour.

Response chains

The green light, when discrimination is established, is repeatedly paired with reinforcement, since the animal comes to respond regularly in its presence, and these responses are reinforced. A stimulus thus becomes a secondary reinforcer at the same time as becoming an SD. If we now arrange a further contingency, making the appearance of the green light depend on the occurrence of some previous response – say the pecking of a second key – this response will also be learned. In this way we can establish a short *chain* of behaviour – pecking one key turns the light from red to green, which provides the go-ahead for the next response, which leads to reinforcement. Actually the chain is already longer than this. The sound made by the food mechanism, itself a secondary reinforcer for pecking, has become an SD for the response of looking in the food tray, where sight of food constitutes a secondary reinforcement for looking and an SD for pecking and eating.

Continuous and intermittent reinforcement

When a response that has become established ceases to be reinforced, it is extinguished. But not at once. If a reinforcement is provided before extinction is complete, this will keep the behaviour going for a while longer, and in this way we can change from an arrangement in which every response is reinforced – continuous reinforcement – to one in which only some are reinforced – intermittent reinforcement. This will maintain the response, usually at an increased rate. Behaviour reinforced intermittently is also much more resistant to extinction, in the sense that the number of responses made after the cessation of all reinforcement is much greater in the intermittent than in the continuous case.

Schedules of reinforcement

We are here dealing with a situation characterized by 'A is followed by B every now and so often.' The rules which determine *when* and *how often* define what Skinner has called 'schedules of reinforcement'. Thus we may arrange that reinforcement is provided only after a fixed number of responses have been made – this is a *fixed ratio* (FR) schedule and produces characteristically very high rates of response. Ratios of one reinforcement to a thousand responses have been maintained with pigeons. On the other hand, we may arrange that after every reinforcement there is a pause of fixed duration during which no reinforcement is given, whether the animal responds or not. This is a *fixed interval* (FI) *schedule*, producing response pauses after every reinforcement, with a build-up in the response rate as the interval draws to a close. *Variable ratio* (VR) schedules maintain a given *average* ratio between responses and reinforcements, but the number of responses required to earn a reinforcement varies, and similarly, with *variable interval* (VI) *schedules*, the interval during which no reinforcement is available changes from occasion to occasion, while maintaining a given average value. Both schedules produce a very steady rate of responding, the rate being much higher for VR schedules than for VI schedules. VR schedules are particularly resistant to extinction and Skinner has pointed out that the reinforcement conditions under which a gambler operates are essentially of this kind. Allowing for the not inconsiderable differences between pigeons and *chemin de fer* players, the notorious persistence of gambling behaviour can at least in part be accounted for in terms of a schedule of reinforcement.

Skinner and his collaborators have made a very extensive study of the effect of different schedules, of their combination and their use in conjunction with stimulus control, whereby a stimulus which has been consistently paired with one particular type of reinforcement schedule comes to evoke the corresponding pattern of behaviour as soon as it is presented. We shall have to consider later the extent to which we can account for more complex forms of behaviour in terms of the interaction of many different schedules and discriminative stimuli to be found in the 'outside world'. (See Chapter 9.) For the moment it is worth noting that in the laboratory the deliberate use of this sort of analysis has been highly successful in developing, maintaining and controlling comparatively simple animal behaviour – suggesting that it is an appropriate analysis at least at this level and under these restricted conditions.

Shaping

We have mentioned reinforcement schedules involving one reinforcement to a thousand responses. Obviously we cannot arrive at such a performance at one go. If we simply put a pigeon into a situation arranged in such a way that the thousandth peck at a key will produce a grain of food, key pecking will never get established, let alone at a high rate. Nor can we change directly from the continuous reinforcement which is most effective in *developing* the response, to this sort of ratio. However, it can be achieved by a *gradual* increase in the response-reinforcement ratio, a gradual shift that is in the exact conditions for earning a reward. As this ratio increases, so does the number of unreinforced responses emitted before extinction. The gradual increase in the ratio thus ensures that the behaviour will not extinguish at any stage of the process, and we are able to arrive at a level of performance far removed from the original one.

In this particular example, the change in conditions involved the *number* of responses required to secure reinforcement. What happens when we change the conditions relating to the *kind* of behaviour that is required?

Skinner has described the process of training two pigeons to play a modified form of ping-pong. This is important, not because there is any particular demand for birds with this sort of skill, but because it illustrates the efficacy of the principles on which the process is based. Although the particular form of the 'game' played uses neither bats nor a net, but simply involves the two animals standing at the ends of a low table, each attempting to propel a ball past its opponent and off the table, it nevertheless constitutes a form of behaviour which is a long way removed from what we ordinarily associate with pigeons. If we consider the principles of operant conditioning, it may at first seem difficult to see how they may be used to achieve this sort of result. Since they involve the reinforcement of the behaviour to be learned, the behaviour must *occur*, before it can be reinforced. If, given a pair of novice pigeons, we impose on them the condition that engaging in a fully fledged game will be reinforced, it is unlikely that either of them will even as much as show interest in a ping-pong ball.

Operant conditioning must necessarily utilize such existing behaviour as has a reasonable probability of occurring. Although at the start of training the final achievement aimed at may be quite certain not to occur spontaneously, the animals' *behavioural repertoire* will contain some components which lie in the direction of this achievement. Thus, if we start with one pigeon wandering about in the presence of a ping-pong ball, it will sometimes be close to, at other times farther away. If we reinforce 'closeness to ball' we soon get a situation in which most of the bird's activity takes place in this area. Under these new circumstances, touching the ball, even pecking it, is quite likely to occur – more likely than it was at the outset. We can now begin to give reinforcement only when the ball is pecked – setting at first comparatively loose criteria for what constitutes a peck, but as soon as this behaviour has become established, tightening conditions so as to reinforce only pecks that move the ball in a specified direction. When the process has been repeated with the other animal, we are obviously a great deal nearer the desired end result and can start on selective reinforcement in the competitive situation. Needless to say, a secondary reinforcer such as a click is used to make possible the very precise timing on which rapid success depends.

This process of 'edging' an animal's behaviour towards a goal, by using a gradual change in the conditions for reinforcement, is known as *shaping*. It depends on selecting at each stage criteria for success, which move the behavioural spectrum towards the goal, and also have a high chance of being met. The concept of shaping makes explicit a principle that is used implicitly in many learning procedures.

When we can in advance map the 'space' between the start and the end point of a learning sequence into a number of overlapping reinforcement conditions, such a sequence of conditions constitutes a *learning programme* and this will be discussed in Chapter 11.

Painful stimulation

In considering the effects of various kinds of A-B relationships to which an animal might be exposed, we have so far focused attention on cases where B is essentially a 'pleasant' event for the animal, a stimulus or situation which it tends to approach, a reward. What if B is a noxious, or *aversive* stimulus, one that an animal will tend to avoid? Painful stimulation gives rise to a whole complex of physiological changes, such as increased heart rate or dilation of pupils, changes which are characteristic of fear but are common to a variety of emotional conditions, and may be regarded as preparing the organism for intense activity of one kind or another. If such a stimulus is used as the unconditioned stimulus in Pavlovian conditioning, the event with which it is paired will come to elicit reactions resembling those of fear, and being anticipatory in character, they are usually referred to as *anxiety*. Anxiety is a conditioned response to whatever stimuli have been paired with the painful event.

As far as instrumental learning is concerned, the situation is rather more complex. When Thorndike first formulated his 'Law of Effect' it contained a section which stated that 'acts followed by states of affairs which the individual avoids or attempts to change, are eliminated.' Such states of affairs, or *annoyers*, were regarded as having an effect opposite to that of satisfiers or reinforcers. However, this part of the law had to be abandoned. Thorndike's own rejection of it rested on experiments involving the use of the word 'wrong' for incorrect choices in a word-association task. Choices 'punished' in this way tended if anything to occur more frequently in subsequent repetitions. One might question the extent to which saying 'wrong' constituted a punishment, but subsequent experimentation has shown that in more straightforward situations also, punishment, even though it usually decreases the frequency of a learned response, does not in fact bring about a reversal of learning. If rats that have been trained to press a lever in a Skinner box are subsequently shocked for doing so, the behaviour is at first suppressed. But after a rest, and provided no further shocks are administered, the bar pressing responses start up again. If allowed to continue to the point of extinction, the total number of responses made does not differ significantly from that made by animals which have not been shocked. The length of pause required will depend on the severity of shock. If sufficiently severe, the 'punishment' may result in a complete withdrawal from normal activity, and require special therapeutic measures to bring the animal back to its usual behaviour. The reflex responses characteristic of fear are incompatible with ongoing organized activity and in this sense seem to prevent the learned behaviour while they last, rather than affect response tendency in the long run.

If, having conditioned an animal to respond on, say, a variable interval schedule involving food reinforcement, we introduce a mild electric shock for every response that is made, but continue at the same time with the VI food schedule, the rate of responding drops initially, but soon regains its initial level. The punishment is effectively discounted. With more intense punishment the response rate drops further and may not entirely recover. Severe punishment can lead, as we have indicated, to a total withdrawal from normal activity, but in no circumstances does the introduction of punishment simply remove or neutralize the effects of reinforcement.

We cannot, from this sort of evidence alone, conclude that punishment is ineffective in preventing undesirable behaviour, though a consideration of our largely punishment-based attempts to control the behaviour of criminals lends support to this conclusion. But if punishment is not effective, why do people continue to use it? The point is that it *is* effective, at the moment at which it is applied, in stopping whatever activity happens to be going on. Where it has less effect is on the *tendency* to behave in that way, if the behaviour continues to be reinforced. Skinner has pointed out however that it is precisely the immediate success in terminating unwanted behaviour that reinforces the *use* of punishment. Because of the importance of timing in instrumental learning, the immediate success of punishment outweighs the effect of the eventual failure, i.e. as far as the *user* of punishment is concerned. By the time an individual reaches adulthood, punishing others as a way of dealing with undesirable behaviour has become so firmly established that even the intellectual acceptance of Skinnerian principles of learning is not always sufficient to counteract it.

We have been considering the effect of punishment on behaviour that has been, and may continue to be reinforced, and which consequently has a strong tendency to occur. In effect, two contingencies – response followed by reinforcement, and response followed by punishment – are being superimposed and their effects do not cancel out. There is comparatively little experimental work on the punishment of behaviour which has not been previously reinforced.

Escape and avoidance learning

Punishment, as we have used the term, consists of the *presentation* of an aversive (or conditioned aversive) stimulus. The *termination* of unpleasant stimulation constitutes a reinforcement, in the sense that responses that are followed by the withdrawal of aversive stimulation, are learned. Thus a rat can easily learn to turn off shock by operating a lever. Reinforcement by removal of aversive stimulation is called *negative reinforcement* by Skinner (although some authors use negative reinforcement as synonymous with punishment). The learning process thus brought about is called *escape learning*, and though it has some similarities to learning with positive reinforcement, there are important differences. In the first place, negative reinforcement requires the presence of noxious stimulation prior to its removal, and this brings with it a reflex emotional response which interferes with the development of all but comparatively simple behaviour patterns. Another difference is that after one escape, the aversive stimulation must again be introduced before another reinforcement becomes possible. Experiments on escape learning typically allow for an interval after each escape and consequently concentrate on the speed of an individual response, rather than on response rate.

A much more important type of learning situation involves the complete *avoidance* of aversive stimulation. Suppose for example that an organism finds itself in a situation in which a signal, say a buzzer, is repeatedly followed by shock. This is straightforward respondent conditioning, in which the buzzer becomes a conditioned aversive stimulus which arouses anxiety. Suppose that in addition we introduce the rule that a particular response, such as lever pressing, will not only terminate the shock once it has occurred, but will *prevent* its presentation if it anticipates the shock. Under these circumstances the animal will first learn to escape shock, then to avoid it altogether. The interesting and important feature of the situation is that once avoidance behaviour has become established, it tends to continue for comparatively long periods, apparently without reinforcement. For consider the sequence of events. At first we have buzzer-shock-leverpress-termination of shock. This is followed by buzzer-leverpress, a situation in which no reinforcement, in the sense in which we have used the term, seems to be involved. Nevertheless extinction can be delayed for long periods. The resistance of avoidance learning to extinction has given rise to much controversy about the appropriate form of explanation. Practically it means that the organism, as long as it continues to take avoidance action, will remain unaffected by any change in relationship between buzzer and shock. If the shock-producing circuit is in fact disconnected, this in no way changes the course of events as they impinge on the animal. If we think of learning in terms of the effect that the characteristics of the environment, including the changes in such characteristics, have on the learner, the interesting feature of avoidance behaviour would seem to be that it insulates the learner from exposure to highly relevant aspects of the environment.

In this chapter we have described various sorts of contingencies, i.e. relationships between events, including the activities of an animal, which may 'hold' in the animal's immediate environment, and we have described the effect that exposure to these contingencies has on the behaviour of the animal. Particular emphasis has been placed on events called 'reinforcements' which have been left largely undefined, but which may be partly identified with the idea of a reward. Attention has also been drawn to the *timing* in the occurrence of events as an important factor in determining their influence on behaviour.

We have taken for granted the idea of a stimulus and of a response in the sense of not inquiring too closely into what the defining properties of these 'units' are – and indeed, in the particular situations that have been considered, their identification may have seemed intuitively obvious. Skinner has further simplified the observational problem by using in many of his experiments an instrument called a *cumulative recorder* – essentially a pen resting on a slowly moving strip of paper, and a mechanism which, whenever a response, such as the pressing of a lever, occurs, moves the pen a short distance at right angles to the paper's motion. When the pen reaches the end of its travel, it flies back and starts moving again with each response made. It is possible also to record on the same graph events such as the occurrence of reinforcement or the presentation of other stimuli. The whole procedure can be automated and in this way the effect of various reinforcement contingencies as well as their combination can be observed over long periods of time.

To the extent to which the experimenter confines himself to the observation of the record, the identification of 'events' is of course quite straightforward. There is no need for embarrassing decisions as to whether what the animal has done does, or does not, constitute a response, or whether a signal that has been delivered has also been 'received'. In a sense we are here investigating the behaviour, not so much of an animal, as of a box with an animal inside it. This does not deprive the investigation of its value – all behaviour does after all take place in an environment which imposes more or less severe limitations on what it is possible to do – but one must be very careful in extending generalizations based on a particular situation to others that may introduce important new elements. It is also necessary to make a distinction between principles which provide a basis for *changing* behaviour in particular ways, and principles which can furnish an adequate explanation of ongoing behaviour.

3. Reinforcement and motivation

The last chapter described some basic phenomena of a number of simple learning situations. Those concerned with instrumental learning involved, as a central feature, the idea of reinforcement. We saw that responses followed by reinforcement gain in frequency, whereas witholding reinforcement produces extinction ; we also considered various schedules of reinforcement and their effect on the pattern of behaviour. But what exactly is reinforcement? Of all the events that could follow an animal's responses, only some are reinforcing. What makes an event into a reinforcer ?

Food or water are frequently used to reinforce the behaviour of animals. The cue to their effectiveness, however, is not simply to be found in the substances themselves – the animal has to be in a suitable condition, hungry or thirsty ; in general we would say it has to *want* the reinforcer if providing it is to be of any use in an attempt to modify behaviour. Thorndike would have been less successful in getting cats to open the doors of his boxes, had they been satiated, and outside the box, at the start of the experiment.

The behaviour of a hungry cat, put into a small cage and in sight of food, is varied, but it is not random – if by random we mean that all the various kinds of behaviour of which cats are capable occur in some sort of incoherent and unpredictable medley. They will miaow, struggle against the bars, bite them, stretch their paws through – what one calls 'try to get out'. Such 'trying' can take various forms – for example, at the end of Thorndike's experiment it involved string pulling in place of the original struggling and biting – yet with either kind of behaviour we retain the notion of a motive, of a goal, which stays unchanged, though the path towards its attainment may vary. The behaviour is 'goal-directed', and it ends in reinforcement. Asking 'what is reinforcement' and 'what is involved in goal-directed, or motivated behaviour' may be related questions.

One's first reaction might be that there is really no problem. To be motivated is simply to want something, and reinforcement consists in getting it. Wanting something accounts for searching, for goal-directed behaviour. Do we not *explain* a man's behaviour by referring to what he is trying to achieve, to his motives? Once we have been told that a man is crossing the road because he wants tobacco, and provided always that there is in fact a tobacconist on the other side, is there any further room for other sorts of explanation?

As we have indicated in the introductory chapter, different types of explanation are appropriate to different types of inquiry. In most everyday situations the conduct of people or animals is explained by reference to what they want, what they are trying to achieve. The notion of wanting something is taken for granted and not further inquired into – though we might occasionally be puzzled by the problem of how an individual comes to want something that strikes us as unusual. Yet if we put the situation into a different focus we might arrive at questions like 'how do people come to want food, or sex, or money or approval?' or 'what, *other than his actual behaviour*, distinguishes a man who is hungry from one who isn't, one who likes women from one who prefers men?' or again 'when a man or animal engages in what we call searching behaviour, *how does he function?*'

Suppose that instead of a man making for a tobacconist, we have a small electronic gadget making for some electric terminals. If in answer to the question 'why is it doing that?' we were told, 'it wants to get itself recharged', we would probably say, 'never mind about the metaphor, how does it work?' Is this type of question only appropriate to machines and robots?

We want to suggest that for a suitably constructed machine to have a purpose, to want something, is not as far fetched a metaphor as it might seem; and that on the other hand, the question 'how does it function' is legitimate when applied to an organism, human or otherwise. This does not blur over or belittle the enormous differences between organisms and what we now call machines. To look at man or animal *as if* he were a machine may be helpful for certain purposes. It does not mean that one asserts their identity.

Motivation and homeostasis

As a starting point for our inquiry into motivation and reinforcement, let us again look at learning situations involving food reinforcement. Hunger is first produced by depriving the animal of food. Providing food will now tend to reduce the degree of this deprivation, and in adequate quantities satiate the animal altogether. Can deprivation, and repairing the effects of deprivation, serve as a model for motivation and reinforcement respectively?

It is necessary to the survival of an organism for many aspects of its physiological and chemical condition to remain in some sort of equilibrium. Blood temperature and pressure must remain within certain limits, as must the balance of its chemical composition, such as its carbon dioxide, or its sugar content. If there is disturbance of any of these, or other conditions, mechanisms are brought into play which tend to counteract the disturbance and restore equilibrium. Sweating and the dilation of the blood vessels in the skin as a reaction to heat is a familiar example. Provided the external temperature does not fluctuate too widely, body temperature can be maintained stable without involving any activity of the *whole animal*. This internal regulatory process is known as *homeostasis* and has a (very much simpler) counterpart in mechanical or electronic devices such as thermostats, governors that control engine speeds, or the feedback circuits in radio-amplifiers.

In many cases, however, the disturbed balance cannot be restored simply by calling on the body's internal resources. If it gets too hot, the individual must get to a cooler place, clothing must be removed or cold substances, such as water or ice cream, must be introduced into the system. The imbalance arising from lack of food can in the long run only be restored by food intake. The individual may be described as being in a state of need, giving rise to characteristic internal stimulation. This stimulation is called a *drive* and corresponds to what we would subjectively describe as feelings of hunger or thirst, or some other form of discomfort. The effect of eating is both to counteract the state of need and to reduce the hunger drive.

This suggests the following generalized account of an animal's behaviour. In the course of normal internal changes a state of need develops, some form of imbalance which the internal homeostatic mechanisms cannot cope with; this condition is accompanied by internal stimulation, or drive, which in conjunction with the external stimulation to which the animal is exposed at the time, leads to more or less directed 'searching' behaviour. The form this takes will depend partly on previous learning and may also involve innate behaviour patterns related to the animal's condition. In the course of this behaviour, something may happen which reduces the drive, e.g. finding food reduces hunger drive. This we equate with reinforcement. It will modify behaviour and in the course of time the hungry animal's response patterns may undergo extensive change.

This model of behaviour, in which the driving force is provided by stimulation arising from internal need and in which reinforcement is equated with drive reduction, is one that was put forward by Clark Hull[1] in his book *Principles of Behaviour* and has exercised considerable influence over learning research since that time. It has the obvious attraction of making it possible to link motivation, and hence reinforcement, to something other than behaviour – to hours of deprivation, for example. When we make a statement, therefore, about learning as a function of reinforcement, we are stating a relationship between variables that may be independently observed and measured. How well does this learning model stand up in a variety of learning situations?

First of all, it seems to take care of what we have called 'escape learning'. Here, too, the animal's activity reduces – in fact removes altogether – strong stimulation, the only difference being that in the one case the stimuli originate internally as a result of gradual organic processes, whereas in escape situations, the stimuli are produced externally, such as in the application of electric shock. The distinction is not clear cut, as can be seen by considering our animal in a high-temperature environment. Whether removal to a cool place is now seen as helping to maintain an internal equilibrium or as an escape from noxious stimulation, is a question of emphasis, related to the degree of heat to which the animal is exposed, and possibly to the rapidity with which the temperature rises.

How does the notion of drive reduction fare in other learning situations? Certainly a great deal of human learning takes place without the related satisfaction of any basic need like hunger or thirst. But we do not have to go as far as this before we come up against difficulties.

Secondary reinforcement and secondary drive

As we saw in the experiment involving rats in Skinner boxes, the click of the food delivery mechanism, having been repeatedly paired with the arrival of food, could be used to bring about learning of a simple response. The click had acquired reinforcing properties and become 'a secondary reinforcer'. On a more complex level, in a much-quoted experiment by Cowles,[2] chimpanzees who had learned to insert poker chips into a slot machine – known as a chimpomat – to gain a food reward, could be taught a variety of tasks using poker chips as reinforcers. This creation of secondary reinforcers out of originally neutral stimuli is a well-established and important phenomenon which Hull recognized and which suggests a mechanism which might, for example, link the subtle and complex factors influencing human learning to some rather more basic or primary reinforcers. It is, however, a phenomenon which does not really fit in well with a drive reduction hypothesis. What drives are being reduced by secondary reinforcers? Not hunger or thirst at any rate – while clicks may help the rat to learn, they do not lessen his appetite, and, taking a human parallel, the signs of approaching meal time tend if anything to enhance the feeling of hunger. It has been suggested that the effect of pairing a neutral event with a primary reinforcer produces a kind of secondary drive – arising from a 'need' for clicks, or poker chips, or the sound of a dinner gong – and that it is this drive which is in turn reduced by the secondary reinforcement.

Certainly, if we consider human behaviour, some such notion seems to be required. Suppose, for example, that I have an appointment to meet someone – let us say for lunch, to get a food motive somewhere into the picture. I am about to leave but cannot find my car keys. I now engage in behaviour which is directed at finding keys. The particular form it takes will depend on previous learning of where they are likely to be, but whatever the sequence of searching or asking other people, this phase of my activity will be brought to a close when the keys turn up, and be followed by going to the car and making my way towards the restaurant. Again, my activity has an aim towards which there are variable routes. I will also have to find a parking place, and a coin to put in the meter and so on. Although my overall behaviour is directed towards the lunch date, there are a whole variety of *sub-goals* which characterize the detailed stages. Motives seem to be ordered in a kind of hierarchy, those lower down deriving their force from those higher up. Any particular route that is taken towards any one sub-goal could be regarded as reinforced by its attainment.

In a similar way the behaviour of an animal in a problem situation, particularly one where a primary reinforcement is attained at the end of a long sequence of behaviour, often has the appearance of being made up of stages. Such stages become explicit in what Skinner has called the *chaining* of responses, referred to in the last chapter. Thus a pigeon may learn to peck at a key when a green light is on, and not in the presence of a red light, by providing reinforcement only in the former situation. Once this response has become established, we can reinforce another response, say, pecking at another key, by changing the light from red to green. In this way we establish a short behavioural chain, which involves response R1 until the light changes, and then response R2 for a primary reinforcement. By making the effectiveness of the first response conditional on yet other prior responses, the chain can be lengthened.

If we regard pigeon or man as being under the influence of successive secondary drives on a journey to some intrinsic or primary reward, we can keep intact the hypothesis that reinforcement consists of drive reduction. Primary reinforcers reduce primary drives, and secondary reinforcers reduce secondary or acquired drives. But we do so at a cost. Our primary drives were closely tied up with various forms of physiological imbalance for which independent measurement procedures were available. The idea of a secondary drive has a much more tenuous status, and can certainly not be assessed in terms of deprivation.

It might be thought that the concept of acquired drive might help to bridge the gap between such basic needs as hunger, thirst etc. and the enormously varied motives that characterize most of human behaviour. But there is another difficulty here. Secondary drives and reinforcements, as we have discussed them, depend for their efficacy on continued association with primary ones. They are only, as it were, stages within a larger motivational system. A satiated rat loses interest in the clicks made by the food dispenser. Even if many of our complex and interlocking motives did develop as a result of association with more primitive ones, we should have to assume that such derived motives can, in human beings at least, become autonomous, i.e. become ends in themselves without requiring the further backing of the needs and rewards that first brought them into being.

The need for stimulation

It also looks as though we shall have to extend our list of primary drives. While in the case of an adult one could conceivably argue that his interest in stamps or motor cars or mountaineering was somehow derived from other 'more biological' motives through a long chain of experience, when one watches very young children playing, examining things and manipulating them, not only is it clear that this is something they enjoy, but it is difficult to account for this enjoyment in terms of associations with some more basic need and form of satisfaction. Is there a primary curiosity drive perhaps?

The tendency to explore, to investigate novel situations is not confined to human beings. R. A. Butler,[3] for example, gave rhesus monkeys a discrimination problem, which involved opening one of two differently coloured opaque windows. Opening the 'correct' window was followed by a brief opportunity to look out at the laboratory from an otherwise dull cage. The discrimination problem was learned. 'What Butler's monkeys saw' acted as a reinforcement, some views more so than others. Looking out at a toy train, for example, was more effective than looking at an empty room.

What is interesting about this situation is that the reinforcement involves if anything a heightening of excitation rather than a reduction, as is essentially implied in the drive reduction hypothesis. This variant of reinforcement is, of course, found frequently in activities voluntarily engaged in by people, where perhaps the majority of situations regarded as enjoyable are essentially stimulating. The possibility of need for heightened stimulation has been most clearly brought out by a series of experiments on *sensory deprivation* carried out at McGill University in Canada. Volunteer students received high pay for remaining completely inactive and shielded as far as possible from all forms of stimulation. They lay on a soft bed, in a small soundproof room, wearing goggles that transmitted only diffused light, and cardboard tubes over their hands preventing touch. Under these circumstances subjects found increasing difficulty in simple intellectual tasks, they became subject to a variety of perceptual distortions and hallucinations, and above all developed a veritable craving for even the most rudimentary forms of stimulation, such as the repeated reading out of a

Stock Market report. In the absence of some minimum of sensory stimulation the condition of these students deteriorated, and in this sense they *needed* stimulation.

Although we have used terms like need and deprivation, we have here moved away from thinking of them in terms of Hull's original ideas, where a need involved actual shortage of some substance. A need for stimulation is a rather more sophisticated notion not so easy to envisage in terms of disturbed equilibria.

The original notion of need, drive and drive reduction got into difficulties as soon as we moved away from situations involving comparatively straightforward reinforcement with food or water. This does not necessarily matter. Explanations do not have to be universal and can be useful even when they are of only limited application. However, looking again at the same situations that we started with and on which Hull's hypotheses are specifically focused, we find that even here there will have to be some rethinking.

We have seen on the one hand that the timing of reinforcement is critical for effective learning. The intake of food is immediately reinforcing, and in adequate quantities will produce satiation. Yet reinforcement will take place, and eating will stop long before the various consequences of food deprivation, e.g. a drop of sugar concentration in the blood, have been restored. It cannot, therefore, be any part of *this* that constitutes reinforcement. It must be some aspect of the immediate impact of food on the organism, as it passes through the mouth and into the stomach – a kind of sensory message produced perhaps by stimulating various membranes in mouth, throat, stomach, by distending the stomach and so on.

It is possible, by means of an operation, to interrupt the oesophagus of an animal, i.e. the pipe through which food normally travels from mouth to stomach, and bring the open ends to the surface. After recovery from the operation, one can now either feed the animal by introducing food directly into the stomach, or alternatively, allow it to eat in the normal way. Normal, that is, except for the fact that the food eaten does not now reach the stomach because of the interrupted food pipe. Under these circumstances dogs have eaten food equivalent to their own weight before stopping. The activity of eating and the passage of food through the mouth and throat are not, by themselves, very effective in terminating eating behaviour ; on the other hand, the direct introduction of food into the stomach is. Something happens when food enters the stomach in sufficient quantities to stop further eating, to produce signs of satiation. This is not simply distension of the stomach, since the nature of the food and not just its bulk determines the point at which eating stops.

If we consider the drinking behaviour of a dog with such an operation, the pattern is very different. If allowed to drink, such an animal will drink only the amount consistent with its period of deprivation and then stop, despite the fact that no water reaches the stomach. After an interval, drinking behaviour again starts and stops after the correct amount. If, on the other hand, water is introduced directly into the stomach, this does not affect the amount drunk if opportunity to drink is given *immediately*. However, with the lengthening of the interval between the instant of injecting water into the stomach and the opportunity to drink, the amount drunk decreases, until eventually the animal is not thirsty.

It must not be forgotten, of course, that although food or water arrives in the stomach after its passage through the mouth, *both* stages precede absorption, and do not constitute restoration of internal equilibrium in the sense in which we have been considering it. Both stages in fact turn out to be reinforcing, even when they occur separately, so that the reinforcing effect of normal eating or drinking is a complex affair. However, it has been found very difficult to produce learning by the injection of nutrient, in a suitable form, directly into the blood stream. The function of reinforcement seems thus to be confined to the 'announcement' of restoration, rather than to restoration itself.

What emerges from this rather complex picture can in part be illustrated by an analogy. Imagine a factory that uses some material for the manufacture of its product. Shortages can arise in a variety of ways throughout the manufacturing process, and reports about these are relayed to an ordering department, which sets out to locate fresh supplies. This searching activity stops as soon as the purchasing contract for the required amount has been agreed. The activity of the ordering department is set off by messages from various parts of the plant, where stocks are running low, but the termination of its efforts is brought about by other 'messages' which *anticipate* the arrival of any actual material in places where the shortage exists. When things are functioning normally in the factory, the activities of the various departments are appropriate to each other's requirements. It is only when we interfere, such as by hi-jacking a consignment after it was promised, or even after it has entered the factory, that we highlight the *specific signals* that in fact regulate the 'behaviour' of the organization.

It has been suggested, notably by Deutsch in a book called *The Structural Basis of Behaviour*,[4] that the activity of organisms is both triggered and terminated by stimulus messages, which are distinct from the more gradual fluctuations about internal equilibrium. The messages signalling 'hunger' and initiating food searching behaviour occur, typically, well before any serious shortage develops, and those signalling 'enough' occur before re-establishment of equilibrium. Indeed, the processes involved in the digestive cycle are so complex that it is doubtful whether one may meaningfully speak of 'a state of equilibrium' having been reached at any stage. These starting and stopping messages are, under normal circumstances, intimately related to the development and restoration of different types of physiological need ; nevertheless, the effective control of behaviour is achieved by means of these signals, rather than directly by the more fundamental processes which they precede. Significantly, it seems to be the advance signals, produced by food or water intake, that have reinforcing properties for the animal, rather than the subsequent, and in a sense more basic, internal changes. It is, as we have mentioned, extremely difficult to produce learning in animals by using, as a reward, the injection of nutrient directly into the blood. On

55

the other hand, normal eating, eating with an oesophageal fistula, and direct injection of food into the stomach, will all do so.

This separation between the immediate, sensory effects of eating – or other forms of need satisfaction – and the later, often more protracted changes, is important in two respects. It helps to clarify the problem of actual behavioural control and provides a basis for the development of models that can simulate specific aspects of animal behaviour. It also provides an explanation for certain instances of 'maladaptive' behaviour, in situations radically different from those in which a particular species of animal evolved. We can, for example, produce 'forgeries' of normal nutrients. Thus saccharine solution, although it has no food value, is consistently reinforcing for hungry rats. It is also preferred to dextrose solution, which does have food value, but not so sweet a taste.

Reinforcement centres in the brain

Perhaps the most powerful demonstration of the possibility of separating reinforcement from biological need comes from the work of Olds and Milner.[5] They found that the direct stimulation, with a weak electric current, of certain specific areas of the brain can act like a reward. By implanting minute electrodes they set up situations in which an animal could stimulate itself by pressing a lever. Given this opportunity, rats, cats and monkeys will rapidly learn to press the bar, and, in the case of one of these areas, which is near a part of the brain known as *hypothalamus*, will persist in doing so for long periods of time, even in preference to eating. The stimulation thus acts as a reinforcer, although it does not in this case appear to be related to any otherwise obvious state of need. Nearby centres, where stimulation has the reverse effect, have also been discovered. These are such that the animal will learn to perform a response which *terminates* the stimulus. It may well be that under normal circumstances these structures are *involved* in the restoration of biological equilibrium. For our present purpose, however, the experiments afford yet another demonstration that reinforcement and the reduction of need *can* occur separately.

Beyond the location of these *reinforcement areas* little is as yet known about their function. It has been suggested recently by Deutsch that stimulation in these areas affects the separate pathways that are normally concerned with signalling need and need termination respectively – i.e. this sort of stimulation both produces a drive and satisfies it at the same time. The term *pleasure centre* has been used in describing them, but although there is some support for this in reports from volunteer human subjects (undergoing brain surgery for other reasons), the variable and complex associations of the word 'pleasure' are almost bound to be misleading.

It may seem that by laying stress on the stimulus aspects of all reinforcement we have removed any basic distinction between primary and secondary reinforcers. Signals from the mouth or stomach are in no fundamental way different from signals received through the eyes or ears. Nevertheless, there may be an important difference. Secondary reinforcers are by definition neutral at the outset and acquire their reinforcing properties by pairing with a primary reinforcer. These latter signals, such as sweetness of taste, appear to be innately reinforcing – i.e. their properties are, as it were, permanently 'wired in' to the organism, they are rewarding in themselves. Since they are associated with other biological processes, we discover their autonomy only in exceptional circumstances. A learned secondary reinforcer also needs, in the long run, the backing of a primary one, otherwise the property is lost. If poker chips stop buying grapes, they fail sooner or later to maintain the behaviour whereby they are earned. Primary reinforcers on the other hand maintain their rewarding property for long periods, even when they are separated from actual need reduction, as in the case of the fistulated animals, or the use of saccharine. The property of being reinforced by a certain kind of sweet taste is something that is genetically built into rats. It is a taste which in a rat's normal habitat is usually produced by sugar, but it is the taste that guides and modifies the animal's behaviour, rather than the nutritional properties.

We began this chapter by inquiring into the nature of reinforcement, and attempted to explain it in terms of its relationship to motivated or goal-directed behaviour – as a signal or event which marked the end point of such behaviour, at any rate temporarily, and in the sense that its attainment was characterized by a marked change of *direction*. At the same time, we tried to account for motivation by the existence of a stimulus condition, arising out of some sort of tissue need, whose presence initiated and helped to maintain motivated behaviour. Such a stimulus condition constituted a drive, and we saw that although many cases of goal seeking were in fact associated with conditions of this kind, nevertheless there were others in which the existence of drive could not be demonstrated except by reference to the behaviour itself. Drives are not therefore a necessary condition of motivated behaviour, which it may be best to regard as a *mode of functioning* of an organism, for the time being unexplained. Drives can contribute towards such a condition, by starting it and helping it to keep in being ; it is terminated, or changed, by other signals, which also have the effect of reinforcing the particular behaviour which leads up to them. In those cases where the existence of a drive, such as hunger, can be demonstrated, reinforcements can be shown to be related to drive by counteracting, ultimately, the condition from which the drive arose – although we saw that they have even then a certain amount of functional independence, by considering certain types of surgical intervention (interruption of the food pipe) or the use of substitutes (e.g. saccharine). Other signals can be made to enter the motivational condition by being repeatedly paired with reinforcements, acquiring on the one hand reinforcing properties themselves, and becoming at the same time subgoals, or stages in the course of motivated activity. In some cases, where secondary reinforcement consists of the sight or smell of the goal, such signals can also exercise a continuously guiding influence over the direction of behaviour.

There is yet another way in which signals from the environment can relate to goal-seeking behaviour, and that is by serving as a 'trigger'. This may come about, on the one hand by interaction with an existing state of need, such as when, as a result of previous learning, a given signal starts off a particular food-searching routine; or when, during the period of mating behaviour, exposure to a particular stimulus configuration, such as a modelled or actual stickleback, *innately* elicits fighting responses in another. (See Chapter 5.) On the other hand, a signal may set off behaviour towards a particular goal in circumstances where it is impossible, by means other than observing the behaviour itself, to specify an internal condition which may be regarded as constituting deprivation or need. An obvious example would be the case where a question like 'what have you done with my book?' starts off a prolonged search.

Frequently a signal associated with reinforcement can also provide the trigger for motivated behaviour. In human beings, sexual behaviour does not bear any relation to any identifiable internal condition, and it is frequently the exposure to conditions associated with sexual reinforcement, broadly referred to as 'opportunity', which can set in motion activities directed at its exploitation. The sight of attractive food or drink can bring about a desire for eating or drinking in circumstances in which, by any biological standards, the individual is in need of neither, and this phenomenon is also observed in animals. Stimuli closely associated with *possible* goals can thus serve to create a condition of goal-seeking.

Fear as a source of motivation

Many of the examples of motivation cited might be accounted for in terms of acquired drives, but we have rejected this 'explanation', since it seems to rob the concept of drive of its main justification – its relation to some independently identifiable state of deprivation. A possible exception is the case of fear or anxiety. Here the use of the term 'drive' is justified, in that fear constitutes a condition of disturbance of the organism without any necessarily associated goals for behaviour. It can be acquired, in the sense that the *occasions* for experiencing fear may be learned. If we repeatedly pair a neutral stimulus with a painful one, such as shock, the neutral stimulus will quickly come to evoke characteristically disturbed behaviour, accompanied by a variety of physiological conditions such as dilation of pupils or quickening of pulse. There is a difference between pairing a neutral stimulus with reinforcement – a signal which is related to the *end* of a motivational condition – and pairing it with a shock or other painful stimulus, which marks the *onset* of such a condition ; and this also makes it appropriate to speak of acquired drive in the latter condition only – though, by analogy, it might be more consistent to think of the originally neutral signal as a *secondary motivator*, comparable to a secondary reinforcer.

Fear, regarded as an acquired drive, has been used to account for avoidance learning, already referred to in Chapter 2. The problem here was to account for the persistence of avoidance behaviour in the apparent absence of reinforcement. For if we thought of reinforcement in terms of escape from the externally imposed painful stimulus, reinforcement ceased as soon as this stimulus was avoided altogether. If, however, we see reinforcement as a termination of the condition of fear, then the avoidance behaviour may continue to be reinforced by reducing a disturbance which is now evoked by the conditioned stimulus. Avoidance learning is thus seen as taking place in two stages – the development of an acquired drive, and the reduction of that drive by suitable behaviour. This kind of two-factor learning theory is associated particularly with O. H. Mowrer. It is not entirely without its difficulties, since it requires the condition of fear to persist in response to the conditioned stimulus, again in the absence of reinforcement. A possible resolution of this problem has however been suggested in Chapter 2.

The measurement of motivation

Since motivated behaviour involves progress towards a goal, the 'strength' of such motivation may be measured in terms of the obstacles that an individual will overcome to reach it – on the other hand, where motivation can be related to a drive condition, we may choose a measure in terms of length of deprivation, or intensity of shock, in the case of a drive induced by this method. These are not, of course, measures of the same 'thing' – as can be seen, for example, by considering that a measure in terms of deprivation will continue to increase through enfeeblement right up to death, whereas a tendency to overcome obstacles increases at first, and then begins to fall off as the organism begins to weaken.

Various obstacles to goal attainment have been used – making an animal pull against a harness and measuring the force exerted, requiring it to cross an electrified grid and counting the frequency with which crossings are made, combining an aversive stimulus with the goal itself – for example, by flavouring food with various concentrations of quinine – withholding reinforcement and measuring how long it takes for extinction of the response to set in, or again by simply measuring the amount of reinforcement required to produce satiation. These measures of motivational strength also do not show any straightforward relationship and there is no reason why they should, since they must each involve the animal's specific reaction to the nature of the obstacles being used. Which particular measure is used must remain a matter of choice, depending on the purposes for which it is required.

There is yet a further complication. Motivational states do not occur singly, but coexist and interact; they also have different time scales of operation. The condition that keeps a student at work to gain a degree exists alongside, now a need for food, now an urge to see a film, or to take exercise. A different kind of measure of 'strength' would seem to be required, taking into account the relevant time scale, and the example really highlights the importance of the period of observation in relation to the study of motives generally. It also points to two aspects of goal-directed behaviour – the tendency to maintain an orientation towards a given stimulus or range of stimulus situations, and the urgency or force with which a goal is pursued at any one time. Urgency and persistence do not necessarily go together.

These problems of quantification make it impossible to discuss in completely general terms the relation between strength of motivation and learning. Animal studies in this area have inevitably concentrated on clear-cut biological drives, the variable of strength being of the urgency type and measured usually in terms of deprivation. P. L. Broadhurst,[6] for example, used oxygen deprivation, requiring rats to solve a discrimination problem under water. The problem involved choosing one of two differently illuminated doors, the 'correct' door being open, and leading to air, the other being locked. Three levels of task difficulty were used, involving greater or lesser differences in the level of illumination. At the same time, the intensity of motivation was varied by keeping the animals submerged for 0, 2, 4 and 8 seconds before being able to swim towards the choice point. The result showed that, in terms of correct number of trials, the optimum level of motivation varied with the difficulty of the task. With the easiest discrimination, best results were achieved after 4 seconds deprivation, with little impairment thereafter. With the most difficult task, optimum discrimination occurred after two seconds, followed by a very marked decline for longer periods.

The result is in accordance with a finding which has been confirmed in a variety of situations, including the use of human subjects, where motivation is usually varied by inducing different degrees of anxiety about the outcome of the learning trials. It is known as the 'Yerkes-Dodson Law', and can be stated as follows: The optimum level of motivation for learning decreases with increasing task difficulty.

A wide variety of experimental investigations support two general findings about the effect of high levels of motivation on the way an organism interacts with its environment. There is on the one hand a narrowing of the behavioural repertoire, i.e. responses made tend to be limited to those characteristic of the motivational condition; on the other hand there is a corresponding restriction of perceptual sensitivity to stimuli or aspects of stimulus situations which are closely associated, innately or through previous learning, with appropriate forms of reinforcement. In human terms, a man who is extremely hungry is likely to show less variety of behaviour than one who is comparatively satiated; he is also likely to notice particularly those aspects of his surroundings that are associated with food, and to ignore others, unless they are particularly salient. This suggests the following explanation for the Yerkes-Dodson Law. To the extent to which behaviour is more restricted in the high-motivation condition, the correct behaviour, if it involves a pattern which is unusual in that condition, will tend to occur less frequently, or may fail to appear altogether. There is hence no reinforcement and no learning. At the same time, even if the correct behaviour occurs and is reinforced, the relevant aspects of the situation may not be attended to, and hence fail to be associated with the response made. If we think of reinforcement as an event which is 'significant' for an animal, increasing motivation will tend to make the corresponding reinforcement more significant and accentuate its effect. At the same time, increasing motivation will tend to restrict the variety of other stimuli which are attended to, an effect which, as far as learning is concerned, works in the opposite direction. The combination of the two leads to a cross-over point which defines the motivational optimum for a given level of perceptual difficulty.

We have tried in this chapter to present motivation as a condition of an organism, characterized by directed behaviour and by a sensitivity to specific cues or stimuli which serve to terminate or guide that behaviour. Such stimuli also have reinforcing properties, as defined in the last chapter. Certain types of motivational condition can be induced by depriving an organism of substances required for its survival, and in these cases reinforcement usually takes the form of providing these substances – but reinforcement, defined in terms of its effect on learning, is not confined to such situations. A motivated condition represents a particular sort of involvement of an organism with its environment, and in this sense reinforcements, being stimuli which are prominent in this involvement, have been referred to as 'significant' events. In the last chapter we described how the relationships that existed between other events, including responses made by organisms, could, by being paired with reinforcement, come to be internalized, producing modified forms of behaviour. To the extent to which this new kind of behaviour now makes its appearance in the context of the corresponding motivational pattern, it may be helpful to think of learning as involving an enlargement or modification of the structures that underlie motivated or goal-directed behaviour. A description of structures having the properties required for producing both characteristic behaviour and its modification under the influence of the environment would then constitute an explanation, both of behaviour and of learning. And this brings us to the topic of the next chapter.

4. Theories of learning

If someone puts a coin into a cigarette machine, and as a result hears a recording of the overture to *Tannhäuser*, he is likely to be surprised. He would be ready to receive a packet of cigarettes, without necessarily having at any time formulated this as a verbal statement about the relationship between coins, cigarettes and certain kinds of machines. The vast majority of actions we undertake – turning the steering wheel of a car, asking someone to pass the salt, boarding a particular train on the way to work – involve expectations and beliefs, usually implicit, about how things work and about the consequences of what we do. Life would hardly be possible otherwise. Sometimes, of course, those expectations turn out to be wrong, and it is mainly on such occasions that we become aware of having in fact anticipated something – as it turned out, something else. But even in the absence of surprises, if we watch people go about their daily lives, particularly when it involves some well-practised routine or a familiar situation, it becomes apparent that there is a general readiness for what happens, whether this is the effect of their own previous 'preparatory' action, or of other external factors.

Having a particular way of dealing with the world is not, of course, the same thing as being able to make verbal statements about it. People who are highly skilled, physically or socially, are often quite incapable of formulating why they do certain things when. Being adapted to one's environment does not presuppose being able to describe it, and this is certainly true of animals. Yet descriptions of the way things hang together can and do provide for human beings the basis for correct as well as false anticipations of events. Such verbal generalizations are the beginnings of theory. In this sense we are all using theory a large part of the time. One essential aspect of a theory is that it consists of statements which make predictions about events;

and this is a feature which scientific theories share with the far less stringent and more widespread generalizations, notions and beliefs which influence our everyday behaviour.

It might be argued that not all theories enable one to predict future events, but those which do not can hardly be said to have the status of scientific theories. Indeed one of the explicit aims of a scientific theory is to be able to predict, if only as a test of its adequacy as an explanation of past events. To predict, and sometimes to control, is therefore one of the reasons for which theories are formulated, in psychology as in other sciences.

The term 'theory', however, tends to be associated with abstract and specialized statements in science. Since to the layman such statements are frequently meaningless, and since in addition highly efficient action is frequently taken without the benefit of verbally formulated principles, theory and practice are often contrasted, with the suggestion that theory is a sort of inessential by-product.

Scientific theories, however, are much more than this. Once written down or recorded in some way they become objects in their own right. They can be used as a guide by other workers, can be tested, discussed or criticized; they have become part of the accumulation of science. As such they have an important directing influence on further experimental work.

A theory must explain more than just the facts it is devised to explain; to be of any use it must be general enough to comprehend situations still untested; it may even contain some surprises. On the basis of such a theory it will be possible to predict the outcome of future events, some of which may be outside the range of situations it was designed to cover. As we saw in Chapter 2 Skinner uses his notion of reinforcement schedule, developed in observing the responses of rats and pigeons, to explain gambling. Whether or not this particular attempt is successful, it illustrates the type of explanatory extension possible with good scientific theory.

Once such theories exist they will be tested. For their authors they provide an organization of data from previous experiments and further work will be carried out guided by the theory. Other experimenters will test predictions of the theory in situations which happen to interest them and sometimes, no doubt, will set out to disprove a theory if their own theoretical approach is different. A large body of the experimental work in psychology has been carried out not to solve some practical problem but because a particular theory predicts a particular outcome.

Some theories are remarkably resistant to disproof, but they are usually amended in the light of contradictory evidence and this dialogue between theory and experiment represents the most important directing influence in experimental psychology. In order to provide a background to discussions of experimental work this chapter gives a brief description of some of the important areas in learning theory.

S-R theories

The most important features of this group of learning – and more generally, behaviour – theories, are contained within the title: the letters 'S' and 'R' and the hyphen between them. S stands for stimulus, R for response, and the hyphen for some sort of connexion or bond. Behaviour is seen as a transaction between the stimuli that impinge on an organism, and the resultant responses. Learning involves more or less lasting changes in the relationships between them.

Any scientific theory must ultimately be translatable into something that can be observed. Since in psychology we are dealing with organisms that act in an environment, behavioural and environmental variables will have to occur somewhere within the statements made by a psychological theory. The name 'S-R' makes this explicit. There is also the further implication that the environment can be described in terms of units called stimuli, the activity of the organism in terms of units called responses, and that these are different, but somehow connected to each other. Such a description is comparatively straightforward, when we are considering situations such as those of Pavlov's dogs, who learned to salivate when a bell or a buzzer was sounded; though even here there are difficulties in arriving at an exact definition. These difficulties increase with the complexity of the circumstances in which learning takes place, and S-R theorists have tended in their experimental work to confine themselves to situations which minimize the problem of definition.

The most influential of S-R theorists was Clark Hull, who published his *Principles of Behaviour*[1] in 1943; a modified form of those principles appeared posthumously in *A Behaviour System*[2] in 1952. Although many further changes have been made in the original conception by subsequent workers, notably Spence and N. E. Miller, Hull can without question be regarded as the central figure in this group of theorists, and possibly in the whole area of learning.

Hull tried to model the form of his theory on that of physics as the senior science, particularly the Newtonian system. Accordingly it is comprehensive, purporting to provide the framework for an account of all mammalian behaviour; it is also highly formalized, being composed of a series of postulates, theorems and corollaries. From these, empirical predictions are derived which serve to check corresponding parts of the theory. If experiment does not support the predictions made, some modification of the theoretical structure is required. In practice, elaborate systems of this kind can be highly resistant to the assault of facts at their periphery.

There are, within Hull's system, three kinds of variable. Two of these are observable, relating to input – such as intensity of stimulation, degree of deprivation of the organism, number of reinforced trials – and to output or response – such as the amplitude, probability of occurrence or *latency* of responses. (The latency of a response is the interval between it and the eliciting stimulus.) The third category consists of *intervening variables,* related by equations to both observable classes, acting as a sort of bridge between them, to facilitate thinking about the relationship between terminal events. For example, *habit strength* is such an intervening variable, symbolized by sHr. It is functionally related to the number of times the joint occurrence of a particular stimulus and a particular response has been followed by reinforcement. The form of the relationship is given by the equation $Hr = 1 - 10^{-aN}$ where 'N' is the number of reinforcements and 'a' is a constant. Habit strength represents the degree to which learning has taken place. Another important intervening variable is *reaction potential* (sEr), a measure of the likelihood with which a given stimulus will in fact evoke a given response. It depends on habit strength, and also on drive, this being a function of the extent to which an organism has been deprived of some requirement such as food or water. Reaction potential is reduced by *reactive inhibition* (Ir) and *conditioned inhibition* (sIr), variables which are most easily thought of in terms of fatigue developed in the course of responding. There are many more variables, and their relationships are complex. Unfortunately the impression of detailed precision that this creates is largely illusory, because of the difficulty of relating the 'observable' variables in the theory to actual observations in any but the simplest experimental conditions.

In Hull's system, the strength of the relationship between S and R depends on reinforcement. This requirement provides one of the major divisions among S-R theories, some theorists like Guthrie maintaining that learning can be accounted for purely in terms of the joint occurrence of stimuli and responses, without the need for a special type of event to strengthen their union. Hull identified reinforcement with drive reduction, a rapid diminution in the stimuli arising from need conditions. He also postulated that the effectiveness of reinforcement in strengthening a particular S-R link depended on the interval of time between response and reinforcement. In this way he was able to account for findings such as that, in maze learning, blind alleys closest to the goal are eliminated first, long blind alleys are omitted sooner than short ones and that there is a general increase in the speed of running as the goal is approached.

As we have already seen in the last chapter, the equation

of drive reduction with reinforcement runs into serious difficulties in the many situations in which learning occurs apparently in the absence of any recognizable deprivation or state of need ; as indeed do all the theorems and postulates when we move away from very simple experimental situations. But it is important to remember that a theory should be judged not only by the accuracy of its predictions, or the range of situations to which it applies, but also by the effect it has in stimulating further research – even if the results of such research show up shortcomings and inadequacies. Hull's system has generated a very large volume of experimental work, with accompanying refinements in experimental technique and design. It is better that a theory should give rise to testable though unconfirmed predictions, than that it should remain intact through failing to make adequate contact with observable events.

Cognitive theories

While the experiments of S-R theorists concentrate on situations in which the identification of stimuli and responses do not create excessive difficulties, and S-R reinforcement theorists on experiments in which this also applies to reinforcement, cognitive theories have emphasized learning and behaviour in more complex circumstances. Here we find attention being drawn to aspects of behaviour which we might ordinarily describe as 'insightful' – in the sense that behaviour appropriate to the situation makes its appearance comparatively suddenly, without evidence of gradually strengthening S-R bonds – or to goal-directed or purposive behaviour – where the result of learning appears to be not so much particular behaviour patterns as the establishment of a goal, towards which a variety of behavioural routes are available. Thus in one experiment, rats who had learned to *run* a maze without error, were found to *swim* the maze correctly, when it was flooded. Such a result – hardly surprising to a layman – is difficult to reconcile with a position which regards learning as the establishment of specific stimulus-response connexions. Cognitive theorists talk about place rather than response learning, about the development of *cognitions*, rather than S-R bonds. Tolman,[3] for example, used terms like *cognitive map, expectancy*, and *means-ends readiness* – a special kind of expectation involving the animal's own behaviour (means) for bringing about a particular result (ends). If this result is attractive to the animal, the means for achieving the result are mobilized, and may take a variety of forms, such as running, swimming, rolling, etc. The animal develops a tendency to approach a particular goal, rather than the movement, in sequence, of specified muscle groups.

We are all familiar with the kind of learning that Tolman is talking about, but unfortunately he does not provide any *explanation* of how cognitive maps in fact lead to appropriate behaviour. Tolman has been accused of leaving his animals 'buried in thought', since he fails to describe any mechanism or functional rules for bringing about behaviour. Cognitive theories serve the important function of drawing attention to learning situations in which a measure of what we normally call 'understanding' is produced; they also emphasize the goal-directed or purposeful aspects of behaviour. They fail, however, to provide any kind of model of how understanding or purpose *works*. Such explanations as they offer consist effectively of an appeal to the familiarity of comparable phenomena in human experience.

If cognitive theories do not manage to explain the features of learning to which they draw attention, they nevertheless cause embarrassment to early forms of S-R theory. Attempts have been made to meet some of the difficulties by the introduction of extra concepts. Thus situations involving 'expectancy' are met by the postulation of an *anticipatory goal response* – a response which is essentially some fragment of the total response made in the presence of the goal, making its appearance prematurely, and mediating anticipatory behaviour. The concept of *afferent neural interaction* recognizes that the immediate neural effects of external stimulation may combine and interact in various ways prior to evoking a response, i.e. it recognizes some sort of perceptual organization as a stage in the production of behaviour. However, no rules are provided for this interaction, nor does it fit in very easily with the rest of S-R theory. Concepts such as these, together with *movement produced stimuli* and *non-overt responses*, constitute a recognition of the need for taking processes within the organism into account, a move towards an S-O(rganism)-R theory. The problem remains to find adequate models for the functioning of organisms, to replace the analogy to a rather complex telephone exchange which still appears to underlie S-R theories, even in their more modern forms.

Behaviour theory and physiology

One way of bringing the organism more explicitly into the picture is by considering the behaviour not only of the whole, but also of its components. The integrated activity of an animal must after all tie up with the more detailed functioning of its parts, i.e. behavioural and physiological descriptions should be able to meet. Although it may be totally impractical to provide a detailed account of an action such as opening a door in terms of statements about nerve impulses and muscle contractions, it may be worth while to see how the physiological components of the organism *could* interact to produce the functions necessary for complex behaviour, without departing (too far) from what is known about their properties. This approach has been taken by D. O. Hebb in his book *The Organisation of Behaviour*.[4] It is obviously beyond the scope of this discussion to provide the degree of physiological background which would allow an account of Hebb's theory in any degree of detail. Nevertheless, an outline of the basic ideas may be attempted.

Nervous systems are made up of large numbers of interconnected nerve cells called *neurons*. In human beings the number is estimated to be around ten thousand million. They are interconnected in the sense that each neuron has many branches which terminate in contact with other neurons. In turn each neuron receives the terminals of many others. The points of contact are called *synapses*, and under given circumstances, neurons may be made to be active, to 'discharge', as a result of the activity of neighbours. Thus activity can be transmitted, and in fact the mass of nervous tissue is constantly active in changing patterns, the complexity of which is suggested by the number of cells potentially involved.

A part of the network consists of cells which are specialized, in the sense that they translate stimulus energies of different kinds – light, vibration of the air, chemical stimulation – into a standard form of activity for the nervous system. These are the *sense receptors,* located in the sense organs, as well as the skin, muscles, joints. Part of the system also *terminates* in muscles and glands, initiating and controlling their activity. There was at one time a temptation to liken the nervous system to a kind of telephone exchange, routing incoming messages to particular muscle groups. This is an entirely misleading comparison, which has, however, deeply infected much of S-R theory.

Consider a pattern of stimulation affecting the sense receptors, such as the presentation of a geometrical shape, producing both a temporal and spatial pattern. Its impact on the organism will be a function, not only of this pattern, but also of the activity that happens to be going on at the time within the organism's nervous system. This in turn depends partly on its more permanent properties, such as differences in the ease with which particular synaptic transmissions take place. To make a crude, limited, but possibly helpful analogy – if water is thrown onto a hillside, the flow that ensues is a function partly of the amount, direction and distribution of the water thrown, partly of the nature of the flow already going on and of the structure of the sloping surface, its grooves and gullies, defining as it were preferential patterns of flow. If we equate perception with aspects of the activity of the nervous system when exposed to sensory stimulation – and we have little alternative – it is brought home forcibly that perceiving is an *interaction* between external events and the organism, which is constantly active and has its own particular properties.

Despite this contribution of the properties of the nervous system on which a particular stimulus configuration impinges, if a given pattern is repeatedly presented – and it is in the nature of our environment for this to happen – certain networks of neurons will be more active than others as a result, and in this sense they correspond to the particular sensory input. If we now suppose that as a result of activity being transmitted across a particular synapse, future transmission is somewhat facilitated, the effect of repeating a given sensory input is to create, within the nervous system, a sort of 'preferred' set of networks, the outcome of repeated inputs acting on previously facilitated paths. In this way there develops within the nervous system a structure, though a flexible one, which tends to play an increasing role in channelling incoming sensory information. The situations to which the organism is exposed will tend to produce within it priority patterns of neural response which correspond to these situations. Since neural activity is intimately related not only to the sensory input, but also to the output of 'instructions' to muscle groups, we have here a basis, though admittedly highly schematic, of the way in which the integration between an organism and its environment might develop.

Hebb's proposal, that the occurrence of synaptic transmission facilitates future transmissions, has not been established by direct physiological methods, but neither has it been shown not to be the case. The hypothesis forms a critical step in Hebb's general theoretical position in regard to behaviour, and at the same time makes testable predictions within physiology.

Within a mass of interconnected units, of the degree of complexity that we have indicated, it is to be expected that there will be a virtually unlimited number of closed circuits, i.e. circuits in which it is possible to start on a particular neuron and, by following along one of its branches to the next, and from there to another, to arrive back at the starting point. It has been suggested by Hebb that such structural circuits might, under the influence of patterned and repeated stimulation, form functional groups, or *cell assemblies,* which can sustain their own activity even without being 'driven' from outside, extending activity beyond actual stimulation, and thus further facilitating the formation of preferred modes of functioning. Hebb has further shown that given the central assumption of synaptic facilitation through use, the simultaneous activity of several cell assemblies will tend to develop yet more complex functional units. If we add to this picture the fact that neural activity occasions in the neuron a brief period, during which it is unexcitable or 'refractory', we can see that the functioning of such circuits will also have important temporal characteristics. Hebb has called such large groups of related cell assemblies *phase sequences.*

The system proposed by Hebb makes possible plausible descriptions of many different facets of the behaviour of organisms. Motivated behaviour, for example, may be seen as being occasioned by a phase sequence kept in activity by the constant input of a particular signal, such as might be produced by a condition of deprivation somewhere in the organism. At the same time, the self-maintaining characteristic of the phase sequence obviates the need for a constant and sustaining 'driving force'. Instead we may think of a circuit which is such that activity within it is most effectively terminated by the occurrence of a particular input into the organism. Such a condition would be appropriately described as a 'search' for that input. As has already been indicated in the chapter on motivation, the conception of a reinforcement as something that 'switches off' an ongoing activity, rather than as something which restores a state of depletion or deprivation within the organisms, is in accord with a great deal of accumulated evidence. At the same time, it must be pointed out that the idea of a phase sequence being more firmly established (i.e. reinforced) as a result of being 'switched off' or terminated in a particular way does not fit in very well with Hebb's system as it stands.

An important feature of this kind of theory which, starting with very small units having comparatively simple properties, describes how increasingly elaborate systems with much more complex functional properties might be developed, is that it lends itself particularly well to computer simulation. We can, that is, build into the computer the proposed properties of the component parts, and discover in a practical way the consequences of exposing such an arrangement to various kinds of 'experience'. The computer makes possible the working out of such consequences in a way that pencil and paper operations cannot attain, in practice if not in principle. By comparing the behaviour of such a simulated organism – or part organism – with that of a real one, we can be led to make modifications in the postulated principles which bring them more into line with actual observation. (Indeed it might be possible in time to hand over to the computer some of this comparison between actual and simulated behaviour, making it into a kind of primitive theorist.) Hebb's theory has been subjected to this kind of treatment (by Milner[5]) and it has been shown, for example, that in order to prevent an unlimited mushrooming of phase sequences, it is necessary to introduce an inhibiting as well as a facilitating elementary unit. There are indications that inhibiting neurons do in fact exist within the nervous system.

B. F. Skinner

In his attitude towards the development of a science of behaviour Skinner represents a complete contrast to Hebb. In the first place he has always insisted that he is not in fact concerned with the construction of theory, claiming that in the present state of psychological knowledge such an undertaking is premature. Instead he has concentrated on discovering what can in fact be done to affect and change behaviour, under circumstances sufficiently limited and restrictive to make prediction possible, and by using a number of well-defined procedures. Again he has been a strong opponent of 'physiologising' in psychology, regarding this as quite unnecessary to the development of methods for controlling behaviour. Along with a number of other psychologists, his position has been described as a 'psychology of the empty organism'. This is by no means a *final* denial of the relevance of physiological observations to the more large-scale behavioural units that are the primary interest of the psychologist, but one regarded as appropriate to the present stage of development.

Although Skinner's is essentially an S-R point of view, there are some deviant features. They lie in his distinction between operant and respondent behaviour. As has already been pointed out, respondent behaviour is produced or elicited by a particular stimulus input – it is completely predictable, essentially a reflex. Operant behaviour on the other hand is 'emitted' by the animal, and it is pointless to look for detailed causal antecedents. It is this concept of 'operant' which may conceal the essential feature of goal-directed or purposive behaviour. However, such operant behaviour may be brought 'under stimulus control' by being repeatedly followed by reinforcement in the presence of some distinctive stimulus. The effect of reinforcement under these circumstances is not only to make the selected behaviour more frequent, but also to provide the stimuli present at the time with the power to act both as secondary reinforcers and as SDs – i.e. as stimuli which are the 'occasion' for reinforcement (signs that reinforcement will occur). If reinforcement occurs consistently in one situation and not in another, the favourable situation will begin to bring about the rewarded behaviour – which will then be under stimulus control. Sequences of responses are produced by 'chaining' – in which the stimulus terminating, and reinforcing, one response in the sequence, is also the occasion, or SD, for the next. By the time that a response has been brought effectively under stimulus control, there is not a great deal to distinguish it from a respondent, except that it is not describable in detail. In so far as we can describe what it achieves – the moving of a lever for example – we could think of an operant as a small goal-directed unit of behaviour, stimulus control being the setting of an objective by means of the controlling stimulus.

Skinner's work on schedules of reinforcement (investigating the effects on behaviour of sustained patterns of intermittent reinforcement, which are more characteristic of the kinds of reward contingencies we might expect to operate in 'real' situations) and on the shaping of behaviour (using systematically varied reinforcement contingencies to guide an animal from one behavioural repertoire to another, a methodology for producing really *new* behaviour in an organism) has given him a unique status among contemporary psychologists. Being quite explicitly *control* oriented, being concerned with the development of methods for changing and regulating what an animal does, he has developed ideas and procedures which actually enable others to do just that. As a result, Skinner has gained a large following, in the U.S.A. and to a lesser extent in this country, of people who are primarily concerned with exploring and refining 'operant techniques' in a variety of situations, and applied to a variety of subjects ranging from pigeons to human sexual deviants.

Skinner's contribution to psychology is best judged by taking his claim not to be a theorist at its face value, and regarding his activity and that of his followers as the elaboration of an effective technology. However, although his concepts were developed in relation to highly controlled and circumscribed laboratory situations, Skinner has consistently extended them to a description of behaviour in more complex circumstances. This is effectively a claim that the development of behaviour in an individual under ordinary circumstances is the result of the joint impact of large numbers of interlocking contingencies of reinforcement and that his behaviour is 'under the control' of a very large number of stimuli acting consecutively or at the same time. In other words, Skinner is putting forward not only a method for influencing behaviour, but an explanation of how all behaviour is brought about. This is a very different proposition. It is as though having discovered that human beings and animals obey the law of gravity, an attempt is made to account for behaviour in gravitational terms. We can always, however complex the system that we are dealing with, find conditions in which its behaviour can be described in comparatively simple terms. Such a description may be of great importance in any attempt we may wish to make to change the behaviour. One must however be very tentative in suggesting that the system can be *completely* described in terms of rules formulated on the basis of its operation in highly limiting circumstances. Skinner has, for example, made a very unconvincing attempt to describe language and the use of language in terms of re-inforcement and stimulus control. As we shall see in a subsequent chapter, the learning of verbal material, indeed of any subject matter, can be influenced, sometimes very effectively, by creating situations which embody Skinnerian principles. But the discovery of a limited number of rules whereby the behaviour of, say, a computer may be affected is not equivalent to a full account of its operation, and the insistence that it is may blind one to other unsuspected potentialities. It may also have the effect – quite unjustifiably – of making people call into question related findings and techniques which have in fact been adequately substantiated.

Models and analogies

A great deal of scientific development takes the form of using analogies. We observe the behaviour of a particular system and it reminds us of certain characteristics that we have observed in another, with whose mode of functioning we are already more familiar. We can now use the mode of explanation that has been successful in accounting for the working of the second system, as a hypothesis, or model, for thinking about the first. We may find that a similar set of mathematical equations provides a predictive model for both cases.

It is important to realize in making comparisons of this kind that it need not imply an indentity, or even similarity, in the *physical components* of the two systems, only in their functional relationships. Thus, for example, it is possible to construct mechanical computers that carry out arithmetical operations of the same kind that can be achieved by electronic means. If we were to observe the output of an *electronic* computer, without knowing anything about its construction, we could, after noting its similarity to the behaviour of a mechanical one, use the type of relationship that was known to exist between the components of the latter as a basis for constructing hypotheses about corresponding relationships within the unknown machine. This does not mean that we would infer the existence inside it of screws, gears and levers, only that we might look for units that had the effect of, say, counting or amplifying a variable, or performing some other kind of transformation between two variables, that we knew to take place within the mechanical model. If our analogy was well chosen, we would find that it put us onto a fruitful track for investigating the structure and function of the unknown system, even though it might be electronic, hydraulic – or organic.

Once we have described a system in terms of 'units' with given functional properties, which can between them account for the behaviour of the total system, this constitutes an important stage – perhaps *the* important stage – in explaining how the system works. It is possible to give such a functional description of the major components of a computer, say, without specifying the particular hardware of which they are composed. A store for binary information can in principle be constructed in an unlimited number of ways, but for the purposes of explaining the operation of the computer it is necessary only to describe the rules for introducing and extracting information.* Thus an attempt to explain the behaviour of organisms in terms of components with specified functional properties does not commit one to a belief in gears or vacuum tubes inside the head, or indeed to any specific *physiological* explanation. This point has been made forcibly by A. J. Deutsch (op. cit.).

One of the outstanding characteristics of organisms is their tendency to maintain or achieve stability, and in a wider sense to move towards goals. At one time, this feature of their behaviour was something that separated them from any existing

* Until the store goes wrong, that is. At that point a knowledge of the construction of the store may become highly important.

mechanisms and machines, which did not include any facility for self-regulation. More recently there has been a great development in machines that achieve stability by noting some aspect of their own performance and using this to influence their subsequent performance in some chosen direction. Such a machine is a *machine with feedback*, the most familiar examples being perhaps heating systems with thermostats, or motors containing 'governors'. In a thermostatically controlled system, the difference between a temperature that has been set as a kind of goal, and the actual temperature at any instant, is made to affect the heat supply in such a way as to reduce that difference. Such an arrangement constitutes a simple *negative feedback* loop – negative, because the effect of the feedback is always in a direction opposite to that of the discrepancy between the internal goal and the current state of affairs. Here, incidentally, we have an example of the way in which a particular function can be achieved with a variety of components. The thermostatic control in a gas oven contains bits and pieces which are quite different from, say, the regulator in an electrical heating system, though its effect might be described in terms of identical equations.

Machines which contain feedback loops are known as *servo mechanisms* and the theory of such systems has been highly developed. Servo systems can be built not only to control highly complex industrial processes – as in automation – but to simulate, in a limited way, the goal-seeking behaviour of organisms. We might, for example, build a machine such that its direction of motion is systematically related to the position of a given light source, relative to that of the machine. Such a machine will be 'light seeking' and there is in principle nothing to prevent one from building into it a facility for responding in a similar way to a variety of different signals. We might further arrange that the machine will respond only to one signal at a time and that the choice of signal will depend on some internal condition of the mechanism. Thus, for example, the physiologist Grey Walter some years ago built a device which abandoned its light-seeking activities when the voltage output of its battery fell below a certain level, and instead returned to its base to be recharged.

If we are going to use machines to provide analogies for the behaviour of animals it will be of obvious advantage to choose such analogies from among systems whose behaviour resembles that of animals as much as possible – little though this may be at the present time. In so far as machines without feedback are not goal seeking, any theoretical description of animal behaviour which is based, either explicitly or implicitly, on such 'open loop' systems will fail to account for this most important feature in their behaviour. One of the fundamental shortcomings of S-R theories of behaviour is that the relationship between stimuli and responses does not contain any feedback. This objection has nothing to do with the insistence that scientific theories must deal with relationships between observables, but concerns the way in which the observables are defined and the *type* of relationship that is postulated as holding between them. Some S-R psychologists (notably N. E. Miller) have advocated the inclusion of ideas taken from cybernetics – the science of control systems – within an S-R framework. Certainly such ideas seem highly appropriate within a theory purporting to account for behaviour and the change of behaviour. What appears doubtful is whether this can be a simple grafting operation, as opposed to something more akin to a total substitution.

5. The development of learning capacity

We have so far been concerned with relatively short-term learning experiences, with pigeons or rats acquiring a specific response such as pressing a bar or running a maze in a comparatively small number of trials.

When we look at, say, the development of speech in humans, from the first babblings of an infant to a budget speech in the House of Commons, it is clear that the scale is vastly different. The most obvious difference lies in the length of the learning experience, years instead of hours, but equally important is the change in the learner during this time.

Every learning experience leaves the learner in a slightly changed state, so that the learning may 'transfer' to new learning experiences, but during the course of learning to speak the development is so general in its effect that it is appropriate to describe it as a change in learning *capacity*. If we compare, for example, a child learning to use the labels 'Mama' and 'Dada' appropriately, with an advocate developing more effective methods of presenting a case to a jury, it is clear that the learning ability is different in kind.

Of course, we also find differences in the level of behaviour between people of the same age. While almost all adults can read, only a small percentage can read and understand papers on advanced nuclear physics. Obviously one reason for this lies in different opportunities to learn, not everyone having studied physics at university. On the other hand, most university departments of physics choose from among the applicants to their course those whom they judge (rightly or wrongly) to be most suitable, most able to learn ; the assumption being that not all people are capable of learning physics even if given the opportunity. To the extent that this assumption is correct, the differences in performance of people of the same age cannot be ascribed solely to different opportunities to learn that *actual performance*, but also to differences, again, in capacity to learn. To differences, that is, in the speed or accuracy of learning or in the level of complexity of skill that can be learned.

Differences in learning capacity can only be effectively tested, of course, by the learning of *specific* skills. There seem however to be general characteristics which involve the ability to learn a large range of skills and there are tests designed to measure this general capacity. People who score highly in intelligence tests, for example, are expected to be better able to learn intellectual skills – any intellectual skills – than people who score significantly less. And there is some basis for this expectation, although the relationship between measured intelligence and intellectual performance, while positive, is far from perfect. The development of capacity with age and the ultimate individual differences in capacity are matters of common experience, but clearly they need explanation.

We mentioned in the Introduction that explanations of the development of behaviour tend to be in two forms, either in terms of structural characteristics, that is, the equipment an individual is born with or develops purely as a result of maturation; or in terms of what happens to an individual during his life. A distinction is often made between 'instinctive' behaviour, which owes nothing to learning and is characteristic of the species, and behaviour which has been modified by experience. Activity serving essential needs – eating, dealing with predators, reproductive and maternal behaviour – is often genetically determined in species which have to fend for themselves from birth or shortly after birth. In recent years considerable study has been devoted to the precise behavioural mechanisms involved in such genetically determined behaviour. It has been shown that activity concerned with care of the young, mating and defending territory boundaries is often initiated by very precise stimuli. Tinbergen,[1] for example, has shown that during the mating period male three-spined sticklebacks attack other males which approach the territory boundary, provided these intruders have the red throat and belly

84

characteristic of males at this period. The fish will attack crude models, provided they are red underneath, with much more vigour than they attack perfect models of male sticklebacks lacking this property. Much of the self and species preservation behaviour of many organisms is controlled by sets of such un-learned 'sign stimuli'. Not all behaviour is of this kind, particu-larly in animals which have a longer infancy (period in which food and protection are provided by older species members, usually parents) and who thus have greater opportunity to learn. In these cases behaviour is less rigidly controlled by innate mechanisms and the resulting learned behaviour is often more flexible and potentially adaptable to a wider range of circumstances.

This is only a general pattern; particular behavioural char-acteristics are often determined partly by genetic factors and partly by the environment. Even those characteristics which are largely maturational in origin are independent only of *specific* environmental effects. Obviously the continued ex-istence of any organism depends on its living in a non-hostile environment and being provided with food. In these circum-stances it is usually possible to discover the contributions of heredity and environment to any given behaviour only by careful study.

An experiment carried out by Carmichael[2] illustrates one particular method of study and provides an example of be-havioural development largely determined by maturation. He raised a batch of tadpoles in an anaesthetic solution until a control group, which had been raised under normal conditions, had developed swimming behaviour. He then transferred the experimental anaesthetized group to fresh water whereupon, within a very short time, they swam as efficiently as the control group. We can assume that in this experiment the genetic constitution was equivalent for both groups and the experi-mental variable was the opportunity to practise swimming, which was denied to the experimental group. The result shows that this does not retard the development of swimming in tad-poles, which is therefore largely dependent on maturation.

Somewhat similar results have been obtained from studies of some types of motor development in children, such as walking and stair-climbing. The Hopi Indians customarily keep children bound to a cradle board for the greater part of the day until they are about one year old. In this position they can move little more than their heads and so cannot practise the limb movements necessary for walking. Dennis[3] studied the time at which walking started in Hopi children from families which still retained this custom compared with those from families in which the procedure was no longer used. He found no significant difference in the average age at which walking started. It seems that the ability to walk develops at a given age largely independent of prior practice in walking.

Talking, on the other hand, is a skill which is clearly dependent on considerable practice and while children may differ in the age at which talking develops on genetic as well as environmental grounds, the opportunity to talk to and listen to other people has a considerable influence on the development of speech. Also the age at which speech is learned and the complexity of its early development may have long-term effects on the development of thinking. In general the early learning of one skill may have effects not only on the later *performance* of that skill but also on the later *learning* of other skills. This relation between early and later learning is one of the most significant aspects of the development of learning capacity and may be regarded as the central theme of the present chapter.

The development of one aspect of general learning capacity – measured intelligence – has received considerable attention. Such studies are often concerned with establishing the *facts* of genetic or general environmental effects on intelligence rather than with investigating detailed relationships between early experience and later intellectual capacity. Nevertheless, they are of interest in giving some idea of the complexity of the interaction of maturational and environmental factors in development, and they also give an idea of the difficulty of establishing baseline facts in this area.

Such investigations are difficult to carry out with humans,

partly because of the difficulty of equating genetic factors; children of the same parents are not genetically identical although they are more similar in this respect than unrelated individuals. Also, it is rarely feasible to adjust the environment of young children for experimental purposes.* A ready-made experimental situation, however, is provided when identical twins, who are genetically identical, are brought up separately. This situation has been exploited in several studies, in one of which, carried out by Newman and others,[4] the environments and intelligence of about twenty such sets of twins was investigated.

It is usually found that identical twins who are brought up together in the normal way have virtually identical intelligence and in the present study those twins raised separately, but receiving much the same amount of education, also had very similar intelligence test scores. As unrelated children of equivalent education would differ on average by about fifteen I.Q. points, this provides strong evidence of the influence of genetic constitution on intelligence. Those twins who received very different degrees of educational experience, however, did differ significantly in intelligence, one pair with very different backgrounds differing by twenty-four I.Q. points. There is also evidence, therefore, of environmental influences on intelligence.

In general such studies show, first, that genetic factors have some influence on the development of intelligence, and second that, if genetic factors are held constant, variations in environment will be reflected in variations in intelligence. They show that intelligence – learning capacity – depends both on environment and on heredity.

The statement that any aspect of a species' structure or behaviour is genetically determined means genetically determined within wide environmental limits; not in the absence of any environment. Carmichael's tadpoles developed swimming behaviour, largely by genetic control, but in an environment

* This has been done, however; see for example Dennis, W. and Dennis, M.G. [1941] Genet. Psychol. Monogr. *23*, 149–155.

which was 'normal' for tadpoles – apart, that is, from the addition of anaesthetic.

In short, every factor of physique or behavioural capacity of every species is controlled partly by genetic pattern and partly by the environment. If it owes very little to inheritance it can vary widely with environment, while if it owes much to inheritance it varies little within the range of environments in which the species can survive. But in every case, the important question is how a particular characteristic develops in detail, i.e. what is the essential process, involving an interaction of hereditary and environmental factors, by which a given capacity develops.

Perhaps the importance of such studies of the development of intelligence is that they lead us to seek optimum environmental conditions for the unfolding of hereditary endowment while indicating that we must accept residual differences in intelligence.

The question of optimum early experience is a very practical one, particularly for parents and teachers, and there has never been any shortage of advice on this topic. Until recently this has been without much basis. We are still only beginning to chart the dimensions along which early experience can be measured, and are a long way from exact prescription.

However, suggestive evidence is beginning to accumulate on the value of rich, as opposed to restricted, early experience, much of it from animal studies. Hebb,[5] for example, has shown that rats reared as pets and allowed to run around a house perform significantly better on a series of maze problems (a rat 'intelligence test') than rats reared in cages in the laboratory. Also the home-reared rats improved more during the course of the tests than those reared in cages. Freedom to move within a large area and explore highly diverse situations (and hence to acquire a wider range of skills) during infancy enables rats at maturity to solve problems more efficiently than rats exposed during infancy to more restricted environments.

There are many further studies of this kind, some involving other animals such as dogs, based on comparisons between deprived and 'normal' animals, or on comparisons between animals in normal conditions versus those with enriched conditions as in the previous experiment. The indications of these are that varied early experience permanently improves later learning capacity. One important aspect of this evidence is that improvement is general: for example, freedom of movement in infancy affects later ability to solve most kinds of location problems.

More recent work is concentrated on two types of problem: first, how does experience during infancy relate in detail to later capacity, and second, does the value of early experience depend on the young animal doing anything in the situation or is passive observation of the environment sufficient. Some results show that response is beneficial and Piaget, for example, bases his developmental theory largely on a notion of interaction with the environment. However, other studies have shown that rats merely *exposed* to a greater range of stimuli perform later as well as rats allowed to *explore* the wider environment.

Although this work on the relation of early experience to later intellectual capacity is comparatively recent, it has long been supposed that early experiences can affect later emotional development and the ability to (learn to) form satisfactory emotional relationships in maturity. Freud, for example, maintained sixty years ago that the basic patterns of emotional interaction are learned by about the age of five, and some of his followers would reduce the age still further. Clear evidence, however, has been difficult to obtain and again the most reliable indications of the importance of early emotional learning have come from studies of animals.

Harlow has shown the importance of early maternal care to rhesus monkeys by separating the young from their mothers and in some cases providing various forms of artificial substitutes, rough models which dispensed milk. Monkeys deprived of maternal care have, at maturity, great difficulty in relationships with other monkeys. They rarely mate and when they do produce offspring the quality of maternal care they themselves provide is very low. Further, when the young monkeys were offered a choice between an artificial mother covered with soft material which did not provide milk and a framework without covering which did, they spent most of their time grasping the soft 'motherly' model and went to the more skeletal food-provider only for milk. The experience of being cared for in the normal way by the mother is clearly very important for the later development of appropriate sexual and parental behaviour and such experiments emphasize the importance in maternal care of bodily contact between mother and offspring. Harlow has also shown, in other experiments, that the opportunity to play with brothers and sisters has significance for the later development of normal sexual behaviour.

It is clear in such studies that the learning of detailed responses is not important. (The responses made by a young monkey when being cared for by its mother are not in any direct way related to the responses it will itself make later in caring for its own young.) The learning that takes place is of a much more generalized kind.

Similar long-term experimental studies of humans are rare, but there are some indications that maternal deprivation during early life both slows down immediate behavioural development and has effects on later social adjustment. For instance, Bowlby has adduced evidence that delinquents often show a pattern of separation from the mother in early life. Implicit in these results is the idea not only that early learning *can* affect later learning but that some things *must* be learned early. The readiness to learn particular skills varies during the life cycle of the individual partly because of maturational processes and partly because the learning of some skills depends on the previous mastery of other skills.

The relationship of learning to particular periods in the life cycle is clearly an important one. Certain abilities can only be acquired during very short periods and not thereafter and, on the other hand, certain skills cannot be acquired until a given stage of development is reached.

Critical learning periods

The most striking example of learning, confined to a particular short period in the life of an animal yet far reaching
in its consequences, is the process known as imprinting. Lorenz[6]
has described how several species of birds, notably certain
ducks and geese, will tend to follow the first moving object
to which they are exposed after hatching, especially if it is
about the right size and makes an appropriate quacking noise.
Of course under normal circumstances this first moving object
will be the mother bird. The effect of substituting at this time a
moving box or even a crouching ethologist are not however
confined to the immediate behaviour. The birds continue to
follow the imprinted object, even in preference to members of
their own species, and will, as time proceeds, attempt to direct
towards the object responses such as mating normally reserved
for other birds. Lorenz has described several 'courtships' involving birds and people and how in particular one jackdaw
fed him continually with worms in an apparent attempt to
gain his affections. In this very short period – a matter of days,
or even hours – the animal learns in effect to 'recognize' a
member of its own species. It is the very dramatic quality
of the phenomenon in some birds that has led to its recognition, but it is very likely that in all animals there are periods
of longer or shorter duration during which there is a
heightened aptitude for certain sorts of learning. If the effects
of such learning are not immediately observable, they may very
well not be detected, and it is an intriguing possibility that the
foundations for people's tastes and interests may be experiences
of comparatively short duration occurring during early childhood.

In contrast to imprinting which occurs in very early life,
more or less immediately on hatching, Tinbergen[7] has described
a situation in which dogs are unable to acquire a particular
ability until a given stage of development has been reached.
Sexually mature Eskimo dogs defend their territory against all

91

other dogs except those of their own group. Sexually immature dogs fail to learn the boundaries of their own or other groups' territories and are continually attacked when they enter the provinces of other groups. In addition they do not assist their own group to defend its territory. At sexual maturity, however, they learn within a few days the boundaries of their own and other groups' territories. They avoid trespassing and they join their own group in expelling intruders. Clearly learning territory boundaries depends on a given stage of maturation. But experiences prior to sexual maturation may well play their part. Although no learning was evident at that time the freedom to move around probably aided them to learn territorial boundaries when the appropriate maturational period for them to do so had arrived. Most learning theories have not as yet taken account of such limited period readiness for learning, but ultimately such phenomena will have to be incorporated. In such cases the most important single factor in the learning process may well be the specific state of the animal, and the environmental conditions under which learning will take place may be capable of wide variations.

Forms of behaviour which appear only at maturity and which occur in all members of a species without prior practice in *those activities*, tend to be classified as unlearned instinctive behaviour. But many such cases can be shown to depend on earlier learning experiences. Riess,[8] for example, has shown that female rats who are raised under conditions in which they cannot learn to grasp or move objects do not build nests when given access to nestbuilding materials during pregnancy. Similarly Birch[9] has shown that female rats reared with collars which prevented them licking themselves, were unable to rear their young. Cleaning the young by licking is one of the typical forms of behaviour associated with maternal care in rats and the experimental group were slow to start licking and continued too long when they did start. Virtually all the pups died, whereas a control group which had worn collars designed not to interfere with self-licking during infancy successfully reared their litters.

It is clear from these somewhat diverse results that learning can depend both on various types or degrees of prior learning and on conditions of the organism associated with a given stage of development. The critical period, the extent of its effect and the type of learning concerned vary from animal to animal and the findings can be applied to man only in the most general way.

Perhaps the greatest similarity between these results and the development of human capacity is the dependence of later learning on the successful acquisition of earlier abilities as this is shown by the work of Piaget.* He has studied the development of intellectual behaviour in children by a method of systematic observation rather than controlled experiment. His methods and his theoretical formulations are very different from those of most other investigators in this field and his work is difficult to compare directly with that of other people; nevertheless it is original and extensive enough to be the most important single contribution.

The work of Piaget

The most obvious characteristic of Piaget's work is his postulation of successive periods or phases of development through which every child passes. There are three main phases, each of which is divided into several stages, but the boundaries between these and indeed between the main periods themselves are not seen as sharp dividing lines but as times when the intellectual abilities are undergoing considerable change. In naming these main phases we run into the first difficulty in relating Piaget's work to more general work in this field – his terminology. The first phase is called the period of *sensorimotor schemata* lasting from birth to about age two. The second is the period of *concrete operations* from two to about eleven and the last the period of *formal operations* from eleven onwards.

* Piaget's publications are very numerous. Perhaps the best introduction to his work is provided by Flavell, J. H., *The Developmental Psychology of Jean Piaget* (D. Van Nostrand, Princeton, 1963).

These names relate to the major types of intellectual activity engaged in during the periods.

During the period of sensorimotor intelligence the emphasis is on immediate perceptual and physical response to aspects of the environment – concept formation is in an extremely concrete, largely pre-verbal, phase. The first few weeks of this period are occupied by the modification and development of coordinations between the reflexes present at birth. The infant gradually begins to follow moving objects with his eyes, to attempt to grasp objects and so on. Between four and eight months a rudimentary purposiveness develops, the child repeats actions which have had interesting results and begins to anticipate. More sustained goal-directed behaviour follows and, after the development of experimentation and exploration, the sensorimotor period ends with the beginning of symbolic behaviour.

The name of the second period, 'concrete operations', emphasizes the fact that during this period the child operates on the environment intellectually – classifies, notes similarities and differences, adds, subtracts, and so on – but still at a concrete level without being capable of much abstraction from the present environment. This period is divided by Piaget into two important *sub-periods*, lasting from about two to seven and seven to eleven. At eleven the child has a fully organized ability to think logically about concrete objects, but not to deal with abstract concepts. This latter ability develops in the period of formal operations. Concrete thinking develops in the sub-period from seven to eleven, while in the phase prior to this the child is still learning to handle symbolic representation and his thought is inadequate in several respects, even for the handling of concrete objects. Thinking at this stage is still *egocentric*, for example the child cannot describe a scene from a position other than the one from which he looks at it, and irreversible, in the sense that the child cannot detach from the sequence of actual events in the environment and is able usually to handle only one property of the situation at a time. For example, a child will say that two containers of liquid of identical shape contain equal quantities, but when the liquid from one is poured into a narrower vessel will say that there is now more because the level is higher. This changes at about seven when the 'principle of invariance' develops and concrete thinking begins to deal adequately with the environment. The period of formal operations terminates when the child has developed adult forms of thought, including the ability to manipulate abstract concepts, set up hypothetical propositions and so on.

The particular classifications used by Piaget are not necessarily the best that could be devised but his observations provide the most detailed evidence we have on the development of intellectual behaviour. Piaget goes on to suggest various processes which underlie this development. He distinguishes between the unvarying *function* of intellectual behaviour, adaptation to the environment, and the changing and developing intellectual *structures* which subserve this function.

Adaptation – adjusting to and dealing with the environment – is seen as the basic role, indeed almost the definition, of intelligence. Two *sub-processes* carry out the basic function of adaptation, assimilation and accommodation. Assimilation is the process by which a new stimulus or experience is absorbed into and responded to on the basis of already existing cognitive structures, whereas accommodation is the change or development of existing cognitive structures to meet new situations.

While these processes are formally opposed they are not necessarily alternatives and may be better thought of as complementary. A situation can only be dealt with broadly by means of available responses, that is, can only be assimilated; but any situation will be different to some extent from all previous experiences and will require some adjustment in current modes of response, will force accommodatory changes. Thus development at a given time will require both assimilation and accommodation but the relation between them alters with age. In the early sensorimotor period, assimilation is probably a 'routine' procedure while situations requiring accommodation may simply present themselves as obstacles. As intelligence develops, the processes are brought into a more articulated relationship whereby the child will seek accommodatory changes – will search for novelty.

This particular method of coping with the environment while continually developing more complex intellectual structures for the purpose brings about, in Piaget's view, a fairly constant order of development from child to child. This is essentially an interactionist view of intellectual development. All children start with the same modes of adaptation to the environment (within certain limits); the characteristics of the physical environment are similarly fairly constant, and so the stages of development are much the same for all children. Ability develops in a fairly constant direction with given abilities inevitably preceding others. An example of the building of more general and more flexible behavioural characteristics on more restricted abilities is provided by Piaget's observations of the development of grasping a visible object. For a child to learn to grasp an object in the field of view it seems to be necessary that a previous skill has been mastered. This is the ability to grasp a visible object when the child's hand and the object are simultaneously in the field of view. When the child is in this stage, a movement of its hand or the object, so that they are no longer both visible at once, will cause reaching for and grasping the object to cease. But once the operations of holding an object in sight and simultaneously reaching for it have been thoroughly 'linked' the child is ready to develop a more general ability in which it will be able to seize any visible object within reach regardless of the initial position of its hands.

Thus the fairly constant order of development is not, for Piaget, evidence of a large maturational component of development as it is for some theorists, but is essentially the result of a process of learning. Maturation may have some effect on the age at which certain stages are reached and on the ultimate level of development, but the development itself proceeds via interaction with the environment.

Piaget may be said nonetheless to be a learning theorist without a learning theory, or rather with an implicit theory rather different from some of those we have previously considered. One of the most obvious differences between his approach and many others is his attitude to motivation and reinforcement. Most theories take account of the relation between the needs of the organism and the system of contingencies characterizing the environment and postulate that learning is conditional on some optimum relationship of these two factors. This generalized law-of-effect approach does not form part of Piaget's view of learning; he sees the operation of intellectual structures – adaptive behaviour – as pleasurable in itself; it is satisfactory to the infant to grasp an object even if it is not edible. This is not unlike the view, discussed in Chapter 3, that a stimulus which is in some way relevant to the organism's state at a given time may function as a reinforcer. It is reminiscent, in particular, of studies showing that being allowed to manipulate objects or look at an interesting view can act as reinforcement.

In general Piaget has given much more attention to the order of development of behavioural characteristics and to their form than to the necessary conditions for the acquisition of a new response. While paying relatively little attention to the nature of learning itself, the whole theoretical system emphasizes the dependence of intelligence on previous simpler, more concrete and less generalized structures. On the existence of previous intellectual structures, that is, and not on the previous acquisition of specific responses.

Much of the other work we have considered has a similar theme, the dependence of later learning on earlier learning and the absence of specificity in the early learning. The general notion in many experiments, while varying enormously in detail, has been that certain types of early experience, rich versus impoverished or general manipulation versus non-manipulation of objects, has beneficial effects on later learning capacity. There seems to be some general change in the learner as a result of certain kinds of early learning, which affects the later learning of a diversity of detailed skills.

A model of this generalized transfer from one learning situation to another is provided by Harlow's[10] work on learning sets. In these experiments Harlow gave his subjects – rhesus monkeys – the task of discriminating between two objects, one of which concealed some food. Both objects were presented to the monkey, the correct object sometimes on the left and sometimes on the right, and gradually (in 50+ trials) they learned to choose the correct object. Once a given discrimination had been acquired the monkey was given another pair of objects, again with the task of learning which one invariably covered food. After two hundred or so different tasks of this kind (i.e. essentially similar tasks but involving different pairs of objects for each task) the monkeys learned to solve a new problem immediately. The monkeys could not know on the first trial of a new task which was the correct object, so chances of success were fifty per cent, but on the second trial the monkeys chose the same object if they were correct on the first trial, or the other one if they were wrong on the first trial, in about ninety-nine per cent of cases. This effect took place within a relatively short time but is a precise experimental demonstration of change of learning capacity as a result of prior learning.

Harlow calls this development the formation of a learning set, a general ability to solve a particular *type* of problem. While it is obviously a fairly restricted ability and formed within a relatively short time, it demonstrates that learning a number of similar tasks can be instrumental in developing a general ability which does not depend on any of the individual tasks learned. The particular characteristics of the objects discriminated were of no importance; given that each pair differed from all other pairs, the conditions were sufficient for the development of a learning set.

Similarly in the more long-term situations we have been considering it seems that the acquisition of certain types of responses, rather than the acquisition of certain specific responses, improves later learning capacity. While in some ways Piaget's is the most comprehensive description of the successive stages in such a learning process, the theoretical approach developed by Hebb, aspects of which have been discussed in the chapter on learning theory, offers a better chance of understanding some of the mechanisms involved. He has developed a theory which relates the different degrees of learning capacity in different species to differences in their brain structure.

Hebb points out first that there are differences in the speed of learning with age and sometimes differences in speed of learning a given task in different species. We normally assume that humans and other primates learn much faster than simpler animals, but this is only necessarily true of complex habits. The more elementary the task the more likely is an animal to learn it as fast as a man. There are also some very specialized skills which an animal will certainly learn faster than a man. Related to this is the comparatively long infancy of humans and the fact that certain skills seem to develop more slowly in man than in animals; perceptual learning, for example, seems to take longer in primates than in simpler species. As a general approximation the higher the ultimate level of learning capacity reached by a species the slower the learning in infancy.

Hebb relates these facts to the different structures of brains in man and other animals. The brains of animals higher in the phylogenetic scale have comparatively less area devoted to dealing with direct sensory input and a larger area concerned with general non-sensory activity than those of lower animals. This relatively larger non-sensory area probably underlies the greater influence on behaviour of central functions – memory, purpose and so on – as opposed to stimuli from the environment. In general, incoming stimuli can be 'processed' more elaborately in the brains of advanced species and any resulting behaviour can be matched more precisely to, for example, very complex environmental contingencies.

But this processing has to be learned. The essential differences between the learning skills of young children and adults are related to the number and complexity of central responses that are available for a given stimulus. Stimulation for adults is almost always more meaningful than it is for young children. This meaning depends on – is – the number of processes activated by the stimulus, the number of associations already learned. Typical adult learning requires only one or very few trials, while infant learning is usually slow and stumbling; special procedures may be necessary in the laboratory to reduce the speed of adult learning, the use of nonsense syllables for example. If we regard, as a necessary condition for learning, the concurrent activation of two or more brain systems, adult learning is faster because stimuli activate large and complex brain processes with relatively constant organizations, and any two such processes will be related easily because they probably have sub-systems in common. In young children stimuli activate brain processes of limited extent and less stability, and association is more difficult. In other words, two stimuli which are to be associated have, for children, less in common already than they would have for adults, and less permanent reality as objects. For example, Hebb notes that brain damage of equivalent extent does not have the same effect on children and adults. There are cases in which adult patients have retained a high degree of intellectual function- ing after suffering injuries to the brain which in young children would produce serious and permanent deficiencies in cognitive ability. The development of intellectual ability depends on the integrity of the brain in a way in which intellectual functioning of certain types at maturity does not. Particular brain areas may play an essential part in the *development* of a particular ability but not be necessary once the ability is *established*.

Hebb suggests that the growth of intelligence may usefully be regarded as problem solving. Once a particular type of prob- lem has been solved – once the phase sequences necessary for its solution have developed – it does not have to be solved again. Similar problems on subsequent occasions are dealt with more easily and do not necessarily involve the same brain areas as the original solution. Hebb has outlined various theo- retical neurological processes which might underlie this type of development, and these have been briefly described in Chapter 4. His theories have great importance also in any considera- tion of perceptual learning and will be mentioned again in that context. While it is convenient for purposes of analysis to discuss learning under various headings it is obvious that the development of perception, for example, is closely related to the development of other forms of behaviour and any such divisions of subject matter are not absolute.

However, while Hebb's approach has brought some order to this immensely complex area and has stimulated considerable research, it is still a pattern for a theory rather than a theory.

Imitation

We take for granted that children will copy both significant and trivial characteristics of adult behaviour; they will walk with their hands behind their backs because their father does and they will also acquire the language and concept system of the people with whom they are brought up. Imitation is important not only for humans: some species of birds, for example nightingales, do not develop the same song as other members of the species if they are raised in isolation, while other species do. It seems that nightingales have to learn their song from older males and indeed, if reared apart from other nightingales, will tend to copy the songs of other species which they happen to hear. Parrots and budgerigars are well known for their ability to reproduce noises of many different types, including human speech.

There may well be inherited differences in the type of behaviour which can be imitated and in the accuracy with which it is reproduced. This seems a necessary assumption in order to explain why some species do imitate human speech, for example, while others, even with the same opportunity, never do. But while imitation is used as an explanation of the acquisition of such behaviour it is in fact merely a description. The problem is whether it is possible to explain imitation on the basis of more general learning principles.

Imitation is said to have occurred when the learner reproduces behaviour which he has seen (or heard) *because he has seen it*. If a flock of birds fly away when disturbed by a loud noise we do not consider that the last birds to fly away are

101

imitating the first to take off (although in some cases they may be). All the birds have been exposed to the same stimulus – the noise – and this would result in their flying off even if they were alone. Behaviour is classified as imitation only when the imitator has not been exposed to an appropriate stimulus for the behaviour except the sight of the 'model's' actions. The presumption of imitation is strengthened if the learner has not shown the behaviour before and if it occurs within a relatively short time of the behaviour which is copied.

Although imitation is widely recognized as important in human learning and to some extent in animal learning, it has been comparatively neglected by learning theorists. Perhaps the main attempt to explain it has been made by Mowrer,[11] whose explanation is largely based on secondary reinforcement. According to this theory the sounds made by a parrot's owner (or a child's parent) become secondarily reinforcing for the parrot by virtue of their association with the owner who provides direct reinforcement such as food. When at some subsequent time the parrot accidentally makes a similar sound this will have reinforcing properties and will tend to be repeated. In the case of children the emission of the copied sound in the presence of the parents will in addition often elicit direct approval.

Foss[12] has tested this theory using Indian myna birds as subjects. A whistle was played to a group of birds regularly when the experimenter was preparing their food and putting it into the cages and another whistle was played in the absence of the experimenter, several hours after feeding. With another group of birds the same procedure was used, except that the reinforced and non-reinforced whistles were switched. When this procedure had been carried out for five weeks recordings were made to determine which whistle the birds had learned to reproduce. Both groups of birds had learned to reproduce both whistles, showing that in this case the presence of the experimenter or food has no necessary connexion with learning to imitate particular sounds. It is in any case difficult to see how a theory of this type could explain all forms of imitation. It is superficially plausible for talking birds and talking humans where the imitated act – speech – is perceived by the imitator in the same way as the stimulus which is being copied. But, as Foss[13] has pointed out, where a child imitates blinking, say, and has never seen itself blinking, it is matching a visual stimulus with a kinaesthetic stimulus and it is difficult to understand this in terms of Mowrer's (or any similar) theory.

It may be that no single theory will serve to explain all examples of imitation. Imitation as such, particularly imitation of parents, may be reinforcing for children regardless of the particular act being imitated. Children are rewarded for copying particular behaviour so reliably that once a concept of imitation has developed it would be expected that imitative responses would generalize. This may go some way towards explaining the considerable degree of uniformity of behaviour in society which shows that imitation is important not merely in childhood learning.

Among adults, imitation – conformity – is not looked upon with the same favour as in children. Values such as self-reliance and independent judgement are opposed to notions of conformity to the extent that non-conformity (admittedly within very narrow limits) is looked upon as a positive virtue. The problem for social man thus becomes that of selecting appropriate areas for conformity and non-conformity, which might be described as non-conformity by consensus.

While there are many interesting detailed results, the present contribution of psychological studies of development to the technology of child raising is still schematic and incomplete. It might be summed up by saying that children should be provided with rich learning opportunities *from* an early age rather than be required to attain high standards of specific performance *at* an early age.

6. Behaviour and perceptual organization

Perception – awareness of the environment – is not a process we readily connect with learning. We tend to take it for granted that, provided the eyes and ears are not defective, people will see and hear whatever there is to see and hear without making special efforts to learn to perceive. Nevertheless, there have for centuries been debates on such questions as what a man blind from birth would see on first recovering his sight. Berkeley wrote in *An Essay Towards a New Theory of Vision*:

Hence it follows, that a man born blind, and afterwards, when grown up, made to see, would not, in the first act of vision, parcel out the ideas of sight into the same distinct collections that others do, who have experienced which do regularly coexist and are proper to be bundled up together under one name.

The problem of whether people have to learn which ideas of sight are bundled up together is still with us.

We recognize that limited perceptual learning exists, although it is not always described in those terms. People whose occupations or interests lead to prolonged inspection of particular objects or situations develop the ability to distinguish between very similar situations and to recognize their particular character. Tea tasters, fly fishermen, stamp collectors or toolmakers can often detect small differences in the taste of tea, the surface of a river, the perforation of a stamp or the finish of a ground steel surface which escape non-specialists, but which have significance for the man concerned. This heightened discrimination is the result of experience and may fairly be described as learned perceptual skill since as a result the world, or one part of it, has different appearances for the novice and the expert. But while it is obvious that perceptual learning of limited extent is possible it is by no means clear how much perception as a whole depends on learning. We may, as a result of experience, learn to distinguish between rectangular objects of very similar size so that ultimately we can readily see differences which escaped us at first, but do we have to learn to see rectangles as such? Before looking at some relevant evidence, however, we have to take up a general point concerning the study of perception.

The study of perception

We described acquired discrimination as a skill and indeed perception is often spoken of as a response by the person to the environment. It is obviously not an overt response which can be observed or measured and it is questionable whether the usage is particularly helpful. Nevertheless, it does emphasize that the perceiver is in some sense active in perceiving; he is not simply registering the state of the environment, but is 'processing' incoming sensory data in some way in order to arrive at a useful impression of his surroundings. For instance, different observers sometimes report having different experiences of the same external stimulus, and one observer may have different experiences at different times. Such variations are related to the complexity and ambiguity of the stimulus. The nature of the variation is to some extent predictable and is related to such factors as differences in the experimental instructions and in the assumptions and purposes of the observer and, as we have seen, to differences in experience between observers. When several observers do not have the same experience of a constant external stimulus they are treating the available sensory information differently. It suggests, at least, that there are selective mechanisms in perception whereby some stimulus elements are preserved and others repressed. Almost certainly the process is more complicated than this but, whatever the details might be, it is this selecting or organizing process in perception which is thought of as responding to the environment and which presumably changes as a result of learning. The problem is that such processes are not readily observable by the psychologist.

From one point of view a study of perceptual learning is an investigation concerned with changes in the appearance of the world for an observer. But perceptual experiences, and changes in these, are not available for experimental observation; by definition the perceiver is the only person who can describe them. We have stressed in earlier chapters that only observable events can form the data of science, in psychology as much as in chemistry or physics, and this poses a problem for the study of perception.

One way of dealing with this might be to develop more elaborate and detailed recording procedures so that some of the physiological variables, which we must assume underlie perception, could be made accessible.

Methods of recording behaviour are improving and physiological measures of such variables as heart-beat rate, speed of respiration, rate of firing of muscle nerves, and so on, are now frequently used. But many of these are measures of 'output' – advance indices of behavioural responses rather than of perceptual variables – and even where this is not the case, detailed studies of eye movements or of the electrical activity of the brain, for example, they pose tremendous problems of interpretation. They are essentially physiological measures used to assess what we would want to describe as psychological activity. Hence we are forced to use indirect behavioural measures of perceptual activity; changes in overt behaviour, including verbal behaviour, which can be related to changes in the perceptual process. This is unfortunate because the complexity of the perceptual organization and the variety of subsequent responses available means that no particular overt act need follow a change in perception and, indeed, no overt act at all may occur. This leads often to the construction of very simplified experimental situations where only a narrow range of stimuli is presented and where the responses of the subject are constrained within a similar narrow range. The extreme type of experiment of this kind is the 'psychophysical' situation in which, for example, two lights of different intensity are presented to the subject and he is instructed to respond only that the second is bright or dimmer than the first.

An additional safeguard sometimes used, particularly in studies of the perception of animals, is to develop experimental procedures in which a particular skill cannot be acquired unless a particular discrimination is made. Suppose the lever in a Skinner box is linked to the food-delivering mechanism only when a red light is shining and not when an equally bright green light is on. If the rat now learns to press the lever only in the presence of the red light we have evidence of his ability to discriminate. Failure to acquire this skill is, of course, not necessarily evidence of failure to distinguish the lights and even success only tells us that the rat can discriminate on the basis of wavelength; we do not know what he *sees*.

However, under such circumstances reasonable accuracy and validity are obtainable but close control of all conditions is necessary. Variations in the degree of control are inevitably reflected in variations in the reliance which can be placed on the results.

The study of perceptual learning thus becomes a study of a subject's ability to respond to particular stimuli at certain crucial periods of his life or after being exposed to certain types of environmental conditions. Essentially the problem is to discover which aspects of perception are innate and which are learned. Subsidiary questions are 'when does such learning, if any, take place?' and 'what are the necessary conditions?' This problem, which is a modern variant of the nativist-empiricist controversy, has received extensive study and a number of different types of evidence has been considered.

The most direct procedure would be to study the perceptual skills of children from birth to maturity, different groups being raised under different controlled conditions permitting experiences of some kinds and not others. In this way it would be possible to discover whether different rearing conditions affect the type of perceptual skill developed and if so what precise relationships between experience and learned perception exist.

While this is impractical, there are some studies of the perceptual experience of young children. The aim in such studies is usually to detect any differences there may be between the experience of young children and adults. Differences would be presumptive evidence of learning in perception. Such experiments, however, are necessarily delayed until the child can make some coordinated response in the experimental situation. We have to infer his experience from his response to selected stimuli, and newly born children in general do not respond in any way which can be classified as evidence for or against a particular type of experience. Such experiments, therefore, are seldom carried out on children under about six months old. Parallel to these experiments are studies of the early perceptual skills of young animals, who can usually be tested at a much earlier age and whose responses are similarly compared with those of adult animals. There are also studies of the effects of special rearing conditions on animals' subsequent perceptual ability.

A rather different approach is to observe the degree of perceptual learning in adult subjects who wear optical devices which cause them to see everything upside down or reversed left to right. This gives some insight into the degree of perceptual learning which is possible for adults exposed to a radical shift in the relationship between vision and other senses such as touch, balance sense and so on.

Berkeley's statement that people blind from birth who are given sight will see differently from other people has also been examined. The usual source of this type of evidence is the post-operative visual experience of patients who have had cataracts removed after having been virtually blind from birth or early childhood.

All these types of evidence present some difficulties of interpretation, the main trouble with the results of child studies, for example, being the time lag between birth and time of testing. The argument in this type of study is that the earlier in life a given perceptual skill is found the less likely it is to have been learned, and if a child cannot be tested before six months old it may, if it exhibits the skill, have benefited from learning during the six months.

Despite some difficulties of interpretation a general picture can be built up on the basis of all the different sources of evidence, and while the main questions 'What is learned in perception?' and 'What are the necessary conditions for the learning?' are by no means answered, certain answers at any rate are ruled out.

Perceptual skills in children

An ingenious experiment on depth perception in young children (whether they can see three dimensions and, in particular, depth) was carried out by Gibson and Walk[1] using a 'visual cliff'. The essential feature of this was a sheet of plate glass supported horizontally above the floor, in other words a glass-topped table. A board was laid across the middle of the glass. Immediately under the glass on one side of the board was fixed some patterned material, while similar material was placed on the floor on the other side of the board (i.e. some distance under the glass). The apparatus now presented the appearance of a solid bridge (the board), on one side of which was a solid patterned surface, while on the other side was a drop to a similar surface – the visual cliff. The thirty-six children used in this experiment ranged in age from six to fourteen months, the aim of the experiment being to discover whether children of this age can detect the depth on the cliff side of the board. Each child was placed on the board. The child's mother then called to him successively from the deep and shallow side of the glass. Twenty-seven of the thirty-six subjects responded by moving off the board and all of them crawled on to the shallow side, but only three crawled on to the cliff side. This demonstrates conclusively that children in general can see depth as soon as they can crawl. As the youngest of these subjects was six months old, however, it still remains possible that some learning of depth perception had occurred during the first six months of life. While it seems entirely appropriate that children should be able to recognize heights as soon as they are mobile, Gibson and Walk point out that this does not guarantee their safety; many of the children supported their weight on the glass covering the deep side while moving around on the board, and would have fallen over had the glass not been there.

These experimenters have also tested various animals on the visual cliff and have found in general that they too can discriminate depth as soon as they can move freely; chickens, for example, consistently choose the shallow side when less than one day old. The possibility of learning in such cases is much less. Gibson and Walk conclude that depth perception develops in animals as soon as they are able to move, whether this is at one day old or at six months old. While learning may play a part in its development in some species, it clearly differs a great deal from species to species.

Using animals in studies of perceptual development makes possible detailed control of the conditions under which they live from birth onwards. Techniques of rearing animals in complete darkness, or wearing translucent goggles so that no patterned vision is possible, or with one eye covered, have been used in a number of studies. The general argument in such studies is that if the deprived animals perform as well as normally reared control animals then no learning is necessary and on the other hand any superiority in performance of the control animals is produced by their richer visual experience.

Experimental studies of visual deprivation

These experiments usually show more positively than the previous type of experiment the benefits of early experience, although there are considerable differences between species. Probably the most relevant studies on which to base inferences about human behaviour are those on visual deprivation in other primates. Riesen[2] raised two chimpanzees from birth for sixteen months in complete darkness. The only light to which they were exposed during this time was for about forty-five seconds several times a day, which was necessary to arrange feeding and so on. When the chimpanzees were removed from the darkness their behaviour indicated that their perceptual ability was very undeveloped. Their eyes were sensitive to light, but they could not fixate objects; even objects approaching the eye failed to provoke the eyeblink response or any response until the object touched the chimpanzees' face. Their feeding bottle was recognized by touch, but no evidence of visual recognition appeared for eleven days and in general their responses to objects in the environment were either absent or imprecise compared with other animals of the same age. They were also deficient in pattern discrimination ability and in visual acuity. This experiment demonstrates that absence of all exposure to light retards the perceptual development of chimpanzees, but it does not indicate that all the retardation is caused by lack of opportunity to learn, since it is possible that degeneration of the optic system occurs in the prolonged complete absence of light.

Later ophthalmoscopic examination of the chimpanzee eyes showed differences in the reflectivity of the retina and optic disc compared with normal chimpanzee eyes. It is unlikely that this difference causes all the perceptual differences between light-deprived and normal chimpanzees, but it indicates that there is a further factor to control. One way to do this is to expose animals to diffused light instead of keeping them in complete darkness. The control animals are exposed to patterned stimuli. The argument here is that absence of light may produce some degeneration in the optic system and this danger will be removed by providing diffused light; on the other hand diffused light gives no opportunity for perceptual learning, which would be dependent on some differentiation of the stimulus. An experiment of this kind was carried out by Riesen and others,[3] who raised one chimpanzee completely in the dark, another in the dark except for one and a half hours each day during which he wore a translucent mask, and another with one and a half hours of patterned (free) vision. This procedure was continued for seven months, at the conclusion

111

of which the chimpanzees were tested and thereafter allowed normal vision.

The completely dark-reared chimpanzee and the translucent-light-experienced one started more or less equal, both being severely retarded in perceptual skill, but the latter acquired abilities of visual pursuit of a moving object, fixating an object and so on in about half the time of the former. The chimpanzee reared with patterned light experience was virtually indistinguishable from normal chimpanzees of the same age.

One must conclude that patterned vision (the experience of seeing things, not just exposure to light) is necessary for normal development of perception in chimpanzees. The experimental animals in these studies ultimately developed most of the perceptual abilities for which tests were made, but there is a possibility that permanent loss of efficiency can result from early deprivation. Some studies have shown that absence of stimulation in a particular sensory modality permanently reduces the efficiency with which response is made on the basis of that sense. We might expect results of this type in view of the general relationship between early and later learning which is discussed more fully in Chapter 5.

An interesting variant among studies of this type is the examination of the effect of learning on the equivalence of the eyes. If we met someone while we were wearing a patch over one eye we would expect to recognize him later even if (by some improbable sequence of events) we were now wearing the patch on the other eye. Under normal conditions such recognition would be possible and the question is whether this functional equivalence of the eyes is innately determined or whether it depends to some extent on learning. Riesen, Kurke and Mellinger[4] raised cats in a dark room from birth to fourteen weeks and then for three weeks they were given half an hour's visual experience per day. During these three weeks the cats wore a translucent cover over one eye, so that both eyes were exposed to light but only one to patterned vision. At the end of this time they were trained to make a visual discrimination with the uncovered eye. When this discrimination was successfully established the translucent cover was put on the other eye and they were tested with the eye which had received no patterned vision. They failed to respond appropriately; the learned discrimination did not transfer to the other eye. Control animals, of course, showed transfer from one eye to the other.

An important further experiment of this type carried out by Riesen and Mellinger[5] has shown that the development of functional equivalence does not depend on both eyes having patterned vision at the same time. They raised cats in the dark except that for one hour per day one eye was exposed to patterned stimuli and the other to light only; then for another hour the first eye received light only and the second patterned stimuli. Later they were trained to make a visual discrimination with one eye only and this discriminating ability transferred to the other eye. This shows that the learning involved in the development of equivalence is of a non-specific kind and this conclusion in the case of learned equivalence may also apply to other forms of early perceptual learning.

Most of the positive evidence for the necessity of learning in perceptual development so far discussed has come from animal studies, but there are two further types of observation of human subjects which are relevant – visual displacement studies and records of post-operative cataract patients' experience.

Experiments on visual displacement

There have been a number of studies of this type, the first of which was carried out by Stratton.[6] He wore a lens system over one eye which reversed the total visual field and inverted it left-to-right; the other eye was covered. He wore this device for three days in order to find out what extent and type of change in perceptual experience would occur from beginning to end of the experiment. At first he had great difficulty in moving about the environment, but as his experience increased he was able to move more freely and to touch objects easily by moving his hands in the correct direction despite the inversion

113

and reversal of the light rays from the objects. He subsequently carried out a similar experiment for eight days which showed a greater increase in re-learned tactual and kinaesthetic correspondence with vision. He never saw the environment correctly while wearing the inverting lenses, but he became able to move about successfully out of doors and even, towards the end of the experimental period, to appreciate the beauty of the scenery, whereas at the beginning he had been unable even to recognize familiar localities.

When the lenses were removed at the end of the eight-day period he had, for some hours, difficulty in carrying out simple activities such as writing or opening doors. He tended to move his hands in the wrong direction or to move his head upwards instead of downwards when attempting to fixate the centre of the field.

The results of this study indicate that some learning of new tactual-visual linkages can occur in conditions of severe disturbance of existing relationships and therefore, possibly, the usual tactual-visual correspondence owes something to learning. There was also some learning of a purely visual type, although it did not extend to learning to see the environment the right way up.

There have been a number of stimulus-transformation experiments of this type and the most extensive series has been carried out by Ivo Kohler at the University of Innsbruck. He has conducted experiments in which subjects have worn inverting and reversing lens systems and mirrors and also lenses for altering the angle of inclination of incoming light rays. He reports considerable development of skill during the wearing of inverting optical systems, but in addition reports much more change in the direction of restoration of the normal appearance of the environment than Stratton and most other workers in this field. One subject, for example, who wore an inverting mirror for nine days reported that at the end of this time upright vision was more or less completely restored, while another who wore left-right reversing prisms for thirty-seven days was said to have seen some objects correctly at the end of the experiment while others, such as letters of the alphabet, were still visually reversed. Those subjects who wore lenses altering the angle of inclination of light rays report eventual correct vision provided that the angle is not too great.

In addition to using goggles involving displacement of the visual image, Kohler[7] has used glasses each lens of which is divided vertically, the left halves being blue and the right halves yellow. A subject wearing these at first sees the world blue when looking left and yellow when looking right, although after a few weeks adaptation occurs and the colour does not change when the eyes move. When the spectacles are removed the subject for a time sees the world yellow (the complementary colour) when looking left and blue when looking right.

These experiments show that a fairly considerable degree of perceptual learning is possible although, apart from the one or two cases mentioned, there does not seem to be complete restoration of normal vision while wearing displacing glasses. The argument is that if adults, who have already developed adequate vision, are able to learn to cope with such extensive alterations to the direction of incoming light rays then learning will be possible to an even greater extent for children. Where learning is possible it is usually necessary, hence the evidence increases the probability of some learning occurring in early perceptual development. It may be, however, that the perceptual learning of adults under conditions of inverted or reversed visual fields is of an essentially different kind from that in young children. Critics of this approach point out that learning in infancy proceeds from a development of general adaptation to later more specific differentiations, whereas a good deal of the adult learning in displaced visual fields seems to be specific without general adaptation, learning to see objects correctly but not letters, for example. Certainly it would be expected that children's modes of learning would differ from those of adults but, while they concern young children only indirectly, these experiments show convincingly that perceptual learning can occur even in extreme circumstances.

Visual experience of newly operated cataract patients

It is appropriate at this point to consider the main type of human evidence which bears directly on the issue, the experience of post-operative cataract patients. Von Senden[8] has collected together a number of accounts of cases of this type, all of which concern patients who had been blind for years, often from birth, and who thus could be said to be seeing virtually for the first time. The importance of these studies is that maturation can be assumed to be more or less complete and therefore differences between their visual skills and those of normal adults can be said to be due to learning. Also, of course, they can report their experience. There are again, however, certain difficulties in interpretation of these results. First, these patients had some slight visual experience, as cataracts do not exclude all light but all experience of form or shape. Also, in some cases the cataracts had formed after birth. The patients also had the advantage of years of experience with other senses, particularly touch, in dealing with the new visual data.

The possibility of this cross-modal transfer, learned recognition in one sensory modality transferring to another, is illustrated by a case described by Gregory and Wallace.[9] This patient had, while blind, learned to read upper-case letters by touch. When the cataracts were removed he could recognize upper-case letters by sight but could not recognize lower-case letters which he had not learned to recognize tactually. His skill in recognition of upper-case letters transferred from touch to sight and this is at least a potential difference between these patients and young children, although this particular degree of cross-modal transfer seems to be rare. This indicates that these patients have advantages *vis-à-vis* young children apart from the completion of maturation, and therefore any difficulties they experience would be less than those of young children. So it might seem that any learning necessary for them would be a minimum and therefore they provide a strong test. But there are certain differences not in their favour.

The operation itself consists in removal of the lens of the eye and so focusing is more difficult for these patients than for those with normal sight; there is often nystagmus and there is always the possibility of degenerative changes in the optic systems such as occurred in the animal experiments. In addition the shock of the operation itself probably interferes with performance, at least in the first days of vision. These differences between the conditions of post-operative cataract patients and new-born children do not totally nullify the evidence, but they indicate the need for caution in interpretation of the results.

Even if there were little learning in perception it could not be expected that the immediate post-operative experiences of these patients would be identical with those of normal people. Their visual experiences could not be very meaningful and would have few of the elements of recognition common to most normal perceptions. But the question is whether these differences are caused simply by an inability to name or recognize objects at first or by an inability to make the consistent discriminations and identifications that normal adults make. It might be expected, for example, that the patients would be able to discriminate red and green without being able to apply the appropriate label or to know that green was the colour of grass. If this were the case, then the only element of learning in the perception of colours would be which name to apply to each colour and the typical colours of common objects. Similarly it might be shown that these patients can make all the discriminations that normal adults make and lack only the name or categorizing response for the items discriminated. In fact this is not the case.

They can more or less immediately differentiate an object from its background and can also discriminate colours, but the discrimination of shape is very difficult and develops only gradually. At first they are unable to recognize by sight even such simple objects as a square and a triangle. They may see that the shapes are different, but, though able to recognize them immediately by touch, without considerable experience they cannot consistently *identify* the shape by its visual appearance. This difficulty is not merely one of recognizing *particular* shapes, but one of recognizing shapes as such. Even after having been told which is the square and which the triangle they may, on subsequent occasions, be able to recognize them only by counting the corners.

It is fairly clear that the visual experiences of such patients cannot be regarded as equivalent to those of normal people; their skill in object or shape recognition is markedly inferior and improves only with weeks or months of practice.

A further difficulty experienced by these patients is of considerable significance. When a particular object has been presented on a number of occasions a patient can acquire the ability to recognize it. But if the colour of light illuminating the object is changed or if it is presented against an unusual background, or at a new angle to the line of sight, it may no longer be recognized as the same object. Another way of describing this problem is to say that the patient's vision is dependent to a much greater extent than that of normal people on the precise nature of the visual stimulus on the retina, sometimes called the proximal stimulus, rather than on the real or permanent nature of the object or distal stimulus.

The function of perception is to enable people to act on the environment in terms of its consistent characteristics. Normal perception enables people to operate in a world of stable objects at varying distances, the properties of which remain constant or change in a systematic way. Perception is a process adapted to the needs of a mobile, active and vulnerable organism. This is of interest when considered in relation to the physical stimuli on which perception is based. Human sense organs register light stimuli of varying area, intensity, wave-length and duration, sounds of varying frequency and amplitude and so on. The incoming proximal stimuli are constantly changing, so that from second to second the person receives differing total physical stimuli from the environment. Despite this, perception is of a stable world of solid objects with few, if any, discontinuities.

An example of the divergence between proximal stimulus and perception is provided by a consideration of the phenomenon of perceptual constancy. This is a characteristic of the visual perception of shape, size, colour, brightness and motion and its general nature is such that the perception of an object which is at an unusual angle to the line of sight, located at a greater distance than usual or illuminated by an unusual colour of light, is a compromise between the typical perception of the object which occurs under more normal circumstances and the perception which would be expected on the basis of the proximal stimulus. The process can be illustrated by an early experiment carried out by Thouless,[10] in which he demonstrated shape constancy.

The stimulus in this experiment was a disc which was placed on a horizontal surface some distance from the subjects. Viewed from this position the disc was at an angle so the projected image of the disc on the retina – the proximal stimulus – was elliptical. The subjects were then given a number of ellipses and told to choose from among them one which best represented the appearance of the disc. These ellipses were of varying minor axis, ranging from below that which would be predicted as the appearance of the disc on the basis of the proximal stimulus, to equal to the major axis. The major axis in each case was equal to the diameter of the disc. The ellipse usually selected by the subjects was not circular but was nearer to a circle than the retinal image. The appearance of a circular disc at an angle is more like the usual appearance of a circle than would be expected on the basis of the retinal image. Similar results are found in many experiments on size, colour and brightness constancy; the perception of an object is usually a compromise between the proximal stimulus and the normal or permanent characteristics of the object.

A common element in these experiments is that the constancy effect is dependent on the presence of certain cues or peripheral stimuli. Maximum shape constancy in Thouless's experiment occurred only under conditions of full illumination in which the exact position of the disc, its distance and its angle to the line of sight could be clearly seen. When the viewing conditions were restricted so that the subject saw less and less of the surrounding area the appearance of the disc increasingly tended to be that expected on the basis of the proximal stimulus. In other words, the constancy effect depends on information about the type of illumination, distance or inclination of the object. If these cues are available they contribute to the processing of the central proximal stimulus, so that the perceptual experience better represents the object. It is not a matter of knowledge or conscious judgment, however, as the constancy effect varies according to the peripheral cues actually present regardless of the subject's knowledge of the real situation.

Perceptual constancy is an example of perceptual response to stimulus properties of a high order of abstraction and is a more advanced perceptual skill than recognition of a particular shape under a variety of viewing conditions which the cataract patients find difficult. There is little direct evidence concerning the degree of learning involved in perceptual constancy itself, although there is some evidence that two-year-old children, while displaying some perceptual constancy, do not seem to exhibit this to the same extent as adults.

The very considerable difficulties shown by the cataract patients in perceiving shape and in responding to higher-order invariants of the stimulus are the clearest evidence that learning is necessary for perception to develop fully in humans, and it is possible to begin to answer the question of the role of learning in perception. It is fairly clear that the cataract patients have more difficulty with form perception than can be accounted for in terms of nystagmus and focusing difficulties, and the animal deprivation studies confirm this. At the same time the results showing that simultaneous operation of both eyes is not necessary for the development of interocular transfer and the partial and specific results of stimulus-transformation studies of adults suggest that the learning involved may be of an unusual type.

As we saw in Chapter 5, certain general types of early experience have important consequences for later learning capacity.

Similarly the learning occurring in early perceptual development seems to be non-specific and to be related to the development of general processes rather than particular detailed skills.
For example, the eyes become functionally equivalent not by
seeing the same things at the same time but by being used in
the same kind of way. Presumably both eyes must acquire
access to the cerebral area in which the visual skills develop. If,
however, one eye only receives experience the brain area
mediating perceptual skills develops, but the other eye does not
have access to it.

What can we say about these visual skills? It seems that a
theory of perceptual development must describe a brain process which changes as a result of experience in such a way that
incoming stimuli can be handled in larger units, categorized
more quickly and responded to on the basis of more abstract
properties of the stimulus. For example, in shape constancy the
response is made not simply to the shape of the object but to
its shape in relation to its apparent angle to the line of sight.

In terms of Hebb's developmental theory the growth of shape
recognition is mediated by the development of relationships between cell assemblies. Repeated experience of a total visible
figure brings about relationships between the cell assemblies
stimulated by the separate sections. Ultimately superordinate
neural structures will develop which underlie the perception of
the total figure. These may be activated by perception of any of
the parts, and finally a flexible arrangement will come about
whereby a person seeing a figure may concentrate readily on
any of the separate sections or on the whole figure. Similarly,
seeing the same figure on different occasions causes, by the
activation at different times of neural structures with elements
in common, the development of processes concerned with
recognition of the figure as essentially the same, despite temporary differences in the angle at which it is viewed, its size
and so on. This aspect of the theory merely indicates that a
possible neural basis has been described for the establishment
of associative learning of perception of a figure and of the
same figure in different positions.

121

We have been concerned so far in this chapter with the perceptual learning over comparatively long periods of time, but perceptual learning within a limited area taking place in a relatively short time occurs throughout life and such changes are of considerable importance. We have already mentioned that special discriminating abilities develop as a result of extensive experience with particular objects and there is no doubt that specialized perceptual abilities are associated with professional competence or expertise in many fields. In the following section some of the conditions for this type of learning will be discussed.

Short-term perceptual learning

Men can discriminate between half-crowns and florins by touch better than women can. This is a hypothesis which has not, so far as is known, been fully tested. It is based on the fact that men carry money in their pockets and often select coins without looking at them, while women carry coins in a purse and choose appropriate coins by sight. Men have been exposed to the stimuli (in this case the tactual stimuli provided by coins), while women have not so often been exposed to this particular range of stimuli.

Whether or not this particular hypothesis would ultimately be confirmed (an informal test of two subjects suggests that it might be), it provides an example of a situation in which perceptual learning might occur. The essential assumption is that different exposure to the stimuli occurs in men and women. If this is unjustified (if, for example, most women select coins from their purses by touch) then no differences in perceptual learning would be found. But the prediction might fail for other reasons. It might be that the tactual differences between half-crowns and florins (differences in diameter, weight and surface design) are so great that the tactual experience of women in handling coins, more limited than men's though it might be, is sufficient for adequate learning to occur. It may even be that no real learning of the difference between half-crowns and florins is necessary. The difference between them may be such that one exposure of each is sufficient for them to be differentiated infallibly thereafter. We do not have to carry oranges and footballs around in our pockets in order to recognize the difference between them by touch. To summarize, two conditions are *necessary* before it is appropriate to talk about perceptual learning: first, the stimuli should originally be difficult to discriminate and, second, they should thereafter be exposed frequently to the learner.

But what are the *sufficient* conditions for perceptual learning to occur? Among other things the reinforcement question arises in the context of perceptual learning. Is it advantageous, or perhaps even necessary, for a correct response to be rewarded during perceptual training? It is clear that the learner must want to acquire the discrimination, should be motivated, that is, either by a desire to satisfy the experimenter or to select the right coins; but it is by no means clear that he must be reinforced for every correct response. Experimental evidence on this point is equivocal and the necessity of reinforcement seems even more doubtful in this type of learning than in others. A more interesting problem centres on the role of response during perceptual learning.

Suppose a subject is learning to discriminate between four objects of very similar shape. He might during training be required to make different responses to the four objects, to call them by different names, for example. At first he would often name them wrongly, but would gradually acquire the ability to give the correct name. Another method might be used in which the subject simply inspects the stimuli without associating any particular names with them or making any other specific different responses. Yet another method would be to use one name for two of the objects and another for the other two.

If three groups of subjects were assigned the task of learning to distinguish the stimuli, were assigned one method per group and were all given the same number of exposures of the objects, would the same kind and degree of learning be expected from each group? According to Gibson and Gibson[11] the answer is 'Yes'. Their view is that perceptual learning proceeds by increasing sensitivity to the stimulus variables, so increasing the ability to distinguish between the actual characteristics of the objects. For this to occur repeated exposure to the stimuli (and attempts to distinguish them) is sufficient and the attachment of different kinds of responses, or none, would have no particular effect. But there are other views. The 'enrichment' view of perceptual learning deriving from Miller and Dollard[12] holds that naming objects distinctively will increase the ability to distinguish between them by the attachment of response-produced cues to the incoming stimuli. Similarly, learning the same name will give stimuli an element in common so they will be more difficult to distinguish than those with different names. In our example, then, this theory would predict that the group using distinctive names would acquire the most efficient discrimination, the no-name group would be next and the group using only two names would find more difficulty in distinguishing objects of the same name than they would have in distinguishing between the members of different pairs.

A recent experiment by Katz[13] tested this hypothesis, using children as subjects. The objects to be distinguished were four complicated visual forms all about four inches square. All the subjects were shown the shapes 150 times for two seconds at a time. After this training series which was equally effective for the four-name and two-name groups (there was no significant difference in their performance on the last fifty trials of the training series – the no-name group made no responses, so could not be assessed) a test of the subjects' ability to discriminate was carried out. They were shown two of the shapes together for two seconds and asked to say whether they were the same shape or different. Twenty-eight such pairs were presented, eight pairs being identical shapes and twenty different. The important comparison between groups was in terms of their responses to ten of the different pairs. These were five presentations each of the two pairs of shapes given the same name by the two-name group. The significant response is the average number of 'same' responses given by the different groups. They were, for the four-name, no-name and two-name groups respectively, 1.94, 3.06 and 4.31 (out of 10). These differences indicate that the group learning a distinctive name for the four shapes discriminated between them best, the inspection or no-name group next and the two-name group had difficulty in differentiating those shapes to which they had given the same name.

Some experiments have shown similar results using instrumental discrimination responses, but others using verbal responses of 'same' and 'different', as in this experiment, have produced negative results. Even if further work confirms these results it does not provide clear evidence for the response-produced cue hypothesis. The problem in such experiments is to separate the effect of making a particular kind of response from the subject's adjustment to the task of making one type of response rather than another. It may be that using names as opposed to not using them or using four names rather than two produces differences in the visual 'style' of the subject, differences in the way he examines the stimulus, which results in his developing sensitivity to alternative aspects of the object. We cannot assume that equal numbers of exposures produce the same type of experience in subjects carrying out different types of task.

There are other research issues in perceptual learning, but many of them derive from particular theories of the nature of perception and are outside the scope of this book. What is clear is that practice with objects can change the perception of them. Many skills usually thought of in terms of the acquisition of competence in making specific responses depend for their successful development on the growth of specific discriminations. While training procedures often concentrate on the control of response-change it may be useful in many cases to train perception explicitly. Even where this is done, as for example in the training of inspectors, the methods used are often haphazard. The use of systematic procedures for producing changes in discriminating ability may well shorten training time and increase the efficiency of final performance. This point will also be taken up in the next chapter.

7. Skill

There are several related uses of the word 'skill' and it is worth while making some distinctions between them at the beginning of this discussion. We may talk about 'skill' in the sense of driving a car, typing or fencing, i.e. we are referring to particular, more or less complex, activities which require a period of deliberate training and practice to be performed adequately and which often have some recognized useful function. The emphasis here is on the activity, on the achievement, frequently on the manipulation of some specialized piece of equipment, though we also talk about social skills, mathematical skills, etc. On the other hand, someone may be described as 'having' skill, being skilled *at* performing a particular task, in the sense of being proficient or good at it, the emphasis being on the level of performance which he is capable of, rather than on the characteristics of the task. In this sense it is possible to talk about having or lacking skill in the use of a sewing machine, but also in the use of a knife and fork – though we would not normally single out the handling of eating instruments as a skill in the *former* sense. The stress is on the activity in one case and on the individual in the other, and we single out those activities as skills in which it is possible for an individual to distinguish himself in some way, showing competence which is not automatically achieved by most members of the population.

In an industrial context, a skilled worker is one who has competence in a given area of work, often specific to a particular manufacturing process and consisting usually of a range of related or independent abilities. Here, however, the criterion for the application of the term is the completion of a required period of training and apprenticeship, rather than the actual degree of competence, even if in fact the two usually go together. A man who has not served the recognized period and form of apprenticeship, and who may have acquired his competence by an unorthodox and possible shorter route, may not be accepted as a skilled worker. Again, many types of activity which, regarded from an independent point of view, might be classified as skills are, somewhat arbitrarily, excluded by convention. Skill in industry is essentially a status term.

In this chapter our concern will be with the individual, with competence, with proficiency. It may manifest itself in the exercise of recognized skills like driving, in the playing of games like tennis, or marbles, also in more widespread accomplishments such as riding a bicycle, the tying of shoe laces or just walking. We want to examine the conditions under which skill develops, the factors making for more or less rapid achievement of a given criterion, and to do this in a way which is only incidentally concerned with the particular type of activity involved.

The characteristics of skilled performance

What are the signs by which we recognize proficiency, what is it that distinguishes the performance of the expert from that of the beginner? To the extent to which there is some sort of product involved, there is of course a faster output of higher quality, and this is the kind of criterion of good performance with which most assessment is concerned. But since output and quality are specific to a given activity, it does not help us in the present inquiry. We are looking for a description of *how* a task is done in terms that might provide an insight into the general features – if there are any – of the change from early to expert behaviour. It will simplify matters if we confine ourselves for the moment to the consideration of *motor skills*, i.e. activities in which physical movement is the predominant, or at least the most obvious, element.

Skilled performance, when compared to its inexpert counterpart, is characterized by an appearance of ease, of smoothness of movement, of confidence and the comparative absence of hesitation; it frequently gives the impression of being unhurried, while the actual pace of activity may of course be quite

1 The goslings in this picture have been 'imprinted' on a man, and treat him
as a kind of 'mother-goose substitute'. Imprinting, which has been observed
primarily in a variety of bird species, usually results from exposure to moving
objects or animals during a brief and highly sensitive learning period shortly
after hatching. Early misdirected following behaviour subsequently often
generalizes to other activities, such as feeding or mating.

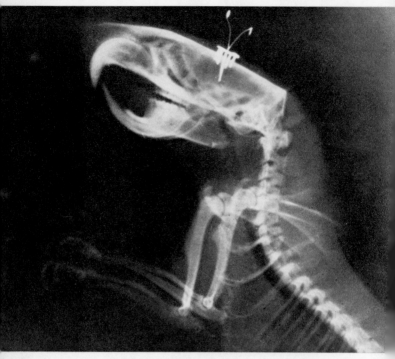

2 This X-ray photograph shows electrodes positioned in a rat's brain, making possible the direct stimulation of highly specific cortical areas. Experiments by Olds and Milner have shown that if selected responses by the animal are followed by direct stimulation in the septal region, such responses are repeated at a high rate and for long periods of time. The septal region may contain a 'reinforcement centre' involved in more usual forms of reinforcement.

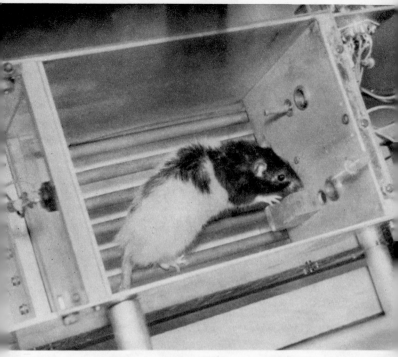

3 A rat in a typical Skinner box. Having pressed the lever visible in the centre of the photograph the animal awaits the delivery of a food pellet into a cup immediately alongside. The comparative simplicity of response and reinforcement involved makes it possible to provide and record long and varied programmes of reinforcement automatically. Provision is also made for additional signals to act as S$_D$s or S$_\Delta$s.

4 The child shown in this photograph is being called by his mother from the 'deep' side of the visual cliff. His reluctance to move from the central bridge indicates that depth perception is developed sufficiently at this age for the deep side to appear threatening.

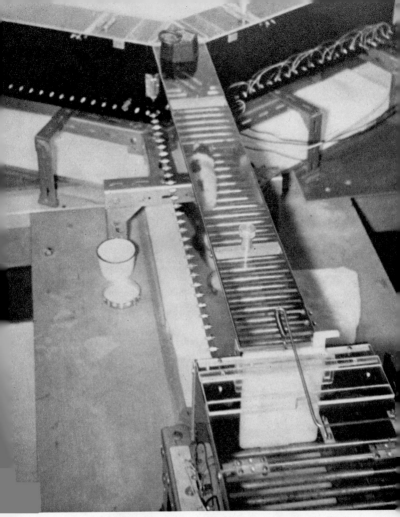

5 A Y-maze used in maze learning experiment with rats. The starting box is shown in the foreground of the picture, goal boxes whose reinforcement can be provided are at the ends of the two arms of the Y. Electrical contacts to the individual bars making up the runway allow for the administration of mild shock, or the detailed recording of movement through the maze.

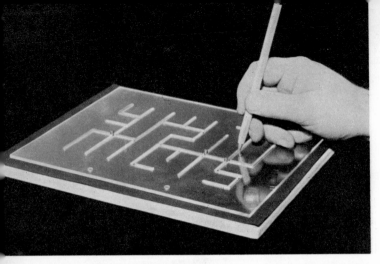

6 Maze learning can also be investigated in human subjects. The illustration shows a 'pencil maze', whose exact path can be varied by the insertion of blocks at choice points. Subjects are blindfolded, and the paper below the perspex sheet retains a record of each attempt made.

7, 8 The term 'skill' covers a very wide range of activities and training devices
and 9 providing information, and recordings of performance accordingly vary in
complexity. The device in plate 7 (*below*) provides an immediate light signal

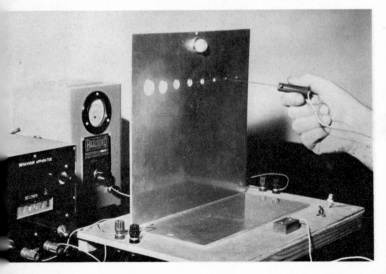

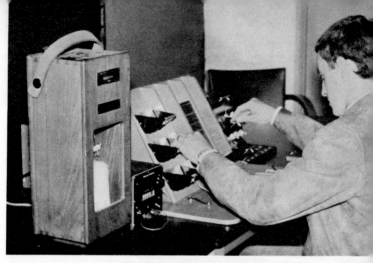

when the subject trying to insert a stylus through progressively smaller holes makes contact with the side. In plate 8 (*above*), providing an example of a simple assembly task, contact with selected components activates a timer which provides the trainee with a cumulative record of his performance times. Using a pen recorder, he can also be provided with a learning curve showing the progressive stages of his training. In plate 9 (*below*) astronaut John Glenn is shown, using a procedures trainer which simulates many of the conditions found in a space vehicle without the hazards resulting from incorrect responses in the real situation.

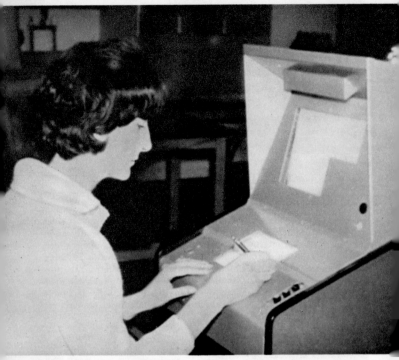

10 The teaching machine shown is of the kind enabling the student to make free
responses to problems or questions posed in the course of the programme.
The student must herself judge the correctness of her answer and then press
the appropriate button, which will determine whether a new or a remedial
part of the programme is next presented.

high. The skilled man 'seems to have all the time in the world' compared, say, to the learner-driver whose progress is more like a sequence of emergencies. In skilled performance there are no surprises, in the sense that surprise involves a lack of readiness for the situation that has arisen – indeed increasing skill involves a widening of the range of possible disturbances that can be coped with without disrupting the performance.

This is perhaps the most striking feature of a high level of proficiency – it involves being ready for a whole variety of events that may occur, *when* they occur – and these events include the consequences of the activity itself. The novice driver is caught unprepared not only by slightly unusual behaviour of traffic, or pedestrians, but initially also by the movements of the vehicle he has himself brought about, by the situation that arises when, having completed one manoeuvre, such as gear change, he is required to begin another, such as turning. The consequences of his actions are also more varied and uneven, and in this respect his task is doubly difficult. He is unprepared for what happens and the range of what *may* happen is greater. The expert, by contrast, somehow always manages to be ready, there are no hesitations. If one watches an adult tying his tie, one can notice how at each stage, as the ends are manipulated, the hands rapidly move into position for the next stage. A good tennis player moves into position much earlier than a beginner, reacting to and anticipating situations which are created in part by himself and in part by his opponent.

The sensory components of skill

We are dealing here with the unfolding of a sequence of movements which bear the character of coordination and integration in *time* – indeed the element of exact timing is highly evident. But what are the components of the sequence, what is it that is being coordinated and organized? We tend to think of skill predominating in terms of movement. In describing a task we tend to concentrate on what is *done*, and task analysis as in motion study takes the form of recording the detailed 'units' of movement into which an operation has been broken down. All this represents the *output* of the individual; what we tend to ignore, partly because it is taken for granted, and partly because it is difficult or impossible to observe directly, is the *input*.

The tennis player takes account of his opponent's moves, the car driver obviously watches the road. These phrases however gloss over the great complexity of what is involved. There are many things about the movements of a tennis player, or about road conditions, on which *attention* may be concentrated. The problem of attention, arises not only in the overt sense of the eyes being directed towards and remaining focused on some things more than others, but also in that of looking at a particular object say, and attending now to its colour, now its shape, now its surface texture, and so on. The information that arrives at the eye can be processed in different ways and the development of new ways of processing information, of perceiving, or a change in emphasis, forms a significant part in the growth of what is more appropriately called a *sensori*-motor skill. The clues to required action lie in some aspects of the environment, and the learning process must involve the development of a selective sensitivity towards them.

It should not be thought that selective attention is confined to seeing. In hearing, we are constantly *listening* to, or for, certain aspects of the total sound pattern that impinges on the ear – in a lecture for example, we might attend, now to what is being said, now to other sounds coming from outside, or inside, the room. Attention may also be divided between different kinds of sensory message, including those arising from within the body, e.g. toothache, or hunger pangs. Confronted with a mass of available information, we learn not only to *attend* to some of it, but by the same token to ignore much that is irrelevant to the task being executed at the time. To the extent to which we are, as trainers, aware of this aspect of developing skill, we may be able to find more effective means of directing the attention of the learner.

It is important to realize that proficiency does not necessarily involve the explicit recognition of the contributing factors, and it is partly for this reason that the man who possesses skill is not always particularly good at helping to produce it in others. Many highly skilled men are unable to explain why they act as they do, and may be quite unconscious of the particular sensory mode that controls their activity. The most effective way of demonstrating the critical role played by incoming signals in a highly practised task, where we are frequently unaware of their relevance, is to eliminate or to distort them. Thus we can illustrate the role that hearing one's own voice plays in speaking, by feeding a noise into the ears of the speaker with the use of earphones. The raising or lowering of the noise-level directly affects the loudness of speech, often without the awareness of the speaker; it is as though the volume control of the noise-generating apparatus is directly coupled to the speaker himself. We know that we tend to raise our voices in noisy conditions, but this is not so much a deliberate act for the benefit of other people, as an automatic one in response to not hearing one's own voice sufficiently clearly.

Although it is the sound received through the ears which is normally utilized to control the level of output, there are other sources of information available which may be used. Sound is transmitted also by bone conduction, and in addition sensations in the mouth, throat and chest bear some relation to the loudness of the voice. It is possible to learn to use these, rather than airborne sound, for controlling volume, though being internal signals they cannot be used to produce continuous adjustment to external conditions. It is a common feature of developing skill that some control of activity is transferred from senses that provide a link with the *external* world, to *internal* senses, thus freeing the individual from interference by the environment, or what is more important, enabling him to accept information from outside to be utilized *later*.

Display-control relationships

It is not enough to attend to particular types of cue, one must also *translate* them into appropriate action. Again, in highly practised skills it is usually not apparent that any sort of translation is involved. The relationship between seeing, say, a light switch and bringing one's hand into contact with it is somehow obvious, the hand just moves in the right way. The need for translation can be brought out in two ways. One is the consideration of the requirements of a robot capable of this sort of achievement – we need not only a motor, or effector, system and a sensing device which is affected by the discrepancy between the position of the moving arm and its goal, but also a unit which transforms the incoming signal into appropriate movement. Alternatively we may arrange to change the 'meaning' of incoming signals which play a part in a well-practised task. In attempting to trace a pattern, where both pattern and hand are seen in a mirror, the automatic relationship between movement and what is seen is disrupted, at times to the extent of complete immobilization, and a conscious translation has to intervene. As practice proceeds, however, a new skill develops in which the relationship between image and movement is changed, becoming again an automatic one. The removal of the mirror then temporarily produces difficulty in tracing under 'normal' circumstances. Watching the groping movements of a child indicates that the direct progress of a limb towards a selected point is learned, even though it may not be obvious what such an achievement involves. Practising mirror drawing can demonstrate that even such a well-established relationship can be temporarily unlearnt and partly reversed, cf. the experiments of Kohler described in the previous chapter.

When some kind of machine or instrument intervenes between movement and the observed result, it is more apparent that the relationship between them has to be learned. The visual picture of car bonnet, road and kerb does not at first lead

132

straightforwardly to the required movement of the hand on the steering wheel; yet the coordination between them is easier to acquire than it would be if, by the use of different gearing, a *clockwise* rotation of the steering wheel turned the wheels to the *left,* and vice versa. Even when the observed consequences of action consist in an artificial *display,* such as a combination of dial readings – as in instrument flying – the *relationship* which exists between the display and the controlling movement can be a relatively easy or difficult one for the operator to learn. To the extent to which it is possible for the designer to arrange this relationship at will, he can contribute to the ease with which the operation of his equipment is learned and thereafter maintained without danger of accidental breakdown under stress. A familiarity with the characteristics of human skilled behaviour can make an important contribution to equipment design and this is being increasingly realized, especially in the military field.

So far we have emphasized two aspects of a developing skill – a change in the sensitivity of the learner to particular features or aspects of the environment in which he operates, including the effects of his own activity, and the establishment of particular relationships between sensory information received and appropriate action. There is, however, a further requirement before a characteristically smooth and unhurried skilled performance is achieved.

The time element in skill

The translation of signal into action takes time, quite apart from that required for the execution of the movement. Even in such a simple task as depressing a key in response to a flashing light, or the onset of a tone, a finite period of the order of 0·1–0·2 [one tenth–one fifth] of a second elapses between signal and *onset* of movement. This is called *reaction time.* We can observe the consequences of this delay in *continuous* performance if we attempt, for example, to track a moving target which is capable of sudden changes of direction. At such times the path

133

followed by the tracker briefly lags behind that of the target, the change cannot instantaneously be translated into movement. Alternately, we may try to sort a pack of cards into red and black suits, using two different methods. In one, the cards are held face down, so that each card is seen only after its predecessor is already in position. In the other method, they are held upwards, but the same turning movement in sorting the cards is used (i.e. they are placed on the table face up in the first case, and face down in the second). Although the movement is identical in both cases, the speed of sorting is far higher in the second case compared to the first. The reader can easily try this for himself.

The reason for this difference in speed is that the time taken for *deciding* where a particular card is to be placed is in the first method necessarily additional to that required for movement, whereas in the second method we place one card into position while at the same time preparing for the next. Information is received in *advance* of the action required. In the example which we considered it was the actual arrangement of the task which in one case prevented the use of advance information – the information about one card was simply not available until the previous one had been dealt with. Frequently, however, the reason why advance information cannot be used is that the operator's total attention is taken up by his current movement. If instead of simply placing the cards on the table we post them into one of two narrow slots, this placing movement must initially be supervised, and the colour of the next card can only be attended to after this supervision is completed. With increasing practice, however, supervision becomes progressively less necessary, and the positioning of each card is, as it were, taken care of by an internal 'programme' which guides the movement to its correct destination. This frees the sorter to attend to signals relating to movements that are required later, so that when the time for them arrives he has already built up an internal programme to carry them out.

The development of larger stimulus and response units

We can perhaps gain a better appreciation of the phenomenon by considering the more complex case of touch typing. At the start, each letter is typed individually, as a separate act. A skilled typist on the other hand will type whole words and even phrases as a *unit* – i.e. the pattern which comprises the whole sequence of movements making up the word or phrase appears to be ready at the outset, the programme simply *runs itself off*. With the arrival of this stage, a copy typist can type *behind* the material that she is reading, building up one programme while executing the last one. Since the execution of movements takes longer than their preparation, the increasing size of internally programmed response units makes for a more leisurely translation process, and removes the element of 'flap' which is so characteristic of an unskilled attempt at speed.

Corresponding to the development of larger units of action there are larger units of perceptual organization. In the case of copy typing these are already established at the outset, in the sense that words and phrases can be read and stored as a whole. The growth of these units can be observed in children learning to read, who progress – depending on the method used – from taking in a sequence of individual letters, through short letter combinations to complete words and phrases. At the adult level, learning to receive morse code shows similar features, and changes in the size of the perceptual unit are accompanied by dramatic changes in the observed rate of learning, as was shown as long ago as 1899 in a classic study by Bryan and Harter.[1]

To summarize, we have emphasized the following features as characteristic of increasing skill: development of selective attention to changes in the environment, including particularly changes produced by the ongoing activity itself; the development of appropriate relationships between received signal and response; the development of perceptual units of increasing size which are translated into internal programmes for activity

135

which may then proceed with little or no supervision, making possible the constant state of readiness for action which is one of the main features of skilled performance.

The acquisition of skill

We must now turn to the question of bringing about skilled behaviour. What factors influence its development? Can the type of learning model that was developed in relation to the behaviour of animals in highly specialized circumstances be used to suggest ways of aiding the acquisition of skill?*

The learning model which we considered earlier stressed the pairing of stimulus – response sequences with reinforcement, as a requirement for developing the appropriate 'connexion': also the pairing of stimuli and reinforcement as a way of making the stimuli in question exercise stimulus control over subsequent behaviour and at the same time turning them into secondary reinforcers which could then to some extent act as reinforcers in their own right. Here stress is laid in the first place on a detailed analysis of the behaviour which it is intended to bring about, including its perceptual components. It is for this reason that we have devoted a comparatively large portion of this chapter to the characteristics of the behaviour aimed at. In the context of many current training practices it is by no means redundant to suggest that a clear and detailed understanding of the objectives of training helps in setting up conditions favourable to bringing them about.

'Knowledge of results'

The insistence on the importance of reinforcement, and particularly on the importance of providing it rapidly, makes

---

* In asking this last question we should like again to emphasize, as we have done in several places in this book, that a learning model may provide a useful guide for bringing about changes in behaviour, while yet remaining unsuitable as a basis for explaining how the behaving organism functions. We shall return to this point later in the chapter.

one look around for events which, in the course of a developing skill, might serve this function. It is clear that when dealing with human behaviour, if we wish to think in reinforcement
terms at all, we must get away from pellets of rat-cake or
drops of condensed milk, and their direct equivalents: yet we
have argued elsewhere that the unlimited extension of the
reinforcement concept robs it of its original usefulness. A very
considerable yet meaningful extension is, however, possible if
we accept the idea of an objective, or goal, as a condition of an
organism which can be 'matched' by external events; and if we
regard the occurrence of such a match as providing reinforcement. This has an important implication for the setting up of a
learning situation, without requiring us to know in detail
what the objectives of the learner are at any one time. We must
provide him with information on the basis of which he is
able to judge whether or not he has achieved his goal, whatever it may be; though it will also be important to help him in
setting himself appropriate goals. The learner should be in a
position to receive information about the consequences of his
own activity, he should obtain *knowledge of results*. And if it
is supposed to act as a reinforcement, it should be provided as close as possible to the behaviour that is to be reinforced.

Let us see what this means in terms of a sensorimotor skill.
In many cases the situation is such that the necessary information is provided automatically. In the case of mirror drawing, for example, the learner can see immediately what the
consequences of his movements are; he also has the criteria
by which to judge the adequacy of that performance. Frequently, however, this is not the case. The only criteria which the
learner understands and can recognize may be a long way, in
time, from his present activity. One might be reinforced by the
sight of a tied shoe lace, but if this is the only available criterion the behaviour leading to it may be a long time in presenting itself for reinforcement.

We have encountered this kind of problem before when dis-
cussing the shaping of behaviour. The procedure involved the

137

systematic change of reinforcement contingencies to 'edge' the behaviour from its starting point to the eventual goal. In the case of an animal, the possibilities of communication are severely limited, and must depend largely on providing carefully timed reinforcement. In the case of human beings it is possible to abbreviate the shaping procedure, not only by providing instructions for what to do, but also by helping to set criteria of adequate performance which may act as sub-goals on the way to the final achievement.

'Demonstration and Verbal Instruction'

This throws an interesting light on two common aspects of teaching or training. The use of verbal instructions is effective only to the extent to which the words used in fact convey the necessary message. The most detailed account of how to move clutch and accelerator in starting a car from rest does not by itself produce in the learner the necessary motor responses. There are aspects of this operation which a verbal description conveys only to someone who has already mastered the skill. What the verbal instruction does do, however, is to get the behaviour approximately right, and this provides an enormous short-cut in the shaping procedure that would otherwise be necessary.

It is at this point that the provision of a usable criterion becomes important. This may take the form of drawing attention to relevant aspects of the situation which are closely related to the activity – for example, demonstrating and emphasizing changes in engine noise, which occur as the clutch is slowly released, or alternatively the use of special instruments, such as a revolution counter, which supply extra information in a form that the learner can easily appreciate. Providing supplementary information of this sort is possible in many cases where we are concerned with learning to operate a piece of equipment, and it is one of the aims at which the design of training devices should be directed.

The second feature of training procedures which may be seen

in a new and useful way is demonstration. In showing a learner how to do something, the demonstrator provides among other things a picture of what correct performance *looks* like. In so far as this can be remembered, this constitutes a criterion which the learner can then use for judging his own performance, it allows him to set himself an appropriate goal. Seen from this point of view, the demonstration, as it appears to the learner, should resemble as closely as possible what he is likely to see when he makes his own attempt. This has obvious implications, for example, for the way the demonstrator should stand in relation to the learner.

The emphasis on speedy reinforcement also implies the importance of comment by an instructor during the stages of a performance, rather than simply at the end or even some time after completion. But there are limits, imposed both by the nature of the task and by the instructor's available time, on the speed and frequency with which such comment can be provided. Criteria of judgement which are directly available to the learner have enormous advantages in this respect; and one could say that one of the most important functions of a teacher or trainer is to provide, where possible, criteria which the learner can himself use to judge the quality of his own performance. The advisability of splitting up a task into manageable sections, each with its own clearly defined goal, is another consequence of this view. One cannot legislate in advance about the optimum size of such a section, it must depend on the nature of the task and to some extent on the individual learner. But the important role played by reinforcement in the form of achieving an objective suggests division into components of activity which end in an easily observable result, in terms of which a criterion can be provided.

This sort of partitioning of performance – concentrating for example on the operation of gear change, in a way that is relatively isolated from the other driving operations with which it will eventually have to be linked – does have its disadvantages. We have emphasized earlier the smooth and rhythmic nature of skilled performance, and the deliberate breaking up of the performance does by itself not favour the development of continuity. It becomes necessary, therefore – and this is an important stage in the learning procedure – to link up the various sections, gradually if there are many, by concentrating on joint performance, once the individual parts have been adequately mastered.

Sequential performance and 'chaining'

We may see some similarity between this linking up procedure, and the development of behavioural chains in animals which have already been briefly described – although this is usually done by starting at the end point of the total chain and work-ing systematically backwards. To restate the method: We arrange for a response, R1, to secure a reward. When this re-sponse is established, we make the provision of reward condi-tional on the presence of a stimulus, S1. This brings the be-haviour under stimulus control of S1 and at the same time makes S1 into a secondary reinforcer. We now arrange a new contingency, whereby a response R2 produces the onset of S1, and this establishes a short chain, R2-S1-R1-reward. Next the R2-S1 sequence is made conditional on a new stimulus S2, which in turn becomes the reinforcer for yet another response R3 and so on. By using this sort of procedure quite long sequences of operations can be established in relatively primi-tive animals such as rats or pigeons.

In a recent experiment, R. M. Gilbert at the University of Aberdeen investigated the effect of modifying the sequence of the controlling stimuli, once a chain has been established. Having taught rats to pull two suspended pieces of chain in sequence, and to follow this by pressing two levers, each operation being followed by a characteristic signal (the last one being food), he changed the order in which the signals occurred. Thus R3, which would normally lead to the onset of S2, might now be followed by S1 or S4. Gilbert found that if this change took place at a time at which the total chain had been performed a comparatively small number of times, he could thereby change the order in which the *responses* occurred, i.e. they remained under the stimulus control of the original signals. However, if a greater amount of practice intervened before the change, it ceased to have any effect, and the response chain R4-R3-R2-R1 would 'run off' apparently without reference to the changed order of the 'controlling' stimuli. The control of the sequence had become internalized, and the finding provides an interesting parallel to the establishment of the larger response units which we referred to earlier.

Knowledge of results and motivation

There is an additional argument in favour of the partitioning of learning tasks. We have in this chapter emphasized almost exclusively the informational aspect of knowledge of results, i.e. the pin-pointing of significant events. But there is also a motivational one. When, in the course of shaping animal behaviour, we set too high a requirement, so that reinforcement is too long delayed, the animal is likely to start doing something else, or just go away if it has the opportunity. This phenomenon is not unknown in the context of training schemes, and it is often the consequence of learners failing to make progress – as far as they are able to observe. Such failure is to some extent, by comparison with other successful learners, a failure of the individual. But it can also be seen as a failure of the training schedule, which has at some stage made reinforcement difficult to attain, leading to a consequent loss of interest in the whole procedure. There is no doubt that a modification of many training schemes in line with this requirement would substantially reduce the 'wastage' that is so frequently involved through learners failing to complete.

The distribution of practice

We must now consider an aspect of learning which is relatively independent of those we have so far considered. This is the question of spacing practice sessions. Other things being equal, what difference does it make to the rate of progress if we vary the length of individual sessions and separate them by intervals of varying length? We are here concerned with the rate of progress measured against the amount of practice, and not against absolute time, since, obviously, when learning sessions are spaced at very long intervals the total time taken to achieve a given criterion will be longer. From a practical point of view, this need not be a disadvantage, provided the intervals between learning sessions can be utilized in some other way, and this does mean that they must be of sufficient length to make this possible.

There is evidence that effectiveness of a given number of learning trials is greater when they are spread out than when they occur closer together. The finding is related to a phenomenon called *reminiscence,* the term being used in a technical sense and having only a very partial overlap with the common usage. It has been found in a wide range of learning studies of both a verbal and a motor skill type, that if the performance is tested immediately after a rapid succession of learning trials the result is not as good as that obtained after allowing a few minutes to elapse. It is this improvement in performance without practice which is called 'reminiscence', and when measured against expenditure in terms of practice it constitutes a sort of learning bonus. Distributed practice may be thought of as benefiting from this effect, and there is in fact little difference between practice with short and practice with long intervals between sessions. In a study of mirror drawing skill, Lorge compared the effect of interposing intervals of one minute, and of twenty-four hours between twenty practice trials, with equivalent continuous practice. He found that while both distributed practice groups were superior to that with massed practice, there was little difference between them.

The relation between the benefits of spaced practice and reminiscence does not of course constitute an explanation of either. A number of theoretical accounts have been offered, of which that in terms of reactive inhibition put forward by Clark

Hull is the most developed, and has also been advanced as an explanation of experimental extinction (Chapter 8). In this theory it is suggested that as a consequence of making any response there is an increment in a tendency *not* to make it. This tendency is called *reactive inhibition* and its strength is regarded as a function of the number of responses made, the interval between them and the effort involved. It constitutes a kind of fatigue variable, and dissipates in time. If reactive inhibition is allowed to build up, failures to respond will be reinforced by reducing what is seen essentially as a *drive* not-to-respond; in this way *conditioned inhibition* is developed, counteracting the response habit which has been built up through the reduction of other drives.

The longer the individual practice session, the more reactive inhibition develops, and the greater is the drive not to respond at the end of the session. This does not necessarily provide an argument for the superiority of short sessions. We might say, for example, that with frequent short sessions, reinforcement for not-responding, though less in 'amount', is more frequent, and that we should therefore get more effective interference with learning. There is in any case evidence that the effect of concentrated v. distributed practice does not survive an exchange of learning conditions – i.e. the performance levels of two groups, that have been trained by the respective methods, will rapidly interchange, if the practice conditions are interchanged. This is analogous to the effect of punishment coupled with reinforcement, which will affect the performance level while it lasts, without apparently changing the degree of learning.

The effect on performance of long work sessions has been demonstrated in tasks which involve very little expenditure of energy, and it would be misleading to think of whatever it is that interferes with performance in terms of physical fatigue. In fact, impairment is particularly pronounced in tasks involving careful observation, such as watching of radar screens for unusual signals, inspection tasks or the repeated adjustment of precision instruments. Thus E. L. Saldanha, in a work not yet published, gave subjects the task of adjusting Vernier gauges to prescribed settings in rapid succession, and found a marked deterioration in accuracy, though not in speed, after periods of as little as twenty minutes. In another experiment, involving a pursuit rotor, in which subjects are required to keep a stylus in contact with a moving target, Adams[2] found that the beneficial effect of rest pauses was significantly reduced if during this period subjects watched *others* performing the same task. Reactive inhibition does not provide a very satisfactory explanation of what may in fact be several distinct phenomena, but unfortunately there is so far no clearly superior account to take its place.

The transfer of training

The activities involved in formal learning and training procedures are inevitably restricted and it is clearly the intention of such procedures that they will make possible or facilitate a far wider range of achievements than those that were actually practised. Certainly this is true of the general education we receive. We expect the consequence of learning one 'thing' to transfer to a variety of others. The question therefore arises to what extent such transfer actually takes place, and whether there are any particular features of learning tasks or methods which bring about widespread transfer.

There has been a reaction away from earlier beliefs in the existence of a limited number of disciplines, such as Latin or mathematics, which would simply 'train the mind', enabling it to cope with virtually any demand that might subsequently be made on it. It is now recognized, and this is particularly true of motor skills, that the effects of training are much more limited by the extent to which elements of skill learned actually form a component of other required achievements. Thus if a man becomes proficient at tightening screws, this will transfer to other tasks which involve the same sort of operation. If a group of tasks have a number of operations in common, the learning of those operations will be of benefit in the whole group. On the other hand, in so far as a particular task involves the performance of a number of operations in a given sequence, the effects of practice in producing a *rhythm* of movement will be specific to the sequence being practised, and will have to be established anew in each case.

We expect facilitation or positive transfer to take place between activities which are similar, and one aspect of similarity is the existence of identical 'elements' in the activities. The idea of similarity, however, requires further analysis. If we consider again the example of mirror drawing, we might think of the operations of tracing the outline of a particular star pattern, with and without mirror, as being highly similar; and yet practice under one condition interferes with performance in the other, i.e. we get negative transfer. Tracing patterns of very different appearance, on the other hand, might be seen as constituting dissimilar tasks; yet there is considerable benefit from practising one pattern with the use of a mirror to being able to trace another under the same conditions. There is also positive transfer from using one hand to using the other.

The important aspect of similarity which this example illustrates is that found in the *relationship* between stimulus input and motor output. This relationship is different as between the mirror and no-mirror conditions, but the same within them; we can in fact expect to find positive transfer between tasks in which the stimulus-response relationships are the same; negative transfer or interference between tasks in which the same stimuli require different and incompatible responses; and little or no transfer between situations involving radically different stimulus inputs.

Our earlier discussion has, however, emphasized the complexity of the idea of stimulus. Identical circumstances may be seen in different ways by different individuals, and one of the important features of training is to encourage attention to those aspects of the stimulus situation that are most relevant to the ongoing activity. The effect of the learning situation on selective attention can also be utilized to facilitate particular sorts of transfer or generalization. Suppose, for example, that we teach an animal a discrimination task, in which blue circles are always reinforced, and red squares are not reinforced, or punished. To what extent will this habit transfer to discrimination between circles and squares of the same colour, or to discrimination between colours, irrespective of shape? What actually happens in this instance will depend both on the nature and experience of the animal, on whether the particular differences of colour or of shape used in the experiment are generally of 'significance' to the animal, or whether they tend to be ignored. We can also, however, use the training procedure to emphasize one or other aspect of the situation by following it with a series of further discrimination problems, in which shape is reinforced irrespective of colour, or colour irrespective of shape, producing a selective attention to the feature which has been singled out. In this way we can develop an ability to respond to shapes, say, which will transfer to others having colours *which have not in fact been used during the learning trials.*

The above is an example of the way in which the presentation of a series of learning tasks can direct the learner to a common feature they contain, and free him from dependence on irrelevant aspects of any particular learning situation. As we might expect, animals vary enormously in their ability to 'catch on to' features of different degrees of complexity. For example, Harlow[3] has shown that chimpanzees can learn to solve 'oddity problems', i.e. problems in which the animal is presented with three objects, two of which are alike, and where the correct response consists in selecting the odd one. Chimpanzees, having been presented with a limited number of such problems, can solve others, in which the actual objects used are not the same as those in the previous learning trials. This is an achievement of which more primitive animals such as rats are not capable. The ability to abstract common features from a limited series of instances is most highly developed in human beings, and will be discussed further in the chapter on concept formation and the use of language. In the sense that the use of language may be regarded as a high-level skill, the ability of human beings to learn the grammar of a language, as a result of being exposed to and using a limited number of correctly structured sentences, may be of particular relevance in the present context. What we wish to suggest is that, nothwithstanding differences in 'abstracting ability' that may exist between different individuals, effective transfer of training to a variety of tasks is best encouraged by an emphasis on *variety* in the training situation, as opposed to concentration on one particular use of skill, or on one particular set of circumstances.

The development and execution of skilled behaviour

We must now return briefly to a discussion of an issue which has turned up at various points in this book – a comparison between accounts of learning and accounts of behaviour. It may have become apparent that we have talked about the nature of skilled performance in terms that are rather different from those used in describing its acquisition. This points to a division in experimental and theoretical work on behaviour which could lie at the root of some of the inadequacies of S-R theories of learning. Investigations of learning have concentrated on the performance of single acts or responses, leading to a preoccupation with aspects of performance which may not be appropriate, or at any rate sufficient, for an understanding of organized activity.

It is not helpful to try to express the skill of a pianist or the quality of an orchestra in terms of volume of sound output, or the speed with which a particular piece of music is completed. Loudness and speed are certainly aspects of a musical performance, and it would be possible, by the use of suitably chosen reinforcement schedules which are contingent on these aspects, to make people play louder, faster or more frequently. This does by no means show, however, that these are the appropriate variables in terms of which to understand the execution of a musical performance. It may be possible to induce a player to produce a sequence of notes by means of a chaining procedure, but this method of production does not necessarily provide an adequate account of the way in which that sequence of notes is subsequently executed. The shift in Gilbert's experiment from external stimulus control of his rats' behaviour to autonomous performance, was something characteristic of the way in which these animals' nervous systems functioned, and there is no reason to suppose that the terms in which *external* control can be described provide a useful description of the nature of *internal* control. The effect of giving reinforcement to an orchestra as a whole will depend on its internal organization, on the presence, for example, of a conductor, and sooner or later we will have to address ourselves to this problem of internal organization if we wish to understand how an orchestra functions. The terms in which we most easily describe the behaviour of the group, regarded as a unit, may well prove totally unsuitable to this discussion. Equally, the organization involved in the pianist's performance is likely to require a different model for its explanation, from that likely to emerge from a concern with the production of single notes.

In talking about the development of integrated 'response units' such as the typing of whole words or phrases 'at one go', and generally in stressing the organized aspect of skilled activity, we have used terms such as 'programme', with the implication that such programmes for activity, including their temporal characteristics, must in some sense *exist* in the skilled organism, even prior to their execution. Miller, Gallanter and Pribram [4] have drawn attention to this programmed aspect of behaviour in general, using the term *plan*. They emphasize primarily the explicit, conscious plan for carrying out a sequence of actions – plans that could, for example, be externalized by making notes, or communicating them to other people. But the concept also covers the idea of an internal and not necessarily conscious reference framework for ongoing activity. The essential notion would seem to be that of *internal reference* – involved both in making a comparison between internal state (representing a 'goal') and some sensory input from outside, the discrepancy between them controlling ongoing behaviour; and also in providing a guide for more rigid and timed sequences of responses, with little or no susceptibility to external influences.

One interesting feature of skilled activity is the possibility of change from 'automatic' to a more flexible and conscious control. Many routine and highly practised activities can proceed quite smoothly with the minimum of attention being given to them. Yet if an unusual situation arises – an odd noise in a machine, for example – the smooth flow of the operation is interrupted, and control passes to a 'higher level': we start thinking about what to do next. External signals can form an integral part in the execution of a skilled activity, but they can also produce a shift in the level of control exercised. One could here make a (guarded) analogy to the transfer of control within an organization, from operator level to that of the foreman, say, if the former encounters a situation he is not competent to deal with. It seems likely that the structure of organisms is hierarchical in character, with control shifting between levels according to the demands of the situation. The analogy between organisms, and organizations composed of many people with different capacities and responsibilities, should not however lead one to assume that control within the organism is the function of clearly demarcated units ; nor for that matter should it be taken as a justification for regarding people within an organization simply as carrying out rigidly prescribed functions towards the furtherance of some higher aim.

In looking for explanations of organized behaviour, it might be best to turn our attention to the structure of other systems exhibiting similar properties. The science of cybernetics, which is concerned explicitly with problems of control in animals and machines, seems likely to provide a language which is more suitable for the analysis of human and animal behaviour, than the terminology of S-R theories of learning. Discussions of skill, in so far as they have been concerned with how a skilled organism *functions,* have in fact increasingly drawn on cybernetic concepts, involving the inter-relationships between the parts of a system. This has not, however, been true of discussions of *learning*; that is to say, both within psychology and within cybernetics, there has been comparatively little attention paid to the properties of systems which are required to make possible changes in their own internal structure, as a result of interaction with the environment.*

Skill should be regarded, not so much as a particular range of activities, but rather as an aspect of all forms of behaviour. The integration of work on skill into the framework of investigations of learning should provoke a significant advance in our understanding of learning phenomena.

* Notable exceptions are the approaches of D. O. Hebb, referred to in Chapter 4, and of J. A. Deutsch in *The Structural Basis of Behaviour*.

8. The retention of learned material

Once an octopus has learned to distinguish between squares and rectangles or a barrister has familiarized himself with the case of *Regina v. Snooks*, either individual is liable, when the occasion arises, to provide some evidence of this learning. At each new trial – if the pun may be permitted – at which the octopus discriminates, or the lawyer quotes, we can say that the original learning is in some way still effective, that something has been *retained*. During the learning period itself the effects of practice are cumulative, there is some retention from occasion to occasion. And there is no fundamental distinction between retention of a learned response from one practice session to the next and retention thereafter. In this sense retention is almost synonymous with learning. The octopus is not to know that the training period is officially over. However, the comparatively long period between test trials, such as might occur once we are no longer concerned with acquisition, highlights such questions as 'What happens to the learned response during this time?' 'Do the events occurring within the period make any difference?' 'Does it matter how long it is?' Many of the standard studies of learning that we have considered are not explicitly concerned with these problems, and this provides one reason for treating them separately. There is another. Both feats and failures of memory are a prominent feature of human verbal learning and as a result retention has been extensively studied in this area. While this chapter is concerned with problems of retention in general, there will be an emphasis on the remembering and forgetting of verbal material.

Before going on to look at some experimental procedures and results, a word of caution about the term 'retention'. When we use a phrase like 'a part of the original learning has been retained' it is easy to start thinking of the process of learning

151

as putting *something* into the learner; of part being kept intact, being retained – the rest being somehow lost. Particularly when dealing with verbal material, there is a temptation to think of memory as being like a record, containing a large number of traces, each item remembered corresponding to a particular trace. Some survive, some are erased. This can be most misleading if we forget that it is only a metaphor. To be sure, learning must produce changes in the organism, which then make possible various sorts of behaviour. But we must not jump to conclusions about the nature of those changes or their relation to the behaviour they make possible.

How do we measure what has been retained? We might consider the criteria that we normally use. The most obvious one is the ability to reproduce, to recall. A measure of how well an actor can remember his lines is the accuracy with which he can speak them. But this is not the only measure. Even though failing to produce the words, he might still recognize them when presented in conjunction with others. This aspect of retention is most clearly evident in the retention of pictorial material, where we quickly learn to recognize but where any sort of reproduction is quite a different matter. While recognition is often possible without recall, recall implies recognition and is, therefore, a more comprehensive test of memory. There is also a third possible indicator. Returning to a part he has not played for some time, an actor might fail to recall any of it. But if we compare the amount of work he has to put into 'refreshing his memory', with the effort that went into the original learning, we would find that in general it was much less. Again, 'something' has been retained. All these – recall, recognition and the saving in the amount of re-learning necessary – are aspects of retention (of learning); and they form the basis of more systematic measuring procedures in the laboratory.

Suppose that the material to be learned consists of a list of words, and that they are presented to the subject one after the other. The apparatus normally used for this purpose is called a memory drum, and consists of a revolving cylinder, turning past a screen with a slit in it, so that words written on the drum are exposed in succession. Sometimes alternative arrangements are used that make it possible to change the order in which material is presented while the experiment is going on. After the first complete presentation, the subject can start trying to anticipate each word before it appears. The presentation is continued until some criterion has been achieved, such as two consecutive perfect sets of anticipations. In order to measure retention after an interval of time, we may now use the same procedure – which is essentially a method based on recall – and score the number of errors. Alternatively, we may count the number of complete presentations required to achieve the original criterion of two perfect lists and compare it to the number of such presentations that were required to achieve the criterion for the first time. This is a 'savings' method. A recognition method would involve the presentation of the words to be learned mixed up with others and asking the subject to identify them. In the present context, which involves the learning of words *in a given sequence*, the result of such a procedure would be difficult to interpret, since the introduction of new words would destroy the sequence. The recognition method is sometimes used in tests and examinations, involving the selection of the 'right' answer from among a number that are wrong.

Results obtained by using these different methods cannot be compared in any quantitative way. As has already been pointed out recall is the most stringent measure, since what is recalled will almost always be recognized, and will not have to be re-learned. The savings method is the most sensitive, but only in the sense that even when nothing is recalled or recognized, this method will often show some retention. Beyond this we cannot go. We are looking at different aspects of the changes brought about by learning. Any investigation which seeks to compare retention under different circumstances – such as using different methods of learning – must use the same measurement procedure for its comparisons.

Why do we forget?

We could, of course, counter this question by asking 'why for that matter should we remember?' And this reopens the whole problem of learning in its full generality. At the moment, however, we are concerned with those cases where there has already been evidence of learning. A man is introduced to someone and later addresses him by name. A student has just translated a prose passage from French to English. A rat finds its way through a maze without errors. Why should any of them fail on a future occasion?

One reason could, of course, be that the occasion is in fact different. Words seen in one context are often easier to translate than when seen in another. We often fail to recall people's names and who they are if we see them under unfamiliar circumstances. If we look for factors influencing retention, we must examine the occasion when retention is being assessed, and also that of the original learning as well as the intervening period. This we shall do later in the chapter.

Forgetting is, of course, a familiar experience, particularly if long periods of time are involved. We talk about memory 'fading' or being 'a little rusty'. These expressions are simply ways of *referring* to the fact of forgetting – but in the choice of metaphor used there lurks a theory. Over a period of time colours fade and iron rusts, unless special precautions are taken. It is not, of course, time itself, but processes happening in time that lead to corrosion and decay – nevertheless, some events require special intervention to bring them about, others will occur unless positive steps are taken to prevent them. One theory of forgetting is that it comes about simply through disuse; that it is in the nature of whatever forms the basis of memory to erode and vanish unless kept in existence by suitable exercise. As an alternative we may suppose that forgetting takes place because of what happens to an individual during the retention period, i.e. interference with retention is produced by specific external influences.

154

If the second of these hypotheses were true we should expect that if, shortly after learning something, an individual is somehow shielded from all experience and then re-tested, retention would be near perfect. Two experimenters, Minami and Dallenbach,[1] trained two groups of cockroaches to acquire a particular form of avoidance response. The experimental group were placed in a 'non-behaving' state by being subjected to contact over a large part of the body surface, which produces immobility in cockroaches. The control group were forced to engage in activity during this time and both groups were then tested for retention of the avoidance response; the immobilized group performed significantly better on this test than the activity group, showing that loss of retention was at least partly attributable to behaviour during the period between learning and test.

Essentially similar experiments have been carried out with human subjects, though the method for bringing about non-behaviour is, of course, rather different. Here the experimental group sleeps after the initial learning, usually of verbal material, while the control group go about their normal activities. Again there is less impairment of retention in the sleeping compared to the active group. What loss does occur is concentrated on the first two hours after learning ceases and might be accounted for in part by the inevitable activity before sleep actually comes about. In any case, the two types of hypothesis do not have to be mutually exclusive. The results confirm that some loss of retention is related to activity and experience during the intervening periods, and the problem becomes that of throwing some light on to this relationship.

Experimental investigations follow the basic pattern already described. Two or more groups learn the same task A to a specified criterion. After this they undergo retest on task A (the original material). Any systematic differences in performance can be ascribed to differences between the effects of the interpolated activities. Such effects are usually referred to as *retroactive inhibition or interference* if they involve impairment of the original performance.

155

Interest has mainly been focused on introducing a second *learning* task between the initial learning of A and re-test. And, as might be expected, the effect of such a second learning task depends on its similarity to the first. Suppose, for example, that subjects originally learn to assign names to ten unfamiliar objects, i.e. they learn to make specific responses to a set of stimuli that are provided. Of the infinite number of possible second tasks we might consider four sub-categories, (a) where both stimuli and responses are identical to those in the first task, (b) where the stimuli are the same, but the required responses are different, (c) where stimuli are different, but the responses are the same and (d) where both stimuli and responses are different. Of these, maximum retention loss is obtained with (b) where in this instance subjects would learn to respond to the same object first with one word, then with another. In the case of (a) the subject is simply continuing to practise the original task and this obviously helps rather than hinders. (c) does not produce interference and can produce some facilitation. (d) produces various degrees of interference depending on the degree of similarity between initial and interpolated stimuli and responses.

There are considerable difficulties in trying to define 'similarity', and attempts to obtain general rules relating degree of similarity between first and second task to extent of interference have not been very successful. It will suffice for our present purpose to salvage the general result that if the responses required in the first and second task are different, then interference increases as the stimuli in the two tasks become increasingly similar. Confusion is greatest when on separate occasions people are called upon to behave in different ways under similar circumstances. This might suggest the following model of what takes place. The first learning session produces a set of stimulus-response tendencies. During the second learning period a conflicting set is built up and during re-test there is some sort of competition between responses, leading to impairment in the production of the first set. S-R bonds are not so much weakened as replaced by new ones. There is some evidence for a process of this kind. During re-test people often make responses appropriate to the interpolated task which are now errors. However, this is not the whole story. Melton and Irwin [2] observed that the number of interpolated task responses made during re-test is not proportional to the total number of errors of all kinds. They found that as the number of trials on the interpolated task was increased the intrusions of interpolated responses during re-test decreased, while total errors did not. They concluded that interference with retention must be attributed to at least two factors and suggest that the additional factor is the partial 'unlearning' of the original task at the time of learning the interpolated task.

As we have seen, where the tasks are to some extent incompatible, the responses appear to compete at the time of re-learning. But there is also competition of responses at the time of learning the interpolated task, and in order that the interpolated task may be learned the responses of the original task must in some way be suppressed. This has the result that at re-test the original responses are less likely to be emitted than they would have been without the interpolated learning, quite apart from the competition factor which interferes with them. They have in effect been weakened.

While this view accounts for the fact that the tendency to omit – or forget – a correct response and the tendency to replace it by some specifically learned alternative do not quite go together, it runs into other difficulties. It is found that the more intensely the first task is learned, the less retention is affected by the second. This is to be expected. But if we increase the amount of effort given to learning the second interpolated task there comes a point where there is no increase in interference; there can even be relative improvement in the re-test performance of the first task. On the model we have just considered, we should expect interference with the first task to increase steadily with the amount of practice given to the second.

A straightforward stimulus-response model does not do justice to the behaviour we are considering. Reports from

157

experimental subjects indicate some of its inadequacies. Frequently, before the emission of the overt response, different possible responses are considered, until eventually one is accepted. Increased learning of the second set of S-R pairs leads to fewer false responses during re-test, since they are increasingly recognized as belonging to the second set, and are in consequence not 'passed'. This process of checking seems to be at least partly independent of the process which produces possible responses for scrutiny – responses known to be wrong can sometimes 'suggest themselves' with irritating persistence.

Obviously an adequate theoretical model must deal with both the process of response production and response checking and must show how the balance of 'correctness' of these processes changes with, among other things, quantity of interpolated material. A theory of Underwood's,[3] for example, which approaches this problem from the point of view of degree of differentiation of the original and interpolated material, deals to some extent with this problem. He suggests that intermediate degrees of learning of both tasks brings about most confusion and hence interference.

Whatever the precise form of the process underlying this form of retention loss, it is clear that interaction with the environment – new learning – in the interval between final learning trial and memory test accounts for a good deal of the forgetting usually found.

Forgetting and extinction

There are many things we learned in school which later as adults we find we have forgotten. As has already been suggested, this may be in part because the circumstances are now different from those that originally evoked the evidence for our knowledge. But we do forget things that had been familiar, even in unchanged situations and over shorter periods of time. Using 'behaviour language' we could say that, in forgetting, responses fail to occur where previously we had come to expect them. And that, after all, is what is involved in extinction.

Here too, the failure is not permanent, there is spontaneous recovery. Could it be that extinction and forgetting are basically the same phenomenon, that we can use the same explanatory ideas in both cases?

We normally use forgetting to refer to response loss in humans and extinction to refer to the loss of a conditioned response in animals, and the question is whether the animal-human difference is the only important one. A comparison of the circumstances surrounding extinction and forgetting respectively shows up some important differences.

A man arriving at a meeting of some secret organization can fail to give the password on arrival because (a) although he once knew it he is at the moment unable to recall it, (b) although he remembers it he can see no point in giving it, not having been challenged on a number of previous occasions, or (c) he is too deeply in conversation with another man to notice that he has arrived.

We would talk about forgetting only in case (a) and perhaps in a somewhat different sense in (c), but not in (b). On the other hand, we have the nearest parallel to extinction in case (b), though if (a) and (c) were a regular occurrence they too would be included. We cannot, of course, tell the difference between the three cases if as experimenters we confine our observations simply to the occurrence of the password, because it is omitted in all three cases. But if we looked at other aspects of behaviour we could easily distinguish between failure to recall the word, and say, disinclination to produce it.

In the case of animals failing to produce a learned response after several non-reinforced trials we are seldom in a position to check whether the response is no longer available (is forgotten), whether the animal is distracted by other stimuli or whether it is simply reacting to a change in the pay-off pattern.

A number of different theories have been advanced to explain extinction and they tend to emphasize one or other of these types of explanation. One group of theories is based on the idea that the animal develops an increasing disinclination to make the response and, in the absence of reinforcement, this is not countered by a positive pay-off, so eventually he stops responding. The main theory of this type is Hull's re-active inhibition theory. Another approach is based on the idea that under conditions of changed reward the animal learns a new response, in practice he learns not to respond in the old way.

There are, in addition, theories concerned with a change in the pattern of the animal's expectancies as a result of with-drawal of reinforcement or with a change in his sensitivity to the appropriate stimuli.

In Hull's theory any response is said to produce a small increase in the tendency not to make the response again – an increase in reactive inhibition. This has many of the properties of fatigue, it accumulates as a result of responding, it dissipates in time if responses stop and it can bring about a cessation of responses even when they are being reinforced if it builds up quickly enough. Normally the excitatory potential generated by reinforcement is sufficient to maintain the response, but when reward is withdrawn reactive inhibition builds up until the animal stops responding.

When extinction trials are resumed after an interval, reac-tive inhibition has dispersed, so the response occurs again – spontaneous recovery. This process would not explain the permanent extinction which is found after several sets of ex-tinction trials, so it is supplemented by a re-learning process. Reactive inhibition is seen as a drive which is reduced when responding stops. Drive reduction being the essential con-dition for learning, the response of 'not responding' or resting is learned and after several sets of extinction trials the response will not occur again, it will be permanently extinguished. So this theory becomes essentially a re-learning theory. The postu-lation of reactive inhibition serves to explain how the response first becomes weakened and also supplies the drive which must be reduced as the necessary condition for acquiring the com-petitive response.

Alternative theories which emphasize re-learning have run into difficulties when trying to explain how the first new response is made (i.e. before the old response has been weakened by competition), and in practice most theories of this type must include some postulate equivalent to reactive inhibition in order to explain the initial weakening of the response to be extinguished. So theories concerned essentially with response loss generally become two-factor theories, with the permanent loss being brought about by re-learning. This process is in many ways equivalent to the processes operating in forgetting.

The primary difficulty with theories such as Hull's, which concentrate on response loss, is that extinction can be shown to occur in situations where no response is made and this has led to the development of theories concerned on the one hand with more 'central' learning, with the acquisition of different expectancies, and on the other to changes in selection of stimuli.

All theories emphasizing re-learning as the main process in extinction have difficulty in explaining the fact that different conditions favour learning and extinction; massed trials, for example, slow down learning but accelerate extinction and this affects expectancy learning as well as response learning. On the other hand, the main theory concerned with changes in susceptibility to the relevant stimuli, Broadbent's [4] filter theory, has difficulty in explaining permanent extinction. The 'filter' is a process which selects stimuli for admission and has a permanent bias in favour of, among other things, novel stimuli. When the conditioned stimulus is presented repeatedly without reinforcement intervening the tendency of the filter to exclude the conditioned stimulus (and hence to stop the response) increases. In this theory the function of reinforcement is seen largely as providing an alternative stimulus input so that the conditioned stimulus has a permanent novelty value. Such a theory can explain extinction within one learning session and spontaneous recovery but, without additional postulates, cannot deal with final complete loss of the response. The situation envisaged in this approach might be equivalent to our case (c).

None of these theories is entirely satisfactory and we are

therefore not in a position to assert that extinction is essentially the same process as forgetting. We have seen in any case that forgetting is not a simple process and indeed probably several factors contribute to the result we call 'forgetting'. This does not mean that the phenomena we have come to know under the heading of extinction and those of forgetting are fundamentally different, but that when we look at the 'extinction of human responses' we find that we have to make distinctions which we cannot usually make when studying animal behaviour. It may be that not only is animal behaviour simpler than human behaviour but our methods of study may simplify our understanding of it still further. If, for example, we regard extinction in animal behaviour not as one process but as perhaps two or three, the reasons for the present multiplicity of theories and lack of complete success of any of them become clearer. It also gives us a partial answer to our general question of the relation of forgetting and extinction; extinction is a concept rooted in the behaviour of the animal and in process terms is wider than – includes – the concept of forgetting.

Qualitative changes in memory

So far we have been concerned with partial retention, with remembering some words from a list and not others. The underlying assumption has been that forgetting is not systematic, more and more may be forgotten as time goes on – as more retroactive inhibition occurs perhaps; but which particular parts of a learned sequence are forgotten is a matter of chance. A little consideration of our own experience convinces us that this does not correspond with the facts. When we return to a town unvisited for some years we may remember very well the general layout, but all the buildings may look smaller. We may have a good memory for names but one particular man's name always escapes us. When we re-read a book or see a film or play for the second time we may be surprised by certain incidents which appear distorted compared with our memory of them.

Some of these apparently qualitative differences in memory may be the effect of conflicting experiences. The man whose name is always forgotten may simply look very like someone else and the names are wrongly assigned. But most examples of this sort of change are probably not caused in this way. The most likely cause of such effects on retention are processes occurring in the person between exposure to the material and the time of remembering it, independently, more or less, of experience *during this interval*. Attempts to specify these processes in the context of ordinary forgetting, however, run up against certain essentially methodological difficulties. For example, most people would accept the proposition that we remember best those things we are interested in and forget those we are indifferent to. Perhaps we also forget most of all those things we actively dislike. And there are psychological theories which predict something of this kind.

The difficulty in testing such a notion is that original learning is seldom equated. If at any given time a person can remember several events or facts which are related to his interests and cannot remember certain others which do not concern him, this is by no means evidence for this theory. To say that he has forgotten certain facts presupposes that he once knew them or was at least exposed to them. But we have no means of knowing that they were ever learned as well as the facts which interested him and which are now remembered. Interest – motivation – will affect the likelihood and efficiency of original learning and without a control on the degree of original learning it is impossible to relate motivation and degree of retention.

While there are many experiments on this topic few, if any, demonstrate unequivocally that motivation affects *retention*; it can fairly easily be shown to affect ease of original learning. Even if original learning is equated (by testing immediate recall), it is difficult, if not impossible, to control rehearsal of the material in the interval between the end of learning and the test. In fact, while interesting material may be remembered better than uninteresting material, to which a person has also been exposed, it is generally the case that the interesting facts have been better learned in the beginning and more often called to mind or used in the interval. So we have no evidence that motivation affects retention as such.

One particular theory of this type, however, deserves special mention. This is the Freudian notion of repression. According to this idea, material which is associated with serious anxiety for the person tends to be forgotten in a special way, repressed. Such material is not completely lost but is not available for conscious recall. Attempts to demonstrate this process experimentally have met with little success and indeed encounter the same difficulties as other studies of motivation and retention. The theory was devised, however, to meet the needs of the clinical situation and there is little doubt that certain neurotic patients do forget material in ways which are not easy to describe in terms other than motivated forgetting. Cases of amnesia, for example, in which a person forgets a large number of facts associated with his personal identity, name, address, and so forth, can often be related to particular patterns of anxiety. Material which causes anxiety to a person cannot be equated with stimuli which are merely unpleasant and this may explain some of the failures of experimenters to reproduce this effect in the laboratory. At the same time this might indicate that repression is not a process which explains much forgetting but is peculiar to certain pathological states.

Some other forms of qualitative memory change are easier to demonstrate. An experiment carried out by Carmichael, Hogan and Walter [5] showed the effect of labelling on the retention of a visual form. They presented their subjects with a series of simple but ambiguous shapes. All subjects were shown the same shapes but half the subjects were given one set of names for them and the other half another set. When the subjects were asked to reproduce the shapes at the end of the experiment the drawings made by the two groups differed and showed the influence of the verbal label. One of these figures, for example, which looked like a reversed 'S' was labelled '2' for one group and '8' for the other group. The reproductions made showed the effect of this labelling, the '8' group producing more closed drawings. Further experiments have confirmed those findings and have shown also that even when a subject is not provided with a label his reproduction tends to be distorted in the direction of his own description of the object.

This effect seems to be a very general one and is not restricted to the assigning of the most likely name to a seen object and the distortion of this object in memory to conform to the name. There seem to be receptive processes which take in and store new information in terms of previously organized material and which result in progressive distortion of the learned material over time. When we read an article in a newspaper – or a book on the psychology of learning – we tend to relate the contents to our own experiences and preoccupations and to remember best those items which fit preconceived notions. Recall of the content of such an article at some future time would be much more a *reconstruction* of the article from a few highlights than any real *reproduction* of the original material.

This particular aspect of memory change has been emphasized by Bartlett.[6] His essential method was to present his subjects with a complex and usually ambiguous stimulus, a folk tale in an unfamiliar idiom or a drawing of an indeterminate animal, allow them to read the story once or twice or inspect the drawing and then, after various intervals, reproduce it. The changes in the material after successive reproductions were striking and certain general processes seemed to operate in the successive reproductions of almost all subjects. The accounts tended to become shorter and simpler and in general more coherent. Unexplained elements of the original story tended to disappear if they were peripheral or be provided with explanation if not. Additions to the story tended to be in line with the subject's own expectations or experience rather than in the terms of the story. The change was not total, of course; striking characteristics of the original served as structure for the reconstruction and sometimes even became exaggerated with time. These changes are not unlike the changes in information content of a rumour as it is passed from person to person, and indeed effects similar to those produced by one person over time can be demonstrated quickly by providing one person with a stimulus and the next with the first's reproduction and so on.

These results illustrate the reconstructive element in recall and certainly go some way towards explaining qualitative changes in memory. They are shown most clearly when the original stimulus is ambiguous or complex or both. This is not surprising, because an ambiguous stimulus is simply one which we find difficulty in categorizing. And it seems that memories are organized, at least to some extent, in terms of pre-existing categories. Whenever there is a mis-match between existing category systems and the properties of a new stimulus the possibility exists of some effect of this kind. It should be emphasized, however, that Bartlett's results imply more than simply that learned material is distorted during learning; the distortion – assimilation to pre-existing structures – continues after removal of the original material.

One important factor in remembering has been ignored so far in this discussion. This is the effect of 'set' or readiness to perform and the relationship of set during recall to that during learning. Set is obviously a property of the learner, but varies with surrounding stimuli as well as with any particular instructions given to, or preparations made by, the subject. We may fail to recognize a person in unfamiliar clothes or in an unusual place while we would instantly recognize him under more typical conditions. Similarly, material learned under one environmental condition may be easier to recall in the same environment than in a different one, even if the surroundings as such have nothing directly to do with the task. Some experiments show that retention loss can be very largely reduced by careful attention to such factors as set and general readiness for the task and this may in fact explain certain failures of memory usually put down to other causes. We sometimes fail to remember items of information if asked for them suddenly while thinking of something else, but can reproduce them correctly once we direct our attention to the task.

Immediate memory

We can usually dial a telephone number correctly after reading it or hearing it only once, provided we dial it immediately. But if we are asked, at the end of the telephone call, what the number was, we might well be unable to give it. This ability would not usually be described as learning, it makes only a very temporary change in our ability to respond, nevertheless the number was stored for a short time. It seems that there is a process of immediate memory which is distinct from longer-term memory processes. It is, first of all, a process of limited capacity, a very small memory store. Studies of the memory span (the number of items, such as digits, which can be correctly repeated after one presentation) show that the average is about seven items for young adults. The memory span is, of course, less for children and also shows a decline with age after about thirty. Immediate memory also shows a rapid decay with time which, as we have seen, is not characteristic of memory in general.

From the point of view of efficiency it would seem desirable to have a short-term store of limited capacity which can handle material which is required for immediate action and which does not have to be placed in the much larger longer-term store; this is a characteristic (perhaps not the only one) which people share with some electronic computers. What is more interesting is that it seems possible to store two sets of items received simultaneously so that they can be processed (reproduced or responded to in some other way) successively.

There is a good deal of evidence that essentially people can only do one thing at a time, they are 'single channel' devices. But this mode of operation does not apply to immediate memory. Broadbent [4] has carried out a number of experiments in which different information was presented simultaneously to both ears or to ears and eyes and, provided that the number of

167

items is small, both sets of information can be responded to. In one experiment, for example, three numbers were presented via headphones to one ear, while three different numbers were presented at the same time to the other ear. In general, the subjects could immediately reproduce all six numbers, although when presentation was fast the numbers were always grouped, the three received from one ear first then the numbers received in the other ear.

This highlights another aspect of the immediate memory process: the material tends to be reproduced in the form in which it is received. Immediate memory conforms much more closely to the idea of a memory trace – something which links reception and recall in a one-to-one fashion – than longer-term memory, which seems to permit reorganization of the material before or during recall. Immediate memory would seem to be a process with a very rapid decay, but we can remember telephone numbers for minutes rather than seconds provided we are free to repeat the number to ourselves, to rehearse it. This suggests that rehearsal of the number amounts to taking it out of the short-term store and then returning it so that on each circuit the elapsed decay time in the immediate memory store is returned to zero. Ultimately this process would result in the material being learned – securing access to the long-term memory store – but if, at any time prior to this, rehearsal is interrupted by an interval equal to the time of decay of the short-term memory, the material will be lost.

9. Concepts and the use of language

When we consider how central language and communication are to human behaviour, how language enters into the large majority of learning situations – at any rate those involving other people – it may seem surprising that one chapter only has been set aside to deal with this 'topic'. Language as an integral part of human behaviour might be expected to form a starting point of any discussion of human learning, and to the extent to which the use of language turned out to be an exclusively human characteristic, a case could be made for making a sharper distinction between people and animals, for showing a greater readiness to find differences in 'the laws of learning', than has been the case in our discussion so far. It is an argument that must be taken seriously. The trouble is that language – as distinct from mere vocalization – is an extremely complicated business and there have been proportionately few experimental investigations of learning concerned with language, except in a purely superficial sense.

Learning and language

We may distinguish a number of different ways in which the existence of language poses problems for any account of learning. There is in the first place the development of the sheer motor skills whereby language can be expressed – the actual production of the sounds and patterns of sound which a particular spoken language requires. In the mixture of noises in an infant's 'repertoire' gradually those particular sounds increase in frequency which characterize the language to which the infant is exposed.

In the normal development of speech it may be difficult to separate the growing skill of being able to make word-like noises from learning the appropriate occasions for their use.

The distinction is a valid one, however – children are obviously able to *pronounce* words without knowing their meaning in even the most primitive sense. It is also well known that certain animals such as parrots are able to make speech-like noises, extending sometimes to a considerable length, while there is a fundamental difference between their use of these utterances, and that of human beings. Since the particular sound pattern produced whether by child or by bird depends on the environment, this is clearly a learned achievement, and the question arises whether it can be accounted for in the same terms that have been proposed for rats in Skinner boxes.

Learning to *use* a language presents a separate and much more complex problem. It is only here that we can begin to speak of *language* as distinct from vocal behaviour. What this distinction amounts to will be discussed a little farther on. For the moment we may simply note that the acquisition of a language in this sense involves a further sub-division – learning to put words together to produce meaningful and acceptable sentences, and learning the relationship between such verbal forms and the situations in which they are appropriately used. Again, in practice these developments tend to go hand in hand, and it may not be possible to separate out those experiences that bring about competence in producing utterances which are acceptable in themselves – which make sense within the language – and those that lead to the ability to *use* such utterances to communicate. But the achievements are distinct to some extent. Language creates its own domain; children will often explore it, making verbal constructions apparently by following *linguistic* rules, and showing surprise and amusement when the result is considered from the point of view of its 'meaning'. 'Butterpups are winking in the paddy-wack' is a construction with the unmistakable form of an English sentence. Its significance, even the significance of its component words may be obscure, yet the correctness of its structure can be recognized independently. The fact that in the playing of such verbal games structure is often preserved independently of meaning – indeed, that it is possible to do so – indicates that this stage of language learning involves at least two types of achievement.

So far we have enumerated aspects of learning language. We may consider separately again the use of language in further learning. Most formal and informal teaching involves verbal communication – and although the effectiveness of this process is perhaps sometimes overestimated, obviously verbal communication *can* and does lead to new performance, both verbal and non-verbal. If someone is given directions to a particular place, there is at any rate a chance that he may successfully arrive at his destination; much more complex instructions are constantly translated into action. Can concepts like reinforcement, discrimination, or stimulus control deal with this sort of thing?

Animals and language

We have already referred to the ability of certain birds to reproduce strings of words, or sentences, yet we do not regard them as being able to speak, as having a language. Some very important features are missing in their behaviour compared to which the sometimes extremely close similarity to human speech of the actual sound patterns produced is quite trivial. A man who looks questioningly and points at his wrist and one who asks 'What is the time?' have something in common which is quite absent from the most word-perfect parrot. Human beings use language – though not always – to achieve an end, to communicate. And they are able to combine component parts of the language for a variety of purposes. These two criteria of language – purposeful use and the possibility of recombination of 'units' for different ends are met only in human behaviour – without even considering the kind of complexities involved in description of present or absent conditions, in imaginary descriptions, in arguments, etc.

This is not to say that we do not find purposive or goal-

171

directed behaviour in animals, involving some communication – such as when a dog brings his lead, wags his tail, and runs backwards and forwards between his owner and the door. The animal's activity is to some extent directed *at* his owner and continues with variations *until* a particular end result is achieved. Again the 'information' that can pass from one animal to another or a group of others is often quite complex, such as when the dance of a bee communicates the direction and distance of a food supply to the rest of the hive. Where such complex information transfer is found, however, it is specialized and non-adaptive. There are no indications that bees can use components of their dance to 'talk' about anything but the location of food.

What happens when we provide an animal with an environment resembling that of a child as closely as possible? Environment does not here mean simply a place with a given layout and containing certain objects, but includes people and the way they behave. Obviously the degree of approximation that we can achieve must depend on the animal. The extent to which we can follow normal patterns of *child* rearing when dealing, say, with a young rat is severely limited. But a young chimpanzee can without too much difficulty be integrated into a household as though he were a child. For example, W. N. and L. A. Kellog brought up a nine-month-old female chimpanzee together with their nine-month-old son exactly as though they were brother and sister. Although at the outset the chimpanzee learned a whole variety of physical skills more rapidly than the child, including response to simple verbal instructions, the child had caught up in most things after a period of nine months, and was beginning to develop language behaviour of a kind that was totally absent in the chimpanzee. The account of the experiment is contained in their book *The Ape and the Child*.

There have been other attempts to teach apes to speak (e.g. by K. J. and C. Hayes[1]), with similar results. After three years of training in circumstances resembling those of a young child as closely as possible, the chimpanzee was able to use a few isolated words like 'mama' or 'cup' in an appropriate context, but that was about the limit of its linguistic achievements.

If we consider the various peripheral aspects of verbal behaviour – the ability to produce speech sounds, the ability to make fine auditory discriminations – we find no reason why, for example, chimpanzees should be unable to learn a language. Again, communication, usually involving alarm signals, occurs in a variety of species, and sometimes, especially in the 'social insects', more elaborate messages are transmitted, though these are cases of one-way communication, where the sender of the message gives no indication that his behaviour *aims* at creating any particular effect. On the other hand, goal-focused or purposeful behaviour is common, particularly in the more highly evolved species, using the term purpose as a description rather than an explanation. Why is it then that a chimpanzee, when he is exposed to a pattern of experiences matching those of a human child as closely as possible, shows no sign of developing even rudimentary speech? The development of a stable language in a *species* would of course require the standardization and transmission from generation to generation of specific symbolic actions (not necessarily involving speech). But even when we present a ready-made culture to a young primate exactly as we present it to a child, he is unable to benefit from it. The difficulty obviously lies in him, he is not sufficiently 'intelligent'. But this is not really an answer, only an indication that we must concern ourselves to some extent with the properties of the animal. Chimpanzees, though in a general sense much more intelligent than parrots or myna birds, do not reproduce speech patterns. This particular way of responding to the impact of the environment is a kind of parrot speciality, as the details of the bee's dance are a specialized reaction to its food-searching experience. It would seem inevitable that any account of learning, if it claims to be comprehensive, must have within it some provision for the differences in genetic contributions to the learning situation. This is not to disparage the search for general laws, only the attempt to make them explain everything. Let us consider such an attempt.

The analysis of verbal behaviour

We have met the concepts of stimulus and response, of reinforcement, stimulus control, secondary reinforcement, schedules of reinforcement, etc. in earlier chapters. The conditions in which these terms were introduced were relatively clear-cut experimental set-ups, involving boxes with levers and lights, and sometimes more complex ones involving pigeons with other pigeons and ping-pong balls. By using the above terms to analyse these situations, and using a number of comparatively simple principles relating them to each other, B. F. Skinner and others have been able to achieve remarkable results in the control of the behaviour in question. In his book *Verbal Behaviour*, Skinner attempted to extend this sort of analysis to human speech and 'language behaviour' generally. The thesis is essentially this: when we consider behaviour in a 'natural', i.e. non-experimentally controlled setting, including such complex situations as people talking to each other, or to themselves, composing poetry or solving a logical problem, the rules whereby the sum total of stimuli impinging on them 'produce' the resultant behaviour are no different in essence from those that operate when, say, a light changing from red to green makes a pigeon switch its pecking from one key to another. The difference is one of complexity. The verbal responses made in a given situation, such as meeting people at a party, looking at a picture, finding that the car refuses to start, facing a class of students – are under the joint 'control' of the many stimuli constituting these situations.

The concept of stimulus is here vastly extended from its use in the operant conditioning experiment and includes 'internal stimulation', which remains undefined. The nature of the control exercised is a function of the particular reinforcement history of the individual in relation to the component stimuli of the situation, as well as of the levels of various forms of deprivation existing in the speaker at the time. Thus, for example, the phrase 'May I have some water?' would be the outcome of a condition of water deprivation coupled with a situation in which such an utterance had previously been reinforced by receiving water.

Skinner has developed a special terminology for sub-dividing various types of utterance according to the way in which they are related to stimulus situation, to the verbal context in which they appear, reinforcement history and so on. 'May I have some water?', for example, would be classified as a *mand*, a mand being defined as 'a verbal operant in which the response is reinforced by a characteristic consequence and is therefore under the functional control of relevant conditions of deprivation and aversive stimulation'. Mands include questions, commands, requests, and although their occurrence must obviously depend to some extent on external stimulation – e.g. the above phrase is more likely to occur at table than, say, on a bus, or while swimming in the sea – it is regarded primarily as a function of internal stimulation arising from some sore of need. A *tact*, by contrast, is 'a verbal operant in which a response of given form is evoked (or at least strengthened) by a particular object or event or property of an object or event'. Virtually any statement, such as 'There is some-one at the door', 'Today is Monday', or indeed a single descriptive or identifying utterance like 'red' or 'elephant' made in appropriate circumstances would fall into this class. There are other categories, such as *echoic operant* – a response which imitates the sound pattern of the evoking stimulus, such as when a language student attempts to repeat a word that has just been pronounced for him – a *textual response,* made when reading written material aloud, or an *intraverbal operant* made in response to verbal or symbolic stimulation, including translations, answers to questions or problems, including mathematical or scientific ones.

Naom Chomsky,[2] in a review of Skinner's book, has demon-strated that the first impression of scientific rigour, created by the use of a specialist vocabulary deriving in part from experimental situations, is unfortunately quite illusory. Terms such as stimulus control, deprivation or reinforcement, which could be given more or less precise definitions in the contexts in which they were originally used, lose their meaning and value when they are extended in a way that makes it impossible to identify what they refer to. If the only way in which we can discover what aspect of a stimulus configuration 'controls' a particular utterance involves taking into account what was in fact said, talking about stimulus control does not add to our understanding of what is taking place. The states of deprivation leading to a mand like 'Let me fix it' or indeed 'May I have some water?' when it is intended for washing the car, bear little resemblance to hunger or thirst. When various activities can be 'self reinforcing', when, for example, it is said that a painter paints as he does *because* he is reinforced by the result, we have not really learnt anything beyond the fact that he paints in a certain way. In previously described animal experiments reinforcers such as food or water or even novelty could be used to produce a *variety* of forms of learning. To identify a particular event as a reinforcer meant that it could be used in this way. This essential character of reinforcement has entirely disappeared in the attempt to provide a *total* explanation of verbal – or indeed any – behaviour. We are dealing not so much with a scientific account as with a *paraphrase* of the ordinary explanations of behaviour, involving terms such as want, expect, like, etc. into a more cumbersome language which adds nothing in the way of understanding or predictive power.

Does this mean that Skinnerian ideas of learning cannot be extended to behaviour involving language? On the contrary, we shall see in the chapter on programmed learning that they are of great practical value in the learning of a wide variety of verbal material. By thinking of spoken or written statements as behaviour we can use reinforcement principles to encourage some and extinguish other statements. We can *use* the idea of shaping to help in developing the sort of complex verbal behaviour that is usually regarded as indicating

The Lifeboat in Weymouth Harbour, Dorset.

Photo: E. Nägele, John Hinde Studios.

3BM34

Published by John Hinde Limited, 6 Rupert St., London W.1. Printed in the Republic of Ireland.

JOHN HINDE
ORIGINAL

that someone understands a particular topic. However, to demonstrate factors whereby learning *may* be influenced under special conditions is not the same as showing that these same factors are sufficient for a complete account. Although it is always worth trying to see how much it is possible to explain with the smallest number of principles, pushing this to extremes is likely to develop a prejudice even against their more limited and justified application. An analysis in terms of stimuli, responses and reinforcements is quite inadequate for describing all behaviour involving language – probably for much more primitive behaviour as well. At the same time, until a more adequate analysis is developed, it can provide us with a useful guide for attempting to modify such behaviour in certain specific and limited ways.

Verbal and other behaviour

The use of language is part of the *fabric* of human behaviour – not simply one kind of activity amongst others, but one that plays a specialized mediating role between the individual and his environment. At a highly complex level we can see this in the use of theoretical language briefly discussed in Chapter 4. Verbal or symbolic statements can be used to describe the world and hence provide a reference and guide for action. At a more mundane level, a great deal of everyday behaviour is related to some sort of verbal formulation – utilizing instructions or descriptions provided from outside, orally or in writing, or generated by the individual himself as a stage in ongoing activity. Quite apart from making explicit plans and referring to them in the verbally remembered form 'What was I going to do next?', many actions are preceded by verbal decision, situations are identified verbally as an integral part of one's reactions to them, and even in the course of highly practised, 'automatically' performed activities, the experience of difficulty frequently generates a burst of verbal behaviour – internal or sometimes overt – in an attempt to sort things out. It is out of this that further activity develops. The use of lan-

177

guage frequently constitutes a stage in the emergence of behaviour and plays an important part in regulating it.

The Russian psychologist Luria[3] has reported some investigations into the development of the relationship between language and other activities in children. Many of the standard learning experiments involving animals, in which, for example, discrimination between objects is slowly brought about by reinforcement or the establishment of conditioned reflexes, are difficult to reproduce with human beings because of their tendency to verbalize the situation. At the same time, experiments with people invariably involve some verbal instructions, which are used by the subject (though not always in the way intended by the experimenter) to set the scene for his activity. Focusing attention on this aspect of the situation, instead of taking it for granted, reveals even the simplest reaction experiments as something a great deal less simple.

In one series of experiments reported by Luria, children of various ages were required to respond to light signals presented to them. Responses were made using a simple device which forms part of the standard equipment of Russian psychological laboratories – a rubber bulb, held in the hand and connected to a pen recorder, providing a continuous quantitative record of the pressure exerted by the subject. Asked to press the bulb when a light appeared, children between the ages of two and five years tended to continue pressing intermittently even in the absence of the signal. Asked to press for a red light, but not to press for a green one, no stable coordination between signal and response developed. On the other hand, with verbal reinforcement for correct response, discrimination was quickly established, though not *maintained* without it. In contrast to this, children of three and four could, after verbal instruction alone, respond *verbally* to the signals by saying 'Go' in one case, and 'Press' or 'Don't press' in the other, showing a *stable* correspondence between signal and response. The dynamics of making verbal responses appear at this age to be more highly developed than motor reactions, which incidentally suggests that different neural systems are likely to be involved.

Children were now asked to combine motor and verbal responses – saying 'Go' and pressing at the same time. The effect of this depended on the age of the children. With the youngest it led to a further disruption or to the inhibition of the motor response. Next came a stage where the making of any verbal response – 'Go', 'Press', 'Don't Press' – *all* facilitated pressing, this time, however, in a controlled way, pressing occurring once only in conjunction with the verbal response. Thus, in the discrimination experiment, motor discrimination could be achieved by pairing pressure with a verbal response such as 'Go', which was made to one signal only. At yet a later age – around four and a half years – the *significance* of the verbal response could be related to action, so that saying 'Press' and 'Don't Press' could be combined with the appropriate movement. In all cases, omitting the verbal response led to the previous instability of the motor reactions.

It appears from these and other experiments that from an early age verbal responses begin to have a greater stability than other types of reaction; that verbal responses made by the subject can be used to mediate between signals and manual (or other) reactions, thus bringing these under greater control; and that the nature of the control exercised changes from a situation where speech acts just as an additional, though more effective 'impulse' to movement, to one where the meaning of the words spoken by the subject can be utilized. At about the same time, control can be shifted from *external* to *internal* speech. The experiments make explicit a process that is likely to occur under ordinary circumstances and Luria argues that the development of speech is closely related to the development of deliberate or voluntary action in general. The experiments also suggest the possibility of utilizing the mediating role of a child's own speech to accelerate control over its activity.

Development of concepts

Many words used to refer to events, situations or objects have more than a single application. Although on a given occasion we may talk about a particular house or about a dog we happen to own, words like house or dog can be used in a wide variety of situations involving houses and dogs of very different shapes and sizes. The words used denote classes or categories of objects or events that are, for certain purposes, treated alike. They give verbal expression to a concept. In fact a concept is defined as a common response (often but not always verbal) made to a category of experiences which have some property in common.

If a child can separate all red objects of varying shapes and sizes from green objects then we accept that he is using the concept red. To take an extreme example, if a rat can learn to approach all triangular objects, regardless of their size, position and colour, and to avoid objects of other shapes, then we could say that the rat had *some* concept of a triangle. The rat, of course, does not call the objects triangles (the child may not call his objects red) but he is giving evidence that he is responding to the common property of having three sides and disregarding all other variations, and this is sufficient for us to say that the animal is using a concept.

It is obvious that possible concepts differ widely in complexity, ease of concrete reference, range of applicability and so forth, and to describe them all as concepts is not to suggest that the same processes of concept formation operate in all cases; it merely emphasizes the general tendency to organize experiences into classes for convenience. We could not handle a world in which we had to learn a response to all the experiences we could in fact discriminate and we reserve precision of response for those situations in which we are especially interested. We usually use about twenty names for colours, for example, while workers in dye factories may use more, but even they do not attempt to name the thousands of colours we can discriminate. Before we consider differences in the types of concepts we can acquire, however, what can be said in general about the process of concept formation?

An early view of Hull's was that all the objects included within a concept must have identical elements, that the concept response is in fact a response to identical stimuli appearing in different contexts. This has frequently been shown to be wrong and perhaps represents the most extreme attempt to explain thinking in the simplest possible stimulus-response terms. Work carried out by Smoke[4], for example, showed that concepts can be developed where the only common characteristic is an invariant internal relationship in the items falling within the category. One of his concepts, labelled 'zif', included all cards on which three dots were marked in such a way that the distance between the two dots farthest apart was equal to twice the distance between the two closest together. It is possible to draw three dots in all sorts of ways which all conform to this requirement, and conversely dots can be located to look quite like members of the concept class without having the correct relationships between their distances. An interesting incidental finding of Smoke's, which has been confirmed in other experiments, is that subjects who successfully learn to respond according to the appropriate concept are not necessarily able to describe it correctly. In one of his experiments, for example, out of fifty-nine subjects who made correct discriminations, twenty-three were unable to formulate the concept correctly in verbal terms. We are familiar with this in non-experimental situations. For example, young children can identify a large variety of different objects long before they can name or describe their distinctive properties.

We have mentioned concepts defining a class of objects with common stimulus elements, or with common internal relationships; but what about concepts like 'edible', 'attractive', 'lethal', or their substantive equivalents? The common feature of the instances which comprise these classes is a particular kind of effect which they have, in this case on people or animals. Subsequently we might discover that they have other properties in common, but in the first instance, many things or situations are grouped together on the basis of evoking a common response or reaction from another group – ultimately, of course, from people. Some concepts, like 'poison', depend on our biological make-up, others, like 'hammer' or 'carving

181

knife', are generated by characteristic activities. Definitions of 'marriage guidance counsellors', 'advertising agency', 'cold war' – indeed all the terms in common usage and the corresponding concepts constitute a reflection of peoples' interaction with their physical and social environment from the most basic to the most complex. Conversely, this interaction will be influenced by the concepts that we have learned to use. The idea of a chair or seat arises naturally in a species predisposed to sitting; the labelling of an object as a chair invites its being treated appropriately. Learning concepts involves a great deal more than simply applying a name to the members of a class.

Concepts differ also in their degree of immediate reference to physical objects, their concreteness. Generally speaking the more abstract they are the more difficult they are to form. Concepts such as 'gene' or 'gravity' come later in the development of a science than 'cell' or 'weight'. Relative difficulty in the development of different types of concepts may usefully be thought of in terms of the relative readiness with which the common associations necessary for the formation of a concept are evoked by the various items. This has been tested directly in experiments in which subjects are presented with a number of single words and are asked to give the most immediate sensory associate of the word; 'mouse', for example, might evoke the responses 'small', 'furry' and 'speedy'. The stimulus words are then grouped and presented to other subjects who are asked which concepts are exemplified by the words. The most frequent response then tends to be a concept which has a high probability of association with all the stimulus words individually. Easy concepts are therefore those formed on the basis of the most likely response to the individual object while difficult concepts are dependent on common responses which have a low probability of association with at least some of the individual items.

If we are required to link a hovercraft and Nelson's monument, we would be unlikely to connect them on the basis that neither has wheels: if the items were a hovercraft and a toboggan we would be much more likely to do so. The skill of course is to arrive at unlikely concepts which are also useful.

Concept formation and concept attainment

A child confronted with a variety of spherical, elastic objects that can be bounced, thrown or rolled, might develop the concept of ball – though it is unlikely that it would spontaneously invent the same – or indeed any – word, or that the category of objects would coincide exactly with that conventionally included under the heading of ball. This would constitute a case of concept invention or formation. It is not, however, the process whereby the great majority of concepts are in fact arrived at. Children are born into a community within which a very large number of concepts already exist and in whose language they are reflected. Thus the child comes across spherical, bouncing objects, which are accompanied by the word 'ball', furry animals called 'cats' and so on. The single word applied to a variety of objects draws attention to them as members of a single class, and helps to create in each new member of the community the same concept structure that is already shared by its existing members. The problem confronting the child is thus not so much one of *forming* concepts, as of *attaining* existing ones, and part of this consists in learning to use the corresponding labels correctly.

In Chapter 7 we referred to experiments carried out by Harlow, involving the solution of 'oddity problems' by rhesus monkeys. When these animals are repeatedly presented with three objects, two of which are identical, choosing the odd object being reinforced, they learn to select the odd item in a set of three, irrespective of the *particular* characteristics of the objects involved. They learn to respond to a relationship. Other species also will respond to relationships – for example chickens, if reinforced for pecking at the darker of two surfaces, will peck at the darker member of other pairs, irrespective of the *absolute* amount of light which they reflect. They cannot, however, learn to respond to 'oddness'. There has been little systematic investigation of the relationship between the evolutionary level of an animal, the type of brain it possesses and the type of learning of which it is capable. Broadly speaking, the ability to respond to features of a learning situation which go beyond its immediate sensory properties, increases with the complexity of the animal and reaches its culmination in human beings. *Naming* appears to be particularly effective in drawing attention to common properties, and as a consequence of having a single name applied to a limited number of objects or situations, people are able to extend it to other, not yet encountered instances.

As in other cases of learning, the learner plays an active role in concept attainment. Children do not simply have examples of cats and dogs pointed out to them, but they select things for identification, and attempt to do their own naming. On such occasions it will often become apparent that the child's concept, such as it is, does not quite correspond to the label that is being used. Thus the term 'bunny' may at first encompass a whole variety of animals of similar size, or possibly of a colour similar to that of the examples to which the name was originally applied. Here we may notice that in general the nature of the first primitive concept formed is likely to depend on the particular characteristics of the early examples that are encountered. If, for example, they happen to be white rabbits of different sizes, white is more likely to become an important feature in identifying other instances of 'bunny' than size. The application of such a developing concept may be likened to the trying out of a hypothesis – though in a young child this is obviously not a deliberate process – which is gradually modified under the influence of the correcting feedback provided by parents and others.

Concept attainment is not confined to childhood but goes on throughout life as new ideas and terms are encountered. Experimental studies in this area share with other investigations of thinking processes the general difficulty that a great deal of what is happening takes place inside the thinker or learner, and the problem is to make as much of this as possible overt and observable, Bruner, Goodnow and Austin[5], in one of a series of experiments, investigated the method adopted by people making a deliberate attempt to arrive at already formulated concepts. They presented subjects with an array of eighty-one different designs. Each design contained some central figures which could be either all circles, all squares or all crosses. The number of figures could be one, two or three; the colour of the figures could be green, red or black; and they could be surrounded by one, two or three borders. Each member of the array was thus defined by one of three values for each of four variables: type of figure, number of figures, colour of figures, and number of borders. This gave $3 \times 3 \times 3 \times 3 = 81$ possible combinations of 'qualities', each such unique combination representing as it were a single object. A concept was now defined by specifying the value of one or more variables. Thus 'red squares' might be a concept, covering all designs containing red squares irrespective of their number or the number of borders. Subjects were started off by being shown one example or 'positive instance' of the concept – such as a design consisting of one red square with three borders – their task being to identify the concept by selecting other designs consecutively and asking the experimenter whether or not it constituted a further positive instance. By analysing the records of successive choices, the investigators were able to distinguish four strategies:

1. *Simultaneous scanning*, involving the systematic trial of hypotheses, full advantage being taken of all the information that the result of each trial provided.

2. *Successive scanning*, again involving the consecutive trial of one hypothesis at a time, but utilizing only that part of the information that was relevant to the hypothesis being tested, so that a certain number of attempts were in fact unnecessary or redundant.

3. *Conservative focusing*, starting with the first positive instance and changing one variable at a time, so that it could be seen at once whether or not its specification was relevant to the concept.

4. *Focus gambling,* again starting with the first positive instance, but changing several variables simultaneously – this could with luck result in the elimination of all of them, if all happened to be irrelevant to the definition of the concept. However, if one of them was relevant, it would be impossible to tell which.

Of these strategies, the first was theoretically the most efficient in using all the information available. However it involved considerable strain in taking in and retaining the information, was seldom adopted and usually ended in failure. Conservative focusing, though somewhat more wasteful of trials, was a much easier strategy to use, and this sort of finding is particularly relevant to any models one may wish to develop for the mechanism underlying concept attainment. From this point of view it is also of interest that *conjunctive concepts* – defined by Property A *and* Property B *and* Property C – were much more easily arrived at than *disjunctive concepts* – defined by having Property A *or* Property B, such as, for example, all designs containing either circles *or* red squares. Whether this preference for additive concepts reflects a basic property of the human brain, or one that has developed as a result of having learned a particular language and its associated concepts, it is not at this stage possible to say.

The Bruner Study is also of importance in introducing the idea of a concept attainment – or more generally, learning *strategy,* i.e. a stable pattern of behaviour adopted by the learner, which plays an important part in determining the information and the reinforcement to which he will be exposed. Strategies differ in their effectiveness, and the use – whether consciously or not – of a particular type of approach to learning situations is likely to have far-reaching consequences for a given learner. This topic will be taken up in Chapter 12.

Properties defining a given concept are seldom as explicit as in the above experiment. When confronted with real objects that are to be categorized, the attributes from which a selection is to be made may remain completely unspecified. What are the properties of a block of wood? Its colour, weight, height, surface texture, shape, density, volume, sharpness of its edges, evidence of dry-rot attack – the list could be extended indefinitely, and it will be apparent that the 'properties' themselves are concepts which may or may not be available to a given individual.

Although it is not necessary to be able to name a given feature of a situation in order to use it as a basis for discrimination, it is a decided advantage. For example Spiker, Gerjuoy and Shepard* carried out an experiment with children between the ages of three and five, who were divided into those who could refer in some appropriate way to the middle-sized member of three stimuli (i.e. who could describe it as 'middle-sized' or by the use of some equivalent phrase) and those who could not. The former group was found to be significantly superior at a concept attainment task which involved choosing the middle-sized stimulus from sets of three, the absolute sizes being varied. Being able to *name* a particular object or attribute does of course imply the ability to discriminate the relevant features of the stimulus situation. But in addition to this, having a name available increases the chance that these features will be attended to.

The concepts which a person uses constitute a kind of filter system for the infinite variety and complexity of the information which impinges on him – there is a strong tendency to see and respond to the environment in terms of available concepts. To the extent that language is the predominant factor in the formation of the concepts we use, it is basic to most of human behaviour, including those cases where spoken or written language as such is not observable. Even though the few examples that have been cited are by no means representative of investigations into language behaviour, some most important questions remain unexplored. Linguists, notably Naom Chomsky, have drawn attention to the *use of rules* in speaking a language, and G. A. Miller has raised the problem

* C. C. Spiker, I. R. Gerjuoy and W. O. Shepard. J. Comp. Physical Psychol. 1956. *49*, 416–419.

of rule-following in more general terms. What is involved in speaking a language correctly, or in the use of linguistically formulated rules to direct and mediate other types of behaviour? We are without a *model* of the language user, without a description of the kind of *system* required to handle symbolic material in anything approaching the way in which people utilize language. Although we speak of *computer languages*, the dissimilarity between the essentially rigid character of existing computers and the flexibility of organisms makes this analogy unhelpful. We are dealing here with a highly sophisticated control system and in this sense the development of models of language users is a problem in cybernetics. As in the case of motor skills discussed in Chapter 7, the control system one is dealing with is one which is capable of progressive modification as a result of interaction with the environment, i.e. it is capable of learning. And although cybernetic theory has so far not concentrated on evolving systems of this kind, nevertheless it is from this quarter that the next step forward in understanding both the acquisition and the use of language is likely to come.

10. Learning theory and abnormal behaviour

In order to enjoy the short-term gains of cigarette smoking smokers accept a much higher chance of early death. Most smokers will agree that smoking is, in the long run, harmful. At the same time they would resist the suggestion that smoking is abnormal behaviour.

In part this is because smoking is not statistically abnormal in our society. A very high proportion of the population smoke, and on these grounds alone we tend not to regard it as pathological. We take a very different view of drug or alcohol addiction; not only are a smaller number of people involved, but the short-term effects are more seriously disabling to the addict. We regard alcoholics as abnormal and in need of treatment both because their behaviour is unusual and because its harmful effects are immediate and obvious.

Similarly we classify as abnormal a whole range of behavioural characteristics many of which would lead people to seek medical help. Inability to remember one's name, fear of entering a room containing more than two strangers or of walking in the open by oneself, the need to touch every lamppost; these are examples of behaviour which are not typical of a majority of the population and which largely incapacitate the person who exhibits them.

People with such conditions are likely to be diagnosed as neurotic especially if the abnormal condition is relatively permanent and if it is accompanied by feelings of anxiety and depression.

In this chapter we are concerned with the relation of processes of learning to the development of neurosis and, more particularly, to procedures for its cure. It will be appreciated that abnormal behaviour can occur as a consequence of brain injury, of certain physical diseases, some types of poisoning and so forth, in short in conditions where a clear organic pathology exists. We are not here concerned with abnormal behaviour resulting primarily from such physical injury or disease, but with the 'functional' disorders, especially neurosis, where no organic pathology is detectable.

Few workers in this area would deny that the development of neurosis depends to some extent on experiences during the life-time of the patient, but views on how the neurotic learning occurs and, even more important, what precisely is learned, differ considerably. Psychoanalysts and related theorists, whose approach stems primarily from the work of Freud, stress the existence of a central state – the neurosis or mental disease – of which neurotic behaviour is the symptom. In this view neurosis is a disease which has symptoms in the same way that a physical disease has symptoms, and therefore the aim should be to cure this underlying condition, generally by psychotherapy, upon which the symptom will disappear. From this point of view attempts to remove the symptoms without curing the central pathological state would, even if successful, lead to eventual reappearance of the symptom or substitution of another.

An alternative view, arising from the development of learning theory, is that neurotic behaviour, including abnormal anxiety, is a learned response and should be removed by procedures based on mechanisms of learning – by *behaviour therapy*. The neurotic condition is seen as one in which certain non-adaptive behavioural characteristics have been acquired and the therapist's task is to set up learning situations in which the behaviour can be changed. Central states such as 'the neurosis' are not required as explanatory devices by the various forms of stimulus-response theory which form the basis for this type of treatment. To the extent that this approach is soundly based, changes of abnormal behaviour brought about by behaviour therapy will be permanent and will not lead to alternative symptoms developing.

We cannot attempt here an evaluation of psychoanalytic theories. Certainly therapeutic methods deriving from them, which often involve hundreds of treatment sessions, are time-consuming and expensive in contrast to the methods of behaviour therapy. On the other hand, therapy based on learning theory may well be based on an oversimplified view of neurosis and may lead to an over emphasis on easily observable behaviour. Nevertheless behaviour therapy has achieved considerable success by its concentration on 'symptoms'. Psychoanalytic approaches, despite their enormous cost in time, have produced entirely unspectacular results, and a more direct attack on symptoms seems wholly justified.

Once a given abnormal behavioural characteristic is regarded primarily as a learned response, procedures for changing it, based on our knowledge of learning in simpler situations, can be devised. Probably the first method to come to mind will be one based on extinction. Learned responses evoked in the absence of reinforcement or of the unconditioned stimulus decay and ultimately disappear. It is not necessary to know the conditions under which responses were first acquired to put this procedure into operation; behaviour can be maintained by reinforcements different in quality and timing from those by which it was acquired. It is only essential that responses are made repeatedly and quickly (in general massed practice is most effective for extinction) in the absence of reinforcement and they will eventually decline.

Several procedures based on the extinction model are used in behaviour therapy. Perhaps the most direct of these, negative practice, involves the patient repeatedly emitting the undesired response throughout a given practice period. As this process continues through several such periods the ability to make the abnormal response voluntarily typically declines. The expectation is that the involuntary emission of the response – the symptom – will similarly decline.

Negative practice

This procedure is most suitable for those cases of abnormal behaviour where the most prominent characteristic is a clearly specifiable overt response. It is inappropriate for dealing with irrational fears or conditions which lead to a large variety of specific behaviours, although there have been reports of its success with more general conditions such as homosexuality. It is best adapted to the treatment of conditions such as tics and has been used successfully for this purpose by Yates[1] and Jones[2] to treat a *tiqueur*.

The patient suffered from four severe related tics, each of which was treated as a separate response and negative practice was carried out in all four of them. No other treatment was given during this period.

Several different detailed procedures were used during the course of treatment (mainly to find the most effective forms of practice), but it is sufficient to indicate the procedure eventually adopted for the stomach-contraction tic, which was the most troublesome.

The patient 'practised' the tic as frequently as possible during a period of one hour, then 'rested' for a week. During the next week the tic was practised for a short time each day. Then another one-hour practice period was held and so on. Seven such one-hour sessions were held and the number of responses made by the patient, the number of voluntary tics emitted during each hour, declined from 259 in the first hour to 12 in the seventh. An eighth session was discontinued after 17 minutes during which no responses were observed.

These results cannot, of course, be attributed to fatigue because of the considerable intervals between practice periods, and they represent the almost complete extinction of the voluntary response. Similar results were obtained with the other three tics. While this demonstrates that negative practice can have a considerable effect on the ability of a patient to make a given response at will the important question is whether or not the involuntary emission of the response declines similarly, whether in fact the symptom is reduced.

Although total behaviour throughout treatment was not quantifiable with the same accuracy as behaviour during treatment sessions, all available evidence indicates that the patient's condition was much improved. The tics declined markedly during treatment, the patient's emotional condition improved and there was no evidence of the development of alternative symptoms.

At a psychiatric examination some time after completion of treatment the patient was classed as much improved compared with her condition prior to treatment and, by all counts, this form of therapy seems to have produced significant amelioration of the condition.

The treatment was carried out within a framework of Hullian learning theory (extinction was seen as the growth of condition inhibition) and many detailed predictions from this theory were confirmed by systematic variation of conditions during the therapeutic process. Whether or not this ultimately proves to be an appropriate theoretical model, the process of experimental extinction seems to have considerable value for those conditions in which it is convenient for the full abnormal response to be made repeatedly under laboratory conditions. Not all behaviour disorders, however, conform to these requirements.

Many neurotic conditions are characterized primarily by anxiety, often anxiety occurring in a wide variety of circumstances and in situations where people in general feel little or no fear. The actual neurotic behaviour in these cases is often avoidance of the feared situation, but it may be impossible, and indeed useless, to treat the avoidance behaviour without treating the anxiety.

To deal with such problems Wolpe[3] has developed a procedure called *reciprocal inhibition*. This does not aim to *extinguish* the response of anxiety but to *replace* it with a new learned response which is incompatible with the development of anxiety. The intention is that this new response will inhibit the development of anxiety so that ultimately the patient will not respond with anxiety in the critical situation.

Reciprocal inhibition

The difficulty in attempting to help patients to learn a new response to an anxiety-producing stimulus is to induce them to approach it. The overt neurosis, as we have seen, consists in a set of avoidance responses which have been developed over time to protect the patient from the anxiety developing in certain critical situations.

The process developed by Wolpe involves systematic 'desensitizations' to anxiety-producing situations starting with relatively innocuous stimuli and gradually moving up the more serious conditions. There are a number of different detailed procedures of reciprocal inhibition in use, but the essential first step is to discover the situations in which anxiety develops and the order of seriousness of these. For example, a patient may be most afraid of addressing a large public meeting and least afraid (while still somewhat anxious) of talking to one stranger. Once these situations are ranked in order of seriousness the therapist's aim is to 'desensitize' them, starting with the least serious, by inducing the patient to learn to respond, when the stimulus is present, in a way which is incompatible with anxiety.

The patient may then be asked to imagine that he is talking to one stranger while at the same time he deliberately relaxes in order to inhibit some of the physical concomitants of anxiety. When this has been repeated several times, the anxiety-provoking properties of the stimulus decreasing all the time, the patient will be induced to imagine the next item on the list of anxiety-producing situations.

From there he may go on to the real confrontation of people, first from a distance, then at close range, ending up with the most difficult, say, addressing a public meeting. Using such a gradual desensitization procedure, people suffering from claustrophobia have been brought to the point where they can remain in a small, dark, locked room without anxiety.

Relaxation is not the only *anxiety-inhibitor* used, although various therapists have found it effective; *assertive* and other types of responses incompatible with anxiety may be used. Nor is it always necessary to use imagined situations if sufficiently low-anxiety real life situations can be found. The details of the procedure obviously depend largely on the pattern of symptoms presented by the patient.

Treatment of a severe phobia by these procedures has recently been reported by Geer,[4] whose patient had an excessive fear of lice. Most people are unenthusiastic about lice, but in this case the patient's abnormal preoccupation with them, and especially her fear of getting lice in her hair, caused her to avoid crowds whenever possible and to resist meeting new people. After a total of sixteen sessions the patient's fear of lice had decreased very considerably and no longer interfered with a normal social life. The first five of these sessions were occupied in constructing the hierarchy of feared situations (these ranged from writing the word 'lice' to being touched on the head with a stranger's comb), training the patient in methods of relaxation and in giving her practice in visualizing scenes suggested by the therapist. During the remaining eleven sessions the list of anxiety-producing situations was systematically desensitized.

Three months after the end of treatment the patient's condition was better than at conclusion of treatment, and no substitute symptoms could be detected. Personality test scores before and after treatment showed a significant swing towards normality. Such generalized improvement after removal, or marked lessening, of a specific symptom by behaviour therapy has been noted in other cases. The general improvement might be explained as a reaction to the removal of an embarrassing symptom or, as is sometimes argued, the therapeutic procedure itself might be more pervasive in its effects, less restricted to the behavioural symptom than is usually accepted by behaviour therapists themselves.

Many kinds of abnormal behaviour involve the patient in a conflict situation, he is both attracted and repelled by the same activity or set of circumstances. In cases of phobia, anxiety has the upper hand, and the patient avoids certain actions or situations, to his own long term disadvantage. Alcoholism, drug addiction and various forms of sexual deviation usually involve conflict in which the *approach*-tendency is dominant, i.e. characteristic activity produces reinforcement whose effect outweighs – at critical times – the misery and distress which associated physical conditions or social disapproval usually produce. Society often tries to deal with conflicts of this kind by intensifying its disapproval – where the activity is classified as criminal increasing the severity of punishment. This is rarely successful even in inhibiting the undesirable behaviour, and certainly does nothing to resolve the conflict. The learning model considered in Chapter 2 gives a clue to this failure.

The effectiveness of reinforcers – both positive and negative – depends critically on their timing. In conflict situations timing can override other considerations of magnitude, and a small reward, close at hand, may loom larger than a distant though more serious punishment. If we try at all to inhibit behaviour by an increase in anxiety, this can more effectively be done by careful timing than by simply increasing the intensity of aversive stimulation. The consequences of 'going on a bender' – even if they follow more quickly and more certainly than those of heavy smoking – are still too delayed to produce avoidance on the next time round. We could expect greater success if disaster could be arranged to follow drinking more closely.

The drug apomorphine produces nausea and has been used in behaviour-therapy approaches to alcoholism. The drug is injected and shortly before nausea develops the patient is induced to drink alcohol. If alcohol closely precedes nausea on a number of occasions, it comes to produce it as a conditioned stimulus, and some limited success has been achieved by this procedure in developing an avoidance of alcohol. It is, however, crude, not just literally but also methodologically, as an example of avoidance conditioning.

Feldman and MacCulloch,[5] using aversion therapy in the treatment of homosexuals, provide an example of how this technique may be applied to a condition involving highly com-

plex behavioural manifestations. Seeing other men is an obvious
and important interest-arousing type of stimulus in the pattern
of homosexual behaviour. Treatment was therefore aimed at
making these stimuli aversive. Voluntary patients, to whom the
treatment was explained in advance, individually ranked a set
of male photographs in order of attractiveness. The least
attractive was now projected on a screen, the patient being able
to switch it off at will. It was explained that he should leave
the picture projected as long as he found it sexually attractive.
If he did not switch it off within eight seconds, however, he
received an electric shock of sufficient strength to make him
switch off immediately. Patients were also asked to accom-
pany switching off by saying 'No'.

Once complete avoidance for a particular picture had been
established, a schedule of intermittent reinforcement was introduced, aimed at increasing resistance to extinction. For
example in some cases the patient's attempt to switch off failed,
the picture remained and he received a brief shock. In others
the picture remained for a variable period, but eventually disappeared within the eight seconds, achieving avoidance. When
the patient reported indifference or dislike of the slide, and
switched it off almost at once on each presentation, the next
slide was introduced and the procedure repeated.

Feldman and MacCulloch also utilized patients' relief when
male slides left the screen in an attempt to make women more
acceptable. Photographs of women were occasionally introduced as the male slide was switched off, thus being associated
with anxiety reduction. Patients were also allowed to ask for
the return of a female slide, this being a kind of guarantee
against the appearance of the shock-producing male. However,
such requests paid off only intermittently and in a random
manner, so as to increase resistance to extinction.

Results were strongly encouraging, even without allowing
for the brevity of the treatment which averaged around fifteen
sessions. Most patients, and particularly the younger ones, reported during follow-up, marked increasing *movement away
from* homosexual interest, and growing interest in the opposite

sex. This is in contrast to other previous attempts to treat homosexuality.

The importance of this and similar work lies in its attempt to integrate therapy more closely and in more detail with complex behaviour. Despite obvious difficulties, the therapists tried to achieve a greater than usual approximation between the treatment and real situations. Photographs of real people, both male and female, and provided by the patient, were used in preference. Attention was given to the scheduling of experience, and to the removal of at least some of the emotional obstacles to the development of alternative behaviour. It is clearly possible in principle to go much further in the direction of analysing the dynamics of this or other types of behaviour and to introduce carefully timed positive and negative reinforcers in an attempt to change the balance of the existing response pattern.

Attempts to evaluate behaviour therapy in general can be of two kinds: the soundness of its theoretical basis can be examined or its success in producing cures can be measured. We have already in previous chapters given some attention to the adequacy of learning theories in explaining the phenomena for which they are specifically designed, and we will not discuss them further here. One specific theory which sets out to explain the development of abnormal behaviour will be described in a later section of this chapter, but its importance to behaviour therapy is only in making plausible, to some extent, the general assumption that abnormal responses (as opposed to more global central characteristics) are learned.

Of much greater immediate significance are the success rates of therapists using such techniques as we have described. The figures claimed vary from quite moderate rates to Wolpe's[6] claim of ninety per cent of patients cured or much improved.

A recent study has shown that 61 per cent of patients receiving behaviour therapy improved compared with 44 per cent of control group subjects showing improvement. Some of this variation may be due to differences in standards of assessment, but what seems fairly clear is that some types of neurotic symptoms respond more to treatment by behaviour therapy than others, and there may be variations in the proportions of these in groups of patients treated by different therapists. In general patients whose symptoms are relatively specific seem to respond best to behaviour therapy. Phobias in particular can be significantly lessened by behaviour therapy, while alcoholism and sexual disorders, among the conditions which would quite frequently be treated by behaviour therapy, seem to respond less satisfactorily, although some reports suggest that these more complex conditions are also becoming more amenable to treatment. There are also, of course, conditions with which behaviour therapy would seldom or never be attempted.

With certain types of cases, then, the success of behaviour therapy seems quite substantial and this is as much as can be said for any method of treating behaviour disorders. Further improvements might follow a more exact specification of what precisely is learned in neurosis, but this might be dependent on advances in learning theory in general.

Avoidance conditioning discussed in Chapter 2 provides a basis for a substantial amount of behaviour therapy and also a model for the development of much neurotic behaviour. The prototype situation is of the 'B follows A unless R' kind, where A is an originally neutral signal, B a noxious, fear-producing stimulus, and R a selected response made by the individual. At first the response brings about *escape* from the aversive stimulus B – as when an animal escapes from one half of a box which has been electrified by clearing a barrier into the other. Later the response *anticipates* the onset of shock, which is avoided altogether, and this type of learning it will be recalled is very resistant to extinction.

Avoidance learning is best regarded as a combination of respondent (or Pavlovian) conditioning, and operant conditioning (or instrumental learning). The originally neutral signal A comes to evoke anxiety as a result of being paired with B, which produces fear as an innate (unlearned) reaction. The emotional effects of highly unpleasant or traumatic experiences become associated with the setting in which they occurred and with the events which preceded the experience. This is a conditioning situation of the Pavlovian type. On the other hand, any action which gets away from or otherwise terminates B will be reinforced, and this is operant conditioning.

There is some disagreement about what happens when eventually B is avoided altogether. Skinner has emphasized *escape*, first from B and then from A, as constituting reinforcement, i.e. even after, say, shock is completely avoided, reinforcement is provided by getting *away from* stimuli which continue to produce anxiety. Others, like Mowrer, simply talk about the reduction of anxiety, producing further reinforcement, without necessarily attributing this reduction to *escape* from any specified stimuli. Provided we use a broad interpretation of Skinner's *conditioned aversive stimuli* there is probably no fundamental difference between these positions. What is important for our present purpose is that the avoidance responses are maintained and keep the individual out of the very situation in which they might be effectively extinguished.

The development of abnormal behaviour

We thus have a model for the development of one kind of neurotic behaviour involving anxiety and avoidance. An original traumatic event, or series of events produces emotional disturbance, which becomes conditioned to situations or events associated with the experience. These events occurring later by themselves produce anxiety and related disturbed behaviour. If the original trauma was sufficiently severe, the conditioned anxiety may be persistent, though repeated exposure to the anxiety-making situation (i.e. the C.S. without the U.C.S.) should lead to eventual extinction.* Indeed a substantial proportion of cases of neurotic disturbance show spontaneous remission. The situation changes, however, if an avoidance

---

* One possibility may be overlooked here: that the experience of intense anxiety may itself constitute a kind of trauma which helps to maintain the effectiveness of the conditioned stimulus – in effect, the development of a kind of positive feedback system.

response develops. If the individual retreats from the C.S. (heights, people, closed rooms, etc.) – a form of behaviour reinforced by anxiety reduction – he never exposes himself to the possibility of extinction, and the avoided situations retain their power to evoke anxiety.

Such conditions may be produced by intensely unpleasant experiences; at the same time, individuals differ in their susceptibility to conditioning situations, and Eysenck regards conditionability as a fundamental personality dimension, deter· mining predisposition to different types of behaviour pathology. Individuals who condition unusually easily will be more susceptible to developing neurotic disorders related to anxiety. Excessive difficulty in conditioning will lead to an under-development of all forms of behaviour which depend on this method of learning. Many forms of socially desired behaviour – cleanliness, restraint of aggression – are learned in childhood partly as avoidance responses for disapproval or other sanctions. Later also, society uses threat for wrong action as a method of controlling behaviour. Failure to condition is thus seen as being at the root of psychopathic behaviour.

An important feature of this type of theory is that it is testable. It also contains immediate implications for therapy. If for example conditionability can be affected by drugs, we have here a very direct way of counteracting pathological learning processes.

Experimental neurosis

It is possible in the laboratory to produce in animals conditions resembling human neurosis. Such similarities as exist may of course be misleading – we can never argue *directly* from animals to men, or for that matter from one species to another. Nevertheless, the conditions that produce such pathological behaviour are of obvious interest, in that they may provide *clues* for the human situation.

One of the earliest observations of experimental neurosis occurred in an experiment in Pavlov's laboratory in which a dog was trained to discriminate between a circle and an ellipse. A salivary response to a circular form was first established. This response generalized to ellipses which were also presented. Ellipses, however, were not followed by the unconditioned stimulus, so ultimately the dog discriminated between circles and ellipses by continuing to respond to the circle and failing to react to the ellipse.

Once this discrimination was established the ellipses were gradually made more circular. The dog continued to respond until the axes of the ellipse were almost equal, when it was almost indistinguishable from the circle, at which point discrimination broke down. It is not clear what a 'rational' response to such a situation would be, perhaps to respond positively to all stimuli or perhaps to none of them, but in any event the behaviour of the dogs in such a situation is more varied and more disturbed than either of these. Some dogs became very aggressive, fighting to get out of the experimental harness and so on, others became very inactive and 'withdrawn'. In some cases the conditioned response could not subsequently be evoked even to stimuli which had previously been successfully discriminated.

This behaviour is similar to that of dogs in extreme fear and has superficial resemblance to some human neurotic behaviour. So experiments deliberately designed to investigate this effect were carried out, many of them containing a similar element of conflict. In some, as in the previous experiment, the conflict was between a tendency to respond and not to respond to a given stimulus; in others, successive stimuli calling for different responses were provided. Such creation of opposing response tendencies has sometimes been seen as the significant factor in experimental neurosis and many experiments on conflict in various animals have been carried out, largely in the United States.

Masserman,[7] for example, used a situation in which cats were trained to lift the cover off a food container on the presentation of a stimulus such as a bell or light. As the cat lifted the lid a blast of air was directed to the side of the animal's head. This did not injure the cat, but was certainly unpleasant. In this conflicting situation the animal did not simply stop eating but exhibited more generalized withdrawal symptoms involving food, the experimenter and the experimental situation.

Masserman found individual differences (as had Pavlov) between his animals, in the extent and permanence of their withdrawal. He was especially concerned to develop therapeutic procedures for the condition that had been induced. One of these, which may be regarded as a forerunner of Wolpe's desensitization procedure, involved calming and feeding the cats, starting in situations greatly different from those in which they had been upset, and approximating by very gradual stages to the original traumatic situation – this time of course without the blast.

Masserman's experiments, and many others, involved the presentation at some stage of an unpleasant and frightening stimulus. Although the cat's subsequent behaviour has been described as due to conflict, it could easily have been the result of the aversive stimulus alone, and indeed similar withdrawal behaviour has been produced by the use of unpleasant stimulation alone. Pavlov's original results cannot be explained in this way, however; there is nothing obviously frightening about objects which are merely difficult to distinguish, when neither of the possibilities is a danger signal. Explanations of this effect sometimes include the assumption that difficult or ambiguous stimuli are inherently anxiety-provoking, and human response to ambiguity is quoted in support of this. Another explanation, suggested by Broadhurst,[8] is that the increased drive produced by the animal, in response to the increased difficulty of the task, mobilizes behavioural responses in addition to those currently appropriate, in particular fear responses which occurred first when the animal was introduced to the experimental situation.

It will have been noticed that some of the situations described provide models both for the development of neurotic behaviour and for its cure. Thus the conflict situation used by Masserman is similar in structure to that used in aversion therapy for alcoholics. There is no inherent contradiction in this – whether the procedure results in breakdown or simply in inhibition of the original response is not clearly predicted by the theory at the present time. Additional variables, more precise quantification and timing may well turn out to be decisive. When we couple a sexually exciting stimulus with shock, theory does not explain precisely why this should make the stimulus aversive rather than provide the shock with erotic significance. When it is therefore claimed that behaviour therapy is directly deducible from learning theory, which can be used to predict its results, this is something of an overstatement. Learning theory does not provide a comprehensive explanation of abnormal any more than of normal behaviour. However, it can suggest some powerful methods for changing behaviour whose details remain to be worked out empirically. This more limited claim, however, still gives behaviour therapy a more favourable scientific status than other methods of treatment.

11. Programmed learning

The advent of programmed learning is likely to be one of the major landmarks in the development of educational practice. Surprisingly perhaps, the ideas on which it is based have their origin in the animal laboratory rather than the classroom. It is surprising especially when one thinks of the essential simplicity, not to say naïveté, of animal learning paradigms, and considers that it is in this area more than in any other that human capacity and performance is quite sharply distinguished from that of our nearest animal relations. Much of the credit for this development must go to B. F. Skinner, not because he is the only or indeed the first psychologist to be concerned with this development, but because he has been prepared to take seriously what is without doubt an imperfect and over-simplified account of learning, and to translate it with a persistent and quite unashamed pragmatism into a variety of practical applications – including the extensive use of programmed texts as part of his psychology teaching at Harvard. In a field where traditionally much attention is paid to the pronouncements of speculative theorists, such faith in the potentialities of ideas based on experimental method is a refreshing phenomenon.

It may be useful at this point to re-state in bare outline the account of the learning process in an instrumental learning, or – to use the Skinnerian terminology – operant conditioning situation. An animal is brought into a situation in which, as a result of both innate behavioural characteristics and previous learning experiences, it possesses a particular repertoire of responses. If now we select some particular response from among these and follow it promptly whenever it occurs with a reinforcement, the relative frequency of the selected behaviour increases, until it dominates all other types of behaviour. At the same time, the whole range of probable responses shifts, becoming centred on the reinforced behaviour.

New and related responses make their appearance and may in turn be selected for reinforcement, leading to still further shifts in the behavioural spectrum, until what the animal does shows no overlap with its previous conduct in the chosen setting, or indeed any setting. Thus the behaviour of two initially quite ordinary pigeons may be 'shaped' by easy stages until they will play a modified form of ping-pong. (See Chapter 2.)

While there is much controversy, as we have seen, about the essential nature of reinforcement and the related state of motivation, the best way of describing the changes that attend reinforcement, and about the adequacy of the whole model in accounting for a variety of learning phenomena, there is at any rate no doubt that, regarded as a description of a training procedure, the model works. This is attested both by the animal training successes of those who have used operant methods – indeed some of Skinner's co-workers have abandoned their careers in psychology to go into the animal training business – and by the success of applications to human learning to be described in this chapter. While comprehensive theories are always a desirable aim, one cannot afford to ignore a point of view that in fact produces results.

For the present purpose, it is necessary to highlight two aspects of operant conditioning: the emphasis on the *occurrence* of behaviour – actual responses – as a crucial component in the development of dispositions to make those responses; and the timing, rather than the nature, of the reinforcement. New behaviour is acquired in essentially two stages. It makes its first, quasi-incidental appearance as a by-product of previously reinforced responses; it is then 'learned' by being in its turn reinforced. The art of training consists in choosing, at each stage of the animal's progress from initial to desired behaviour, those responses whose reinforcement will edge the behavioural spectrum towards the chosen final achievement. This choice may be made with some precision. As has been shown in Chapter 2, the critical events in the reinforcement schedule are not so much the actual occasions of food delivery or consumption, as the signals which have repeatedly been paired with it (such as clicks in the supply mechanism), which may be regarded as having acquired 'informational value' for the animal. It is the recognition of the potentialities of such secondary reinforcers that has made possible the various remarkable training achievements that have been described. While there is inevitably a time lag of variable duration between the occurrence of some particular response, and the delivery, let alone the consumption, of a food pellet, clicks or other signals may be arranged to follow the selected response immediately. In this way it becomes possible to 'point out' to the animal, consistently and unambiguously, a particular aspect of its behaviour. It is the achievement of this consistency which is at the root of greatly increased learning speeds and which is sometimes a condition of particular responses being learnt at all.

It does not follow that because certain principles make for effective training in pigeons or rats, they will therefore be equally applicable to university students. If, however, a particular approach to the analysis of the learning process has been successful with a variety of different species, it is at any rate worth bringing the same approach to bear on the learning of yet another species, however highly evolved, to see if it will be successful. Inevitably there will have to be much translation of detail, and we may well find that there are forms of human learning for which animal work has provided no equivalent. On the other hand, the very complexity of human behaviour may have obscured basic learning patterns that are shared with simpler animals, and that become more readily apparent through an initial study of the latter.

When we come to translate operant ideas into human terms, two important differences from animal conditioning become apparent. In dealing with animals, the trainer has a problem of communication. He has to rely entirely on the occurrence of 'correct' responses, to manoeuvre the animal gradually towards a goal, the nature of which he knows explicitly from the outset. When dealing with human beings the use of language makes possible the condensation of much elaborate 'shaping' of behaviour into a few verbal instructions or explanations. When it comes to reinforcement, the much greater complexity of human motives makes it unnecessary in most cases to use either direct, tangible reward or to develop special reinforcers which may be more easily manipulated. The achievement of understanding and the associated correct behaviour may in most learning situations be regarded as a goal the learner wishes to attain, and any indication that a correct response has been made thus acts as a reinforcement. This information about the appropriateness of a response may come to the learner via the comment of a teacher, or it may be possible for him to assess his performance by himself. When throwing darts at a target, immediate 'knowledge of results' is provided as an integral feature of the situation. Whether or not a mathematical problem has been solved correctly may be conveyed either by the teacher, or by the correct answer being independently available, or it may be discovered by using other criteria appropriate to the problem (e.g. alternative methods of solution) with which the student has previously been made familiar.

It may appear that the use of verbal explanation obviates the need for positive action on the part of the learner. Although lip-service is often paid to the importance of active student participation, a look at educational practice reveals an emphasis on the purely receptive and passive aspects of learning, and does not suggest that the activity of the learner is regarded as a vital component of the learning process as such. While the need for practice is inescapable in the acquisition of a motor skill, it is frequently suggested that learning a fact or gaining insight into the nature of an argument is an altogether different process, requiring only exposition and explanation. Yet it should be recognized that the criterion for the possession of knowledge of whatever kind is the ability to produce some sort of appropriate behaviour, including of course speech, and that the criterion for depth of understanding lies in the variety and complexity of the behaviour that becomes possible. If we extend the operant conditioning model to human beings, the implication would be that we should aim constantly, whatever the subject matter being taught, *to produce criterion behaviour,* to reinforce it by indicating its correctness, and to regard this alternation between the activity of the teacher and that of the student as the basic unit of the learning process.

The analogy may be followed further. The 'space' that separates the learner's initial state of knowledge from that which he is to attain may be mapped out in a detailed series of items of information and explanation, student responses to test questions, and comment on those responses, edging the student towards the behavioural goal of a particular programme of instruction. The difference between this and a more conventional teaching plan, which, it may be felt, does precisely this, lies in the degree of detail with which the material is prepared, each step being designed to make possible the tackling of small new problems, and in making further progress dependent on the successful completion of each stage by the student.

Here we come up against a difficulty; if the teaching programme is to be prepared in advance in such a way as to incorporate and make allowance for the students' responses at the many test points of the programme, it is necessary to make some predictions about those responses. Is this ever possible? While we expect a competent teacher to be able to cope with most problems that a student may raise – supposing always that the method of instruction used is such as to give the student this opportunity – to what extent is it possible to say in advance what those problems will be and when they will occur? The teacher possesses a degree of flexibility, of *potential* behaviour, to which it may be impossible to do justice in a predetermined programme without making it quite hopelessly unwieldy. There are, however, many situations in which the full extent of this flexibility is scarcely called upon. It is possible to exaggerate the unpredictability of human, even of student, behaviour. The programme of instruction including the particular questions asked at each stage exercises a strongly limiting influence on the responses made. If the ground covered by individual steps is small enough then we may be virtually certain of what the response to a question covering a particular step will be – it will be the correct answer. The larger the steps and the more comprehensive the questions, the greater will be the variety of misunderstandings that might arise, and in consequence, the likelihood and variety of wrong answers.

The importance of arranging things so that the learner will make nothing but correct responses throughout the whole course of instruction, and receive, as a consequence, nothing but positive reinforcement, has been emphasized by Skinner. Programmes embodying this approach are called *linear*. It is possible, however, to make allowance for one or more categories of wrong response at some or all stages of a programme, by making the instructional path followed by the student at each stage depend on the answer he has given to the immediately preceding question. Thus a wrong answer may lead to an alternative, and more detailed, explanation of the previous stage, incorporating further test questions before returning the student to the 'main stream'. Alternately, a part of the previous instruction may be repeated, with an explanation of why the answer given was wrong. This is called *intrinsic programming* or *branching*, usually associated with Norman Crowder and developing out of an emphasis on multiple choice testing and teaching devices first introduced by Pressey.[1]

Cutting across the question of linear versus branching programmes is one involving the nature of the response to be made by the learner. On the one hand he may be called upon to *compose* or *construct* answers to questions freely – i.e. the only clue provided is contained in the question that is asked – on the other he may be presented with a number of alternative answers and asked to choose between them. These two approaches are again associated with Skinner and Pressey respectively; they are also usually found in conjunction with the two types of programme structure previously mentioned – linear with free response, branching with multiple choice. However, when the relative merits of different kinds of programme are discussed, it should be remembered that the theoretical issues raised by the two dichotomies – linear versus branching, and free versus multiple choice response – are logically quite independent, although in practice they frequently tend to get confused.

The argument put forward in favour of using minimal steps and ensuring success at each stage, is that learning takes place only with positive reinforcement. Certainly the information conveyed by being told that a given response is correct is usually much greater than by being told that it is wrong. There is, however, a possibility here that the analogy from animal training has been taken too literally. With human beings one is not confined to simple statements of right or wrong, but can build further explanations and reasons into these statements. There are two types of function that the information provided by a programme fulfils – part of the information gives a basis for making the *next* response, and part provides a comment on the last one. These functions need not be kept entirely distinct. Thus the comment on a wrong answer may involve a detailed explanation of how to correct it, i.e. provide a preparation for the next response. This also means that the discovery that a wrong response has been made need not necessarily have aversive properties comparable to shock in an animal training situation. However, it is generally agreed that in a programme as a whole the frequency of correct responses made should outweigh that of wrong responses.

On the other hand, using nothing but very small steps in a programme may have positive disadvantages. First, there is the danger of boredom in the more intelligent student. One might expect that the reward value of being successful decreases with the triviality of the problem. Secondly, there is to date insufficient evidence on the question of whether the response involved in making a large learning step is always equivalent to making a number of small ones. The real situations for which the learner is preparing will certainly involve occasions on which it is necessary to withhold responses until quite a large amount of information has been taken in. In the absence of direct evidence, it may be argued that minimal-step training *may* have disadvantageous second-order effects, in failing to prepare the student for learning situations which cannot be programmed in this way.

The issue of free versus multiple choice responses is quite distinct. Two arguments may be brought against a *teaching* procedure which involves the selection of one of a number of provided answers. One is that the learner is quite gratuitously introduced to a whole series of wrong responses. To the extent to which the wrong alternatives are plausible, this may be quite seriously confusing. If they are not plausible, the achievement in selecting the correct one is insignificant. Secondly, the response of recognition is different from that of spontaneous construction. Given that we wish to produce and reinforce the sort of behaviour which is the desired end product of the teaching programme, the use of constructed responses is clearly indicated. They have the further advantage of *including* the response of correct recognition, whereas the converse is not necessarily true.

If the construction of a detailed and predetermined learning programme is possible – the size and sequence of steps being adjusted to produce either a virtually one hundred per cent rate of correct response, or allowing for various degrees of branching – it follows that the instructional process may be mechanized. Although the whole topic of programmed learning is usually associated first and foremost with teaching machines, mention of such machines has been delayed until now, because they are in fact conceptually quite incidental, however great their practical importance may be or eventually become. The essence of programmed learning is in the programme – the nature of the information provided, the size of informational units, the sequence of presentation in relation to different possible responses – not in the particular *means* that may be employed to present the information or take note of the learner's responses. In considering the potentialities of mechanical teaching devices it is as well to recognize that the sophistication of the engineer cannot compensate for the possible inadequacies of the subject specialist who writes the programme.

Existing teaching machines employ two main types of information presentation: filmstrip, projecting the material on to a ground glass screen; and typescript on continuous paper roll, which can be moved past an aperture. The former arrangement is more expensive, but better suited to a branching programme, being more flexible in use. The use of branching programmes usually also involves a multiple choice type of response – not only because of the historical development, but also because this type of response can be more easily mechanized. Thus a machine may possess a series of numbered buttons. A multiple choice question will then direct the learner to press one of these, according to the choice he has made from the alternative answers presented, leading either to the appearance of a frame which confirms the correctness of the answer and presents the next item of information, or one which indicates that the answer was wrong, explains the nature of the mistake and continues with a *remedial sequence*, followed by re-testing. On the other hand, free responses which involve the writing of answers into a space provided, must inevitably rely on the student judging the correctness of his own answer when subsequently provided with the right one. Machines using this kind of method usually ensure that the act of bringing the correct answer into view moves the space available for the written answer behind glass, where it can be seen, but no longer changed! Thus a faithful record of performance is available at the end of the instructional sequence. A machine developed at Sheffield University under H. Kay, and sponsored by the Department of Scientific and Industrial Research, combines provision for free response with a limited degree of branching. Two programmes are written in parallel: an 'A' programme which proceeds in comparatively large steps and asks correspondingly comprehensive questions, and a 'B' programme which covers the same ground but spells out each point in more explanatory detail, posing more, and smaller, problems. To each frame in the 'A' series there correspond several frames in the 'B' series. Answers are written on cards and 'posted' where they can be seen, but not retrieved. The correct answer is then displayed. If the learner's answer is correct, he presses a button which presents the next 'A' frame. If wrong, another button diverts him to the 'B' sequence leading up to the last 'A' question which he failed to answer correctly. The 'B' frames take him through a detailed *linear* sequence before returning him to the 'A' stream. The programme thus allows for the possibility of large steps, while providing more detailed explanations, should they be necessary, and combines this with a facility for free responses. This approach may well turn out to be the most satisfactory of those developed so far.

Is it necessary to have mechanical devices at all? Clearly a teacher could carry out the functions of the machine by following the programme, but this would be a wasteful use of a human being. However, text books can be written so as to allow the reader to formulate the answers to questions without at the same time being confronted by the correct answer – which is, however, provided immediately afterwards so that the reader's response may be checked. This involves a rather unorthodox layout (e.g. that in Holland and Skinner[2]). Two kinds of book are available, embodying respectively linear and branching programmes, the latter being referred to as 'scrambled' books. Here, according to the answer given by the reader – which of course he checks himself – he is referred to an appropriate section of the book, which either takes him to a further stage or clarifies a previous point. This way of dealing with programmes has the great advantage of cheapness, and can be used particularly by the mature learner who can be made to understand the self-defeating character of 'cheating', and for whom the 'toy' aspect of the machine is of less decisive importance.

How effective are these methods? This is a very difficult question to answer. In the first place one cannot really evaluate programmed instruction independently of particular programmes – any more than one can evaluate 'conventional' methods without reference to particular teachers and particular presentations of a given topic. The idea of programming is an *approach* to learning, and as such capable of developments the detailed nature of which cannot be foreseen. When it comes to an evaluation of existing programmes presented by means of devices currently available, one has to recognize that the assessment of *any* kind of educational procedure is a formidable task. What are the criteria that should be used? One method is to rely on a limited set of tests and examinations at the end of a course of instruction, such as are at present almost universally used. Used, that is, to assess the quality of the *learner*, though they inevitably also reflect on the quality and appropriateness of the instruction. The real objects of education and training, however, are different from and go beyond the passing of examinations, and the adequacy of the examination system in providing a measure of the wider and more long-term effects of a learning experience is frequently questioned. If a comparison of different teaching methods gives similar results in such a conventional type of test, it may still be objected that important differences in the character of the learning produced simply fail to show up under these circumstances. Programmed learning may enable people to pass tests, but how will they be able to cope with the more varied demands that may be made upon their knowledge subsequently? We shall have a limited answer to this question only when a substantial number of people, part of whose learning experience has been of the programmed variety, pass into the working population. In the meantime it is worthwhile to consider the results of some of the evaluative studies that have been carried out.

Three such studies have recently been reported in this country (by Cavanagh [3]), carried out under the auspices of the Royal Navy, the Royal Air Force and British European Airways. The first two involved short programmes in elementary trigonometry, the third a specially written programme on 'load control'. All three studies used learner groups drawn from

215

the respective establishments, and matched for intelligence and initial familiarity with the subject being taught. In each case the main objective was a comparison between the effects of conventional instruction and the use of a particular teaching machine and programme. The first study also included the use of a 'scrambled' text. One of the criteria of achievement used in all three cases was a conventional examination of the kind normally employed in testing knowledge of the relevant subject matter.

The results may be briefly summarized as follows.

1. Achievement with the teaching machine was as good as that with conventional instruction.

2. This same level of test achievement was brought about in a substantially shorter time by means of the teaching machine compared to classroom instruction.

3. Retention of learned material was better after machine learning than after conventional instruction.

4. The machine was more effective in both these respects compared to the scrambled text.

5. There are indications that the advantages of the teaching machine are most pronounced with the more intelligent students.

The size of the validation problem can be appreciated when one considers, on the one hand, the elaborateness of the experimental designs involved, and on the other, the inevitable limitations of the results obtained – limitations of subject matter, of course-length, of type of programme and of the particular nature of the classroom instruction used for comparison purposes. Many 'trials' of teaching machines, some of which have been reported in the press, have been conducted without any appreciation of the methodological problems that such comparisons involve. On the basis of the competently obtained evidence published so far – Kay and Warr [4] have summarized the results of forty-two other such studies – one may safely claim that teaching machines and programmes generally have justified at least a much more extensive experimental use.

The great majority of programmes written so far have been confined to comparatively straightforward factual or logically well-structured material. It is impossible to say at the present stage of development whether this is an essential limitation of the whole approach. It is not difficult to see why factual material has been favoured: the desired behavioural consequences of 'knowing a fact' are – apparently – comparatively easy to define. Even if this is a limitation, it still opens up vast areas for the application of programmed methods. There is in every subject a great deal of quite straightforward *information* which it is necessary for the student to hold if he is to be able to make sense of subsequent developments. A considerable portion of the time currently used in classroom instruction is devoted to the imparting of this sort of information. Not only should a well-thought-out programme be able to cope with *conveying* such information, but by requiring the student to use it at once in a variety of situations, it should ensure a more *effective* comprehension of the material than mere confrontation can achieve.

Subjects with a clear-cut logical development like mathematics would seem to lend themselves to programmed treatment, indeed the logical development itself suggests the programme. We must recognize, however, that the logical structure of the material does not necessarily coincide with the sequence of presentation which is optimum for developing the student's understanding. This is an area in which more research is needed.

We must now turn to some of the objections to the whole concept of programmed learning, particularly in connexion with teaching machines. The idea of the machine in education is sometimes regarded as an affront to the dignity of man, particularly that of teaching man. What becomes of the role of the teacher? Is he to be replaced by a machine? It is a type of question that has been asked, part scoffingly, part anxiously, in many areas of human activity. Here, as in other cases, the answer is quite clear. There is little sign of *people* being replaced by machines. It is what many people *do*, or are *expected* to do, which can sometimes be taken over by machines. It has been suggested that any teacher that can effectively be replaced by a machine *deserves* to be replaced. This may be rather unfair when one considers that much educational tradition, and the institutions that embody it, encourage and sometimes constrain teachers to engage in such replaceable activities. The incursion of machines into human preserves only highlights the extent to which people carry out tasks that are not worthy of their potentialities.

It can also help to clarify the particular nature of those potentialities. In the first place, teaching machines can only *carry out* programmes; they can neither discover the information that is to be presented, nor structure it in such a way that it is effectively learned. The explanations that a programme provides and the degree of specificity with which those explanations can be fitted to the needs of a particular learner are severely limited; a teacher has much greater flexibility. There is within the larger education unit scope both for the almost unlimited adaptiveness of the instructor, and for the comparative rigidity of the prepared programme.

When one considers the whole potential function of an educational experience, in which a student might hope not only to be presented with carefully selected, well-structured material, but also to receive some attention directed to his own specific difficulties, and which, apart from subject content, could be expected to transmit the interest and enthusiasm of people deeply involved in their particular discipline, the distinctive contribution of the teacher becomes clear. If much of his time has been taken up with a recital of factual information, he can only welcome the development of teaching aids which promise to achieve the objects of this essentially inhuman activity more efficiently than he can.

We are at the present time in the middle of an educational crisis. The overt *demand* for training and for trained people exceeds the capacity of existing facilities. If one takes the wider view of seeing the purpose of an educational system as providing facilities for the maximum intellectual development of the population irrespective of actual clamour for school and university places, then it is a crisis that has been with us for a very long time and one whose proportions are, if possible, even vaster than is at present officially suspected. It is to be hoped that among the various proposals that have been made to remedy this situation, the long-term benefits of research and development into programmed learning will not be neglected. While there is undoubtedly a need for having a larger number of teachers, there is also a strong case for using the time and ability of those we have to better purpose.

Teaching machines should not however be seen as simply taking over some of the traditional activities of teachers. Their use is likely to have wider repercussions. Teaching machines make learning a much more individual activity than being a member of a class permits. People are able to work at their own pace – which, from the available evidence, is in any case faster than normal progress in a classroom. This may mean that a correlation between ability and achievement may to some extent be turned into one between ability and time taken. While it is most unlikely that all individual differences can be ironed out by enabling some people to take longer over their studies than others, the cumulatively damaging effect of having fallen behind at some important stage of what is essentially a 'paced' system can probably be avoided. A contrasting result of the use of machines could be a widened gap, at any particular *time*, between people of different abilities, since there are indications that the more intelligent students benefit disproportionately in the change-over from conventional to programmed instruction. Orthodox notions of what the proper age is for the learning of different types or stages of subject matter may have to be quite radically revised, once we get away from the idea that a particular class of children or students must progress together as a unit over long periods of time. Another most important claim that is made for teaching machines, or more generally, for any methods of instruction that constantly require and reinforce the students' responses, is that they produce and maintain a high level of activity – behaviour which we should normally wish to describe in terms of interest and good motivation. The motivation produced by the programme's pattern of reinforcement does not depend on comparisons made with other members of a class, comparisons which for a substantial proportion of any group of pupils are likely to be *dis*couraging. The widespread practice of trying to produce in non-cooperative pupils a semblance of learning behaviour, by the infliction of penalties *additional* to those the educational experience already contains for them, is thus given a more promising alternative. The development of programmed instruction and associated devices should aid the reappraisal not only of the teacher's role, but of the whole conception and organization of the educational system.

If the impact of an idea makes people look at what they are doing more critically and from a different point of view, this is clearly an advantage. The more direct value of programmed learning will depend on how it is used. Teaching machines are likely to become big business, as indeed they already are in the United States, and the interests of business do not necessarily coincide with those of the consumer. There is a danger, not only of hurriedly constructed, untested programmes coming onto the market, but of a restriction of programming developments and explorations through premature investment in particular types of machine and the associated type of programme. There is a need for a rapid development of consumer sophistication in this area. Above all there is a need for large-scale and well-planned research into the use of techniques and machines which, paradoxically, promise to return to education some of the concern for individual development that is at present in danger of disappearing.

12. Learning and education

In the opening chapter it was pointed out that learning processes extended well beyond the predominantly formal situations that are ordinarily associated with the term; and that for the most part psychological research on learning was concerned with the establishment of general principles. What implications do methods and results of this kind of work have for the practical problems of teaching and training? While a concern with practical application is not necessarily advantageous – and may sometimes even be detrimental – to the activities of individual scientists, it is reasonable to look for points of contact between the laboratory and the 'real' world outside. The work of theoretical physicists frequently does not have any obvious practical relevance, yet it has resulted in a complete transformation of our way of life – and indeed of death. What are the actual and potential consequences of work in the social sciences, and specifically of psychological work on learning?

The application of psychological theory

Comparisons between psychology and the physical sciences, both from the point of view of theory and of its application, often lead to the observation that psychology is several hundred years behind in its development. The implication is that given sufficient time we may expect psychology to approach physics in the coherence of its theory, and in the manner of its utilization. We believe that such a view is, at least in part, misleading.

Experimental work in psychology, as in other sciences, aims at achieving controlled circumstances, situations in which it becomes possible to focus attention on a small number of factors influencing our observations and to ignore the rest. Given the sorting out of a great deal of conceptual and linguistic confusion that persists in psychology, one may indeed hope that such a procedure will in time lead to more comprehensive theories and to more effective prediction of behaviour than is possible at present. However, with regard to application, we must recognize an important difference. The application of physical theory to 'real life' nearly always involves the construction of special circumstances in which the laws discovered in the laboratory can in fact lead to predictable results. Machines and specialized equipment, whether they be transistor radios or nuclear reactors, reflect the circumstances of the laboratory and are deliberately designed to achieve a desired outcome. Such application of physical theory involves the *building* of a portion of the world, in which the effect of undesirable variables is eliminated, and things are arranged in such a way that the remainder operate according to plan. It is in such artificial 'islands' that events can be predicted and controlled.

One implication of this comparison is that to reap the benefit of work in the psychological laboratory we must develop a technology of learning. Much of Skinner's work has in fact been directed at the creation of technology. For example, a 'box' for babies has been designed, and is commercially available, which makes possible the detailed control of the child's physical environment, and also the provision of reinforcement contingencies for a variety of different kinds of behaviour.[1] It is a specially designed substitute for the usual cot, and it is claimed to produce a more rapid and generally more satisfactory development of a young child than is possible with more traditional methods and environments. Such devices, together with teaching machines discussed in Chapter 11, constitute a move towards creating practical situations in which such regularities of behaviour as have been observed in the laboratory can be utilized. Circumstances are deliberately arranged to resemble those on which existing principles and generalizations are based. There is undoubtedly a great deal of scope for technological developments of this kind, and they need not be based exclusively on the work of Skinner;

though his analysis of learning situations lends itself more easily to such developments than that of other theorists.

There are, however, serious limitations to an approach which involves the extended use of circumstances which closely resemble those of the laboratory. On the one hand, any particular set of restricted conditions on which a given theory is based are unlikely to make full use of all the factors which can influence learning. On the other hand, people are often ready to accept restrictions on their freedom of action in the context of an experiment, which they are not prepared to put up with in everyday life. Because we are dealing with people rather than with inanimate matter, the application of any theory of learning or of behaviour in general must allow for a large measure of uncontrolled variation, while the application of a physical principle would aim at the elimination of such disturbing factors. However carefully we structure the educational experience, a school remains a complex community in which social interactions among children, and between children and teachers, will influence the learning process and are likely to influence different individuals in different ways. At the same time, a large portion of a child's experience lies outside the school, yet will affect the way in which events within it are re-received. The gap which inevitably exists between controlled laboratory experiment and its application is very much greater in psychology than in the physical sciences.

The need for educational research

In such a situation, theory cannot provide a detailed, authoritative guide for action. It can, however, make a valuable contribution if the practitioners – teachers, trainers, educational administrators – have a more extensive grasp of research methods and results than is usually the case and if they are in fact given the opportunity to approach their work in the spirit of experiment. In a recent book, Michael Young [2] has argued strongly for such a change in attitude among educators and for a far greater volume of educational research. Despite the impression of experimental ferment within education that is sometimes given by the press, the rate of expenditure on educational research stands currently at about £250,000 per annum or 0·03 per cent of total spending on education. This compares most unfavourably with a research budget of about 1 per cent in the U.S.A., or in absolute terms, with £6 millions annual expenditure by the Agricultural Research Council, for example. It represents a lamentably small investment in the discovery of better methods for bringing about learning and of assessing the effectiveness of methods in current use.

What kinds of educational research are needed? There is in the first place the *assessment* of educational innovations. These might be specific and limited in their objectives, such as for example, the introduction of a new alphabet like the initial teaching alphabet aimed at facilitating the process of learning to read, devices like cuisenaire rods, which are claimed to bring about a more rapid understanding of arithmetical operations, or particular ways, developed by an individual teacher, of putting over ideas, procedures or notations, such as, for example, the use of specialized techniques to demonstrate the relationship between geographical contours and their representations in ordnance survey maps.[3] On the other hand, there are innovations with much more widespread implications, such as a change to comprehensive schooling and the abandonment of the 11 + examination, or the 'sandwich' method of education used by many of the new technological universities. Many such changes are brought about as the result of ideological and political considerations; others come in on a tide of fashion, comparable to those for particular surgical operations, like removal of the tonsils or the appendix, or for the use of particular drugs. Because of the gap between laboratory experiment and theory on the one hand, and application on the other – a gap which exists in medicine as well as in psychology – there is a need for extensive evaluation and assessment of new methods 'in the field'. To many people the idea of such large-scale experiments involving human beings is inherently repugnant, but it has to be recognized that this is the only way in which we can ever hope to find methods for treating people – physically or mentally – which are reliably better than those currently in use.

The assessment of innovations

What is involved in the assessment of an educational or training procedure? If the objectives are limited, clearly specified, and observable within a short period of the completion of the learning experience, the problem is comparatively simple. For example, the effectiveness of a training method aimed at producing skill in valve assembly can be measured in terms of quantity of output meeting some specified qualitative standard. Even here, care must be taken in designing the measurement procedure to ensure that the results obtained may be validly ascribed to the method of training used rather than, say, to characteristics of particular trainers, or trainees, or to some generalized improvement in morale which frequently occurs when people are explicitly involved in trying out something new. When dealing with educational practices of wider application, problems of assessment become more intractable. How does one measure the effectiveness of different approaches to university education? Even if we were agreed as to what the outcomes of such an education should be, such outcomes manifest themselves over a graduate's entire life span. We cannot look at the performance of people, say, ten years after the completion of formal education and attribute differences in professional competence to particular differences in their educational experience. Success in examinations provides an intermediate measure, but even to the extent to which such success is a guide to subsequent performance – and there is little documented evidence for this – it may at least in part be the result of further opportunities that follow from good examination results rather than a validation of the examination system.

If we cannot hope to obtain conclusive evidence for the relative effectiveness of different educational practices there are, nevertheless, indirect sources of information which can provide a guide for action. For example, a study, by means of interview and observation, of what does happen to a student during his academic or industrial training, is an improvement on making assumptions about it. Such a study, carried out by Marie Jahoda[4] at Brunel University, was concerned with students' attitudes to the academic and industrial parts of their educational 'sandwich'.

The sandwich method of education involves students in alternate six-month periods of academic work in college, and relevant practical work in industry or other appropriate work settings – the whole process extending over four years. This procedure is intended to produce graduates better prepared to translate academic knowledge into practical application than is usual with those following the more conventional educational pattern. On *a priori* grounds this approach seems reasonable enough. Yet like other educational innovations, however plausible, it can only be justified by its results, or at least by such indications of its likely results that it is possible to obtain.

One outcome of Professor Jahoda's study was a documentation of the wide variety in the nature of the first industrial experience. Some students were given opportunities by the firm in which they worked to carry out projects on their own, others spent most of their time in an apprentice training school, or on a 'perambulatory course', involving constant movement from department to department, watching rather than being actively involved in what was going on. Many students were engaged on routine work at various levels of skill, including some which made very little demands on their ability. On the whole students described their work experience as 'good' to the extent to which it provided scope for individual and responsible activity – bad experiences being primarily those in which students were involved in routine production work. Interviews with managers and industrial training officers revealed wide discrepancies in how different firms saw their contribution to the students' education and the students' contribution to the work of the firm. Often such discrepancies existed between people at different levels within the same organization. Given that a college has some influence over the type of experience provided by a firm – and if any real integration between academic and practical work is to be achieved, this is clearly desirable – what type of opportunity should it ask for? Excluding routine production work at the lowest levels, a plausible case could be made out for any of the different types of experience being offered. While the Jahoda study did not demonstrate directly which kind produced the most appropriate learning, it did show that the students' own assessment of their experience – and hence their general motivation throughout their industrial period – is significantly related to clearly specifiable types of activity. As a result of this and similar studies we know more about how to look at the industrial experience offered to students and can make more informed choices and recommendations.

Information based on interview and verbal report cannot have the status of physical measurement, though much is known about interviewing and the general design of investigations using such methods which makes the data obtained as reliable as possible. Where more direct observational methods are not available, information gained by such means provides a great improvement on uncoordinated judgements based on individual and usually unspecified experience. This particular study documents in a systematic form some of the problems involved in attempting to integrate academic and industrial experience. Investigations of this kind, carried out in the context of an ongoing educational process, can provide advance indicators of likely success or failure. They can reveal differences between assumptions about what is going on and what does in fact happen. They can also provide clues, forming the basis for other, more detailed investigations, to factors operating in the total educational experience which might otherwise remain unsuspected, or at any rate ignored.

Research into 'complex' learning

A second type of research aims, like much of the work that has been described in this book, at the formulation of general principles, but takes as its starting point material and situations more closely related to school or university. This may give prominence to aspects of learning which do not force themselves on the attention of investigators who concentrate on highly simplified learning situations. An investigation directed by L. F. Thomas and sponsored at Brunel University by the Department of Education and Science may serve as an illustration.

The work of Skinner has emphasized the careful structuring of the learning situation so as to guide or shape the student's behaviour towards some specified achievement. The learner is seen as being under the control of external influences, and it is the teacher's or programmer's objective to arrange these influences in such a way that they will lead the learner along a prescribed path, irrespective of individual characteristics. What happens, however, when a student is faced with material that is less precisely structured, such as a book or article, as opposed to a programmed text? To some extent the conventional layout of written material determines the path that the reader will take through it. Individual lines – unless they can be taken in at a single glance – have to be read from left to right, and *on the whole* the development of the subject matter leads people to follow it through from beginning to end; but within this general framework there is considerable variety in the precise route taken by different people in the extent to which they review what they have read, in the location and frequency of points in the narrative at which they stop to do so, and in the extent to which they concentrate their attention on detail as compared with the broad outline of an argument. On a larger scale, people differ in the organization of their work, their use of lecture notes, books and articles, their methods of revision – and such differences depend to some extent on the objectives which they set themselves in relation to their work, in separate parts and as a whole. Thomas's study is concerned with describing and developing a model for different *strategies of learning*, in so far as these may be characteristic of the individual learner.

The discovery of such strategies presents observational difficulties. Thomas has used a device which under the control of the student presents written material a line at a time, and which records a complete protocol of the path followed. Such paths are then systematically related to the amount and kind of information that has been retained. In this way it is hoped to establish characteristic strategies, and to discover the relative goodness of such strategies with regard to the learning which they achieve. Using a rather different kind of material, methods adopted for learning binary code have been studied.* The learner is presented with twenty cards, bearing a decimal number between 0 and 19 on one side, and its binary equivalent on the other. He is asked to learn the code by selecting cards in any order he chooses, including repetitions, and a record is kept of the sequence of choices made. This procedure reveals wide differences in approach from the (apparent) individual memorizing of all twenty equivalents, to the systematic choice of 'key' cards, which confirm or refute the learner's developing hypothesis about the principle involved. The performance of any particular individual in one such learning task is compared to performance in others, and there are indications of consistencies in approach. (At the time of writing, this research project is still in progress.)

Given that different strategies are more or less advantageous for the achievement of learning, the development, in students, of appropriate strategies presents a challenge for teaching methods. The assumption here is that it is possible to teach

---

* Binary code used primarily in computers represents numbers by the use of two characters only – 0 and 1 instead of the ten characters 0 to 9 used in the decimal system. Thus 0 is written for 0, 1 for 1, 10 for 2, 11 for 3, 100 for 4, 101 for 5, etc.

students, explicitly, methods of learning, as distinct from specific subject matter.

The purpose of education

This raises an issue of fundamental importance for the objectives of education. It will have become apparent that the emphasis of the different kinds of experimental work that have been described in this book is on learning as a process, on the activities of the learner rather than on those of the teacher or trainer. A clearer understanding of what happens to the learner can on the one hand provide methods for achieving a more direct and effective control over the details of an individual's learning progress – this is the direction in which Skinnerian thinking has developed. We may, however, aim to hand over, progressively, the control of the learning sequence to the learner himself. Such an approach has far-reaching implications.

It is a commonplace notion that we are living in a rapidly changing environment. New scientific discoveries and related technological developments are appearing at an ever-increasing rate. Individual industrial concerns as well as whole nations are benefiting to the extent to which they are able to come to terms with the opportunities that this provides. It requires constant reconsideration of production methods and of organization and this in turn requires adaptive change by individuals – the development of new skills, the review of problems and of methods for their solution which have been taken for granted, the re-evaluation of objectives. This imposes severe strains on both organizational machinery and on individuals, and there is widespread resistance to change. There is no shortage of exhortations, but it appears not to be enough.

In the context of the educational system we are faced not only by an explosion of the eligible population, but also by an explosion of knowledge. It is no longer possible for a single individual to gain a detailed familiarity with anything but an increasingly narrow section of what is to be known. The growing tendency towards early specialization is met – not too successfully – by an increase in the time allotted to formal education; the argument seems to be that since there is more information available a student must take more time to assimilate it, before he can be let loose on the real world.

We believe that this involves a fallacy. Knowledge does not simply accumulate, it also becomes obsolete. Much of the detailed information acquired during formal education is out of date shortly afterwards. An acquisition of more knowledge, in the sense of facts and specialized techniques, may simply mean that more has to be put aside and re-learned closer to the time of its application. The amount of unlearning to be done may even prove a positive obstacle to the subsequent adaptation.

We have here the clue to the proper objective of formal education. It is primarily to enable people to learn and adapt more easily without the aid of such formal guidance; to *extract* from those situations in which they will find themselves what is to be known – whether this situation is that of the academic researcher or that of the industrial worker. If we recognize that specific knowledge will constantly go out of date, then we must concentrate on enabling every single individual, within the limitations of his intellectual capacity, to deal with new situations ; enabling him on the one hand to absorb, without guidance, new, already formulated knowledge presented in books or in other symbolic forms, and on the other hand to create new knowledge for himself. If it is accepted that the function of schools, colleges and universities is not the handing out of a self-contained and complete parcel of knowledge and professional competence, but rather the preparation for a process which is intended to continue throughout life, the necessity for cramming an increasing amount of subject matter into the period of formal education disappears.

There are several factors which militate against this indefinite extension of the learning period. It is generally accepted that the learning of new material is easiest in childhood and adolescence and becomes progressively more difficult with increasing age. But there is no conclusive evidence to suggest

231

that, prior to the beginning of senility, this is the result of maturational processes. However, the conviction that old dogs cannot learn new tricks is in itself an obstacle to change. A belief in the impossibility of success does not provide the best motivation for its achievement. To the extent to which learning is identified with childhood, with classrooms and teachers, the need for further learning in maturity is often regarded as an admission of failure – we talk about going *back* to school. Also, the working conditions of most people provide little occasion or encouragement for re-training and review. Given family responsibilities and sheer fatigue, only exceptional individuals will take advantage of such opportunities for further education that evening classes and libraries may provide.

We need a national change of attitude towards adult learning, and the creation of government re-training centres is one small step in the direction of bringing this about. The opportunities provided by the mass media, and in particular television, have hardly begun to be used. It is not enough to provide the odd educational programme. The ingenuity and effort which goes into persuading people of the individual supremacy of several indistinguishable washing powders, or the prestige to be gained from smoking a particular cigarette could be utilized towards achieving more desirable objectives. There is no reason why we should not have a small boy announcing some suitable equivalent of 'My dad uses the local library – and it shows'.

Industry could provide more explicit incentives for its employees to undergo periodic re-training, which should become part of the normal pattern of working life at all occupational levels. With the increasing trend toward automation and shorter working hours, the institution of paid sabbatical periods might be extended to non-academic professions. But whatever opportunities for learning are provided during people's working lives, these will not achieve their aim unless the first educational experience constitutes an explicit and deliberate preparation for taking advantage of them. The difficulties which older people experience in this respect may in part be due to the approach to learning which their early schooling developed in them.

The conception of school, as providing a progressive preparation for learning also has implications within the educational system. It is a common experience in dealing with students at university levels to find that many have difficulty in coping with the greater degree of responsibility which is placed upon them – responsibility, that is, for organizing their own learning. Compared to most schools, work at university level involves a much greater dependence on books, articles and unstructured laboratory work and less detailed guidance by the teaching staff. Students are often ill prepared for this sort of change, having become accustomed to a syllabus that is 'covered' in lessons, to prescribed homework and detailed preparation for examinations – having in general come to regard the teacher and the school as carrying the full responsibility for their own progress.

Universities and individual teachers within them vary in their ways of dealing with this situation. Some do not recognize the problem, or choose to ignore it. Students are simply left to sink or swim with the system. It has led to a move at other places towards a greater attention being given to teaching as opposed to formal lecturing. This may, however, simply prolong the dependence of students on the teaching staff, and postpone the moment when they find themselves on their own. A tutorial system, whereby each student, either alone or accompanied by at most two others, regularly meets a member of staff who helps him to maximize the use he makes of the facilities – including lectures – which the university provides, is probably a more satisfactory solution. But even this should be seen as a remedial activity, a somewhat belated 'weaning' process which aims at making students increasingly independent.

Educational weaning could begin much earlier, indeed the whole system might be designed, from the earliest beginnings in primary school, to place an increasing emphasis on *learning by the child* rather than on *instruction by the teacher*. It was suggested in the chapter on skill that one of the most important functions of a teacher is to provide criteria, which the student may use to assess his own performance. This may now be generalized by saying that teaching should be aimed at making much of a teacher's currently accepted function progressively redundant as the child moves through school and university.

The achievement of independent learning

Stating objectives still leaves the question of their realization. We have all sorts of methods for presenting information and there is still much room for improvement by means of the more extended use of visual and other aids. But how do we make someone into an active learner – i.e. someone who has the ability to organize his own work, select and find his own sources, and who has the desire to do so? How do we help someone to become the sort of person who can in later life scrap obsolescent ideas and adopt or develop new ones?

There are two, not unrelated, aspects of this problem: the discovery on the one hand of increasingly efficient learning strategies which might themselves form one of the objectives of teaching and, on the other, of ways to produce a general motivation to learn. Existing learning theories cannot supply ready solutions to either of these quesions; but they do provide a background against which such questions can be turned into more clearly formulated research objectives.

Investigations such as those of L. F. Thomas are primarily concerned with learning strategies. We will here consider the problem of getting people to develop any strategy whatever, i.e. the problem of generating motivation. The need for motivation in students is widely recognized, but there is little detailed understanding either of the effects of various artificial goals, such as test and examination results which are introduced into the course of the learning experience, of the interaction between coexisting short-term and long-term goals which may be incompatible, or indeed of the nature and range of motivational factors which enter into the learning activities of students.

The Achievement of Independent Learning

Skinner has described procedures for developing in animals high response rates with very infrequent reinforcement, and this is at any rate superficially similar to what we would call 'behaviour with a long-term goal'. What happens when two or more reinforcement contingencies coexist, some with a short-term but small, others with a large, long-term pay-off? We may certainly expect innate species differences, but are there in addition shaping procedures which can lead to distant rewards taking precedence over near ones? This raises, at a primitive level, issues of great interest in relation to individual differences between people. Is 'singleness of purpose' at least to some extent a function of early reinforcement history, or of other environmental influences? With human beings there exists of course an important complication, in that many of the objectives which people set themselves have never previously been realized. The student who wants to become a doctor has at no time been reinforced for being one, yet the contemplation of this objective can affect current activity. We know very little about the aetiology of such aims, the extent for example to which 'identification' with other people is involved, or for that matter, the circumstances that bring about identification.

When an attempt is made to assess a new teaching procedure or device, such as, for example, the use of the initial teaching alphabet (I.T.A.), factors such as the 'atmosphere' of the school in which children learn, or the personal characteristics of the teachers involved, constitute 'error factors' which the experimental design must cope with. One of the criticisms that has been made of the claims for I.T.A. is that the enthusiasm of the teachers using this new method may in itself be an important factor in producing successful results. At the same time, the importance of the teacher's behaviour is acknowledged – variables which are a nuisance in testing the effectiveness of one particular factor can themselves become the object of investigation. Many people, thinking back over their educational experience, may trace their interest in a particular subject, or even more generally in the activity of learning, to the personal influence of individual teachers or tutors, to a kind of

235

contagious transmission of enthusiasm. It should not be impossible to analyse the type of behaviour that brings about such a result, as a step towards making it an explicit objective of teacher training.

Curiosity as a motive

There is no shortage of evidence showing that animals, especially primates and human beings, will engage in exploratory and manipulative behaviour for its own sake, that – in different language – novelty can act as a reinforcement. Although there is thus no *need* for independent rewards to bring about exploration, such rewards will nevertheless influence the extent to which an animal engages in this type of activity. If it is frequently followed by punishment or discouragement, behaviour will tend to become less adventurous – it has been pointed out in Chapter 3 that in general punishment and the associated anxiety lead to rigid and stereotyped behaviour. If, on the other hand, a wide range of 'investigations' produce satisfactory results additional to the sheer novelty which they introduce, we may expect to see a general increase in inquisitiveness. If we accept the equation, at a basic level, between curiosity and the desire to learn, this suggests a policy of encouraging acts of exploration or inquiry *as such*, as distinct from the particular results which this behaviour may occasionally achieve. When children are sometimes praised for 'trying' – as distinct from succeeding – such praise usually contains a strong element of patronage which is easily detected. To some extent, the ability to sustain search – or research – depends on an enjoyment of the activity itself, as well as on the importance which is attached to its eventual outcome. It could well be that the relative emphasis placed on trying and on succeeding in childhood has far-reaching consequences for the inclination, in later life, to engage in activities without prospect of immediate pay-off.

At the same time, the frequency of success or failure is bound to influence the readiness with which attempts are made.

Skinner has argued that our present teaching methods involve strong punitive elements for a large proportion of children. This is a result of an emphasis on competition which by definition condemns a proportion of each class to relative failure, and hence an argument for more individual work, with self-contained criteria of success. However, Skinner's stress on very small learning steps to insure that a prescribed path will be followed with frequent successes, does not provide the only solution. The application of an *effective* learning strategy, relatively independent of particular subject matter, will also produce reinforcement and hence motivation, but for a higher level of activity than that involved in following a carefully structured programme. If we *can* develop such strategies and transmit them to the student, their success will help to maintain a more general motivation for learning.

The difference between a child copying letters from a blackboard and a student working on a thesis or an industrial research worker trying to solve a production problem is not simply one of complexity of subject matter; it is also one of control. The child receives constant and detailed guidance, the research worker is relatively speaking on his own. Our educational methods focus attention on the development of subject matter, and the increasing emancipation of the pupil from external control, which inevitably takes place to a greater or lesser extent, is rarely an explicit objective of teaching or a subject for research. As a result, the extent to which an individual can take charge of his own learning activity tends to be ascribed too exclusively to some inherent ability or capacity. There may indeed be an innate component, but the extent to which such a capacity may be *developed* by carefully phased external influences has hardly begun to be explored.

The training of teachers

Two suggestions have been made: that developing an *ability to learn* should be a primary and explicit objective of education; and that the application of theory and research within education is *itself* a kind of research activity. The implication of these suggestions is that the training of teachers – as well as the organization of their professional activity – should enable them to meet these requirements. This would involve a far greater emphasis on the process of learning as such, and a deliberate preparation for teaching regarded in part as a research activity. A concern with the psychology of learning, less in terms of supposedly definite findings, but rather as a methodology and an attitude, would seem to be an appropriate focus for teacher training. Increasing emphasis on subject matter, as a preparation for teaching at more senior levels, should be paralleled by even greater concentration on learning processes by those who intend to teach in primary schools. Given that the latter are responsible for laying the foundations for later achievement, their relatively low status within the educational hierarchy, coupled with low training requirements, is one of the most serious shortcomings of our educational system.

The development of ability in people, and especially of the ability to become educationally self-supporting, is an enterprise which ranks at least equally in importance with the development of the natural sciences and associated technologies – if only because it is on the availability of competent people that achievement in these areas depends. There is a strong case for a determined attack on problems of human learning and development on a scale much larger than existing priorities allow. Inevitably this kind of work takes time to bear fruit, and governments, like laboratory rats, prefer short-term reinforcements. However, investment in better learning is likely to produce returns on a compound interest basis, and an administration prepared to take the long-term view could lay the basis for a significant breakthrough in education.

Notes

3

1 HULL, C. L., *Principles of Behaviour: An Introduction to Behaviour Theory* (Appleton-Century Crofts, New York, 1943).
2 COWLES, J. T., 'Food tokens as incentives for learning by chimpanzees', *Comparative Psychology Monograph* (1937), Vol. 14, pp. 1–96.
3 BUTLER, R. A., 'Discrimination learning by rhesus monkeys to visual-exploration motivation', *Journal of Comparative and Physiological Psychology* (1953), Vol. 46, pp. 95–8.
4 DEUTSCH, J. A., *The Structural Basis of Behaviour* (C.U.P., 1960).
5 OLDS, J. and MILNER, P., 'Positive reinforcement produced by electrical stimulation of septal area and other regions of rat brain', *Journal of Comparative and Physiological Psychology* (1954), Vol. 47, pp. 419–27.
6 BROADHURST, P. L., 'Air deprivation as a motivational technique in the rat, and its application to the problem of emotionality as a determinant of drive', *Bulletin of the British Psychological Society* (1957), Vol. 32, p. 23.

4

1 HULL, *Principles of Behaviour*, op. cit.
2 HULL, C. L., *A Behaviour System* (Yale University Press, New Haven, 1952).
3 TOLMAN, E. C., 'Cognitive maps in rats and men', *Psychological Review* (1948), Vol. 55, pp. 189–208.
4 HEBB, D. O., *The Organisation of Behaviour* (Wiley, New York, 1949).
5 MILNER, P. M., 'The cell assembly: Mark II', *Psychological Review* (1957), Vol. 64, pp. 242–52.
6 DEUTSCH, *The Structural Basis of Behaviour*, op. cit.

5

1 TINBERGEN, N., *The Study of Instinct* (O.U.P., 1951).
2 CARMICHAEL, L., 'The development of behaviour in vertebrates experimentally removed from the influence of external stimulation', *Psychological Review* (1926), Vol. 33, pp. 51–8.
3 DENNIS, W. and DENNIS, M. G., 'The effect of cradling practice upon

the onset of walking in Hopi children', *Journal of Genetic Psychology* (1940), Vol. 56, pp. 77–86.

4 NEWMAN, H. H., FREEMAN, F. N. and HOLZINGER, K. J., *Twins: A Study of Heredity and Environment* (University of Chicago Press, 1937).

5 HEBB, *The Organisation of Behaviour*, op. cit.

6 LORENZ, K., *King Solomon's Ring* (Methuen, 1952).

7 TINBERGEN, N., quoted in Thorpe, W. H., *Learning and Instinct in Animals* (Methuen, 1956).

8 RIESS, B. F., 'The isolation of factors of learning and native behaviour in field and laboratory studies', *Annals of the New York Academy of Science* (1950), Vol. 51, pp. 1093–1102.

9 BIRCH, H. G., 'Sources of order in the maternal behaviour of animals', *American Journal of Orthopsychiatry* (1956), Vol. 26, pp. 279–84.

10 HARLOW, H. F., 'The formation of learning sets', *Psychological Review* (1949), Vol. 56, pp. 51–65.

11 MOWRER, O. H., *Learning Theory and the Symbolic Processes* (Wiley, New York, 1960).

12 FOSS, B. M., 'Mimicry in mynas (Gracula Religiosa): a test of Mowrer's theory', *British Journal of Psychology* (1964), Vol. 55, pp. 85–8.

13 FOSS, B. M., 'Imitation' in *Determinants of Infant Behaviour*, Vol. III, ed. B. M. Foss (Methuen, 1965).

6

1 GIBSON, E. J. and WALK, R. D., 'The "visual cliff" ', *Scientific American* (1960), Vol. 202, pp. 64–71.

2 RIESEN, A. H., 'The development of visual perception in man and chimpanzee', *Science* (1947), Vol. 106, pp. 107–8.

3 RIESEN, A. H., CHOW, K. L., SEMMES, J. and NISSEN, H. W., 'Chimpanzee vision after four conditions of light deprivation', *American Psychologist* (1951), Vol. 6, p. 282.

4 RIESEN, A. H., KURKE, M. I. and MELLINGER, J. C., 'Interocular transfer of habits learned monocularly in visually naïve and visually experienced cats', *Journal of Comparative and Physiological Psychology* (1953), Vol. 46, pp. 166–71.

5 RIESEN, A. H. and MELLINGER, J. C., 'Interocular transfer of habits in cats after alternating monocular visual experience', *Journal of Comparative and Physiological Psychology* (1956), Vol. 49, pp. 516–20.

6 STRATTON, C. M., 'Vision without inversion of the retinal image', *Psychological Review* (1897), Vol. 4, pp. 341–60, 463–81.

7 KOHLER, I., 'Experiments with goggles', *Scientific American* (1962), Vol. 206, pp. 62–72.

8 VON SENDEN, M., *Space and Sight* (Methuen, 1960).

9 GREGORY, R. L. and WALLACE, J. G., 'Recovery from early blindness – a case study', *Quarterly Journal of Experimental Psychology Monographs* (1963), Supp. 2.

10 THOULESS, R. H., 'Phenomenal regression to the real object I,' *British Journal of Psychology* (1931), Vol. 21, pp. 339–59.

11 GIBSON, J. J. and GIBSON, E. J., 'Perceptual learning: differentiation or enrichment', *Psychological Review* (1955), Vol. 62, pp. 32–41.

12 MILLER, N. E. and DOLLARD, J., *Social Learning and Imitation* (Yale University Press, New Haven, 1941).

13 KATZ, P. A., 'Effects of labels on children's perception and discrimination learning', *Journal of Experimental Psychology* (1963), Vol. 66, pp. 423–8.

7

1 BRYAN, N. L. and HARTER, N., 'Studies on the telegraphic language', *Psychological Review* (1899), Vol. 6, pp. 345–75.

2 ADAMS, J. A., 'A source of decrement in psychomotor performance', *Journal of Experimental Psychology* (1955), Vol. 49, pp. 390–4.

3 HARLOW, A. F., MEYER, D. R. and SETTLAGE, P. H., 'Effect of large cortical lesions on the solution of oddity problems', *Journal of Comparative and Physiological Psychology* (1951), Vol. 18, pp. 44–50.

4. MILLER, G. A., GALANTER, E. and PRIBAM, K. H., *Plans and the Structure of Behaviour* (Holt Rinehart and Winston, New York, 1960).

8

1 MINAMI, H. and DALLENBACH, K. M., 'The effect of activity upon learning and retention in the cockroach', *American Journal of Psychology* (1946), Vol. 59, pp. 1–58.

2 MELTON, A. W. and IRWIN, J. MCQ., 'The influence of degree of interpolated learning on retroactive inhibition and the overt transfer of specific responses', *American Journal of Psychology* (1940), Vol. 53, pp. 173–203.

3 UNDERWOOD, B. J., 'The effect of successive interpolations on retroactive and proactive inhibition', *Psychology Monograph* (1945), 59, No. 3.

4 BROADBENT, D. E., *Perception and Communication* (Pergamon Press, 1958).

5 CARMICHAEL, L., HOGAN, H. P. and WALTER, A. A., 'An experimental study of the effect of language on the reproduction of visually perceived form', *Journal of Experimental Psychology* (1932), Vol. 15, pp. 73–86.

Notes

6 BARTLETT, F. C., *Remembering: A Study in Experimental and Social Psychology* (C.U.P., 1932).

9

1 HAYES, K. J. and HAYES, C., 'The intellectual development of a home-raised chimpanzee', *Proceedings of the American Philosophical Society* (1951), Vol. 95, pp. 105–9.

2 CHOMSKY, N., 'A review of *Verbal Behaviour* by B. F. Skinner', *Language* (1959), Vol. 35.

3 LURIA, A. R., *The Role of Speech in the Development of Normal and Abnormal Behaviour* (Pergamon Press, 1963).

4 SMOKE, K. L., 'An objective study of concept formation', *Psychology Monograph* (1932), 42, No. 191.

5 BRUNER, J. S., GOODNOW, J. and AUSTIN, G. A., *A Study of Thinking* (Wiley, New York, 1956).

10

1 YATES, A. J., 'The application of learning theory to the treatment of tics', *Behaviour Therapy and the Neuroses*, ed. H. J. Eysenck (Pergamon Press, 1960).

2 JONES, H. G., 'Continuation of Yate's treatment of tiqueur', *Behaviour Therapy and the Neuroses*, op. cit.

3 WOLPE, J., *Psychotherapy by Reciprocal Inhibition* (Stanford University Press, 1958).

4 GEER, J. H., 'Phobia treated by reciprocal inhibition', *Journal of Abnormal and Social Psychology* (1964), Vol. 69, pp. 642–5

5 FELDMAN, M. P. and MACCULLOCH, M. J., 'The application of anticipatory avoidance learning to the treatment of homosexuality', *Behaviour Research and Therapy* (1965), Vol. 2, pp. 165–83.

6 WOLPE, J., 'Reciprocal inhibition as the main basis of psychotherapeutic effects', *Behaviour Therapy and the Neuroses*, op. cit.

7 MASSERMAN, J. H., *Behaviour and Neurosis: An Experimental Psychoanalytic Approach to Psychobiologic Principles* (University of Chicago Press, 1943).

8 BROADHURST, P. L., 'Abnormal animal behaviour', *Handbook of Abnormal Psychology*, ed. H. J. Eysenck (Pitman Medical Publishing Co. Ltd, 1960).

11

1 PRESSEY, L. S., 'A simple apparatus which gives tests and scores and teaches', *School and Society* (1962), Vol. 23, pp. 373–6.

2 HOLLAND, J. G. and SKINNER, B. F., *The Analysis of Behaviour* (McGraw-Hill, 1961).

3 CAVANAGH, P., 'The autotutor and classroom instructions: three comparative studies', *Occupational Psychology* (1963), Vol. 37, pp. 44–9.

4 KAY, H. and WARR, P. B., 'Teaching by machine', *Chartered Mechanical Engineer* (1962), Vol. 9, pp. 472–5.

12

1. SKINNER, B. F., *Cumulative Record* (Methuen, 1959)

2 YOUNG, M., *Innovation and Research in Education* (Routledge & Kegan Paul, 1965),

3 MARSHALL, S., *An Experiment in Education* (C.U.P., 1963).

4 JAHODA, M., *The Training of Technologists* (Tavistock Publications, 1963).

Further Reading

BROADBENT, D., *Behaviour* (Eyre & Spottiswoode, 1961).

BUGELSKI, B. R., *The Psychology of Learning* (Methuen, 1956).

HEBB, D. O., *The Organisation of Behaviour* (Wiley, 1949).

HILGARD, E. R., *Theories of Learning* (Methuen, 1958).

HOLLAND, J. G. and SKINNER, B. F., *The Analysis of Behaviour* (McGraw-Hill, 1961).

HULL, C. L., *A Behaviour System* (Yale University Press, 1952).

HUNT, J. MCV., *Intelligence and Experience* (Ronald Press, New York, 1961).

MILLER, G. A., GALANTER, E. and PRIBRAM, K. H., *Plans and the Structure of Behaviour* (Holt Rinehart and Winston, New York, 1960).

OSGOOD, C. E., *Method and Theory in Experimental Psychology* (O.U.P., New York, 1953).

SKINNER, B. F., *Cumulative Record* (Methuen, 1959).

Index

More about Penguins and Pelicans

Penguinews, which appears every month,
contains details of all the new books issued by
Penguins as they are published. From time to time
it is supplemented by *Penguins in Print*, which is a
complete list of all books published by Penguins
which are in print. (There are over three thousand
of these.)

A specimen copy of *Penguinews* will be
sent to you free on request, and you can become
a subscriber for the price of the postage – 4s. for
a year's issues (including the complete lists). Just write
to Dept EP, Penguin Books Ltd, Harmondsworth,
Middlesex, enclosing a cheque or postal order, and
your name will be added to the mailing list.

Some other books published by Penguins are described
on the following pages.

Note: *Penguinews* and *Penguins in Print* are not
available in the U.S.A. or Canada.

The Psychology of Interpersonal Behaviour

Michael Argyle

Looks, gestures, and tones of voice may be powerful factors when people meet. Moreover these rapid and subtle messages are highly co-ordinated.

Experimental techniques have recently been developed for studying the *minutiae* of social behaviour scientifically: these are described here by a social psychologist. The study of social interaction demands a 'language' of its own, to which Michael Argyle supplies a clear key. But the reader will not be slow to grasp that 'the motivation of social interaction', 'the synchronization of styles of behaviour' between two or more people, and 'the presentation of a self-image' refer to things we encounter every day.

Certain specific skills, such as interviewing, group leadership, public speaking, and even child-rearing, are discussed in the light of the latest research, and the author devotes a good deal of space to mental health and to training in social skill. His outline of what amounts to a break-through in psychological analysis makes this a book which the student of psychology may well find indispensable; and the relevance of his material to everyday life offers irresistible reading to the plain man.

The Psychology of Human Ageing

D. B. Bromley

Infant and adolescent psychology have been very
thoroughly explored: but the study of ageing lags behind.

A gerontologist, who is scientific adviser in this field
to the Medical Research Council, fills a gap in the
literature of psychology with this new introduction to
human ageing and its mental effects. Dealing with the
course of life from maturity onwards, Dr Bromley
examines many biological and social effects of human
ageing; personality and adjustment; mental disorders in
adult life and old age; age changes in the organization of
occupational and skilled performance; adult intelligence;
and age changes in intellectual, social, and other
achievements. A final section on method in the study of
ageing makes this book an important contribution for
the student of psychology as well as the layman.

H. J. Eysenck

Uses and Abuses of Psychology

In this book H. J. Eysenck indicates both to what extent
the claims made for psychology are justified, and to what
extent they fail to have any factual basis. The discussion
is very fully documented by references to the most
important and relevant researches carried out in this
country and abroad.

Know Your Own I.Q.

This was the first book to permit the reader
to determine his own I.Q. In the first part of it the author
describes clearly what an I.Q. is, how it can be applied,
and what the shortcomings of this system of rating may
be. The second part of the book contains eight sets of
forty I.Q. problems each. There are tables for converting
results into an I.Q. rating, and explanations of the
problems, together with the right answers, at the end
of the book.

Check Your Own I.Q.

Know Your Own I.Q. was a best-seller. It also provoked a
mass of critical comment and correspondence.

In this sequel, *Check Your Own I.Q.*, Professor Eysenck
answers these criticisms fully and provides five new tests
of the standard (omnibus) type as a check. He has also
added three specific tests which are designed to sort out
whether the reader shows more ability in verbal,
numerical, or visual-spatial terms.

also available
Sense and Nonsense in Psychology
Fact and Fiction in Psychology

The Senses

Otto Lowenstein

It is doubtful if a red rag means much to a bull, and
certainly cats and dogs see only in black and white.
A fly tastes with its feet. Fish can smell. Bats employ
echo-sounding. And man has more than the five senses
he is credited with.

Such are some of the more surprising details to be
found in this new introductory study addressed to student
biologists and general readers. Professor Lowenstein
explains how animals, in order to keep themselves
accurately posted about the world outside, are
continuously receiving 'information' along the pathways
provided by the sensory receptors. Sensory stimuli are
today known to be of three kinds: electro-magnetic
(sight), mechanical (touch, sound), and chemical (taste,
smell). The author therefore treats the classical 'five
senses', along with the senses of posture, balance,
temperature, and others of which we are hardly
conscious, under these three headings.

His book gives an authoritative outline of a field of
biology in which the speed, sensitivity, and ingenuity of
nature make automation and computers look like
toddlers' toys.